QBasic
The Language of DOS
2nd Edition

Mike James

I/O PRESS

I/O Press

First Published 1994
©I/O Press
ISBN 1-871962-40-4

British Library Cataloguing in Publication Data
A catalogue record for this book is available from the British Library

All Rights Reserved. No part of this publication may be reproduced, stored in a retrieval system, or transmitted in any form or by any means, electronic, mechanical, photocopying, recording or otherwise, without prior written permission.

Products mentioned within this text may be protected by trade marks, in which case full acknowledgement is hereby given.

Although every effort has been made to ensure the correctness of the information contained herein neither the publishers nor the author accept liability for any omissions or errors that remain.

Typeset by I/O Press
Printed and bound in Great Britain by Cromwell Press Limited,
Broughton Gifford, Wiltshire.

Table of Contents

Preface

Using the Disk

Chapter 1   Getting Started   1

What is a program?; Starting QBasic; Installing QBasic; Using the editor; QBasic with Windows; Edit control keys; Keywords and syntax checking

Chapter 2   Multi-line Programs   15

What is a variable?; Using variables; Finding out what's in a variable - PRINT; Arithmetic; Why arithmetic goes wrong - the order of evaluation; Variables and constants; A short program; The INPUT statement; Input prompting; Print Hello and Print "Hello" a warning!

Chapter 3   The Flow of Control   29

The flow of control; The infinite loop - DO and LOOP; Indenting; Getting out of a loop - EXIT; Thinking about loops; The WHILE-WEND loop; UNTIL and WHILE; Exit points; Counting - the simple FOR loop; C=C+1; Finer details of FOR loops; Step; When does a loop finish?; Negative steps; Making choices - simple IF; The block IF; The shape of an IF; Five easy pieces; An example - the bubble sort; Relics of the past - GOTO

Chapter 4   Modular Programs   59

Windows of the mind; The subroutine; Subroutine structure and the editor; Step by step programming; Interaction; Parameters; Value and reference - out and in; Local, shared and global; Dynamic and static variables; Scope and existence; Functions; Modular problems; Relics of the past - GOSUB

Chapter 5   The Importance of Data   79

Types of simple variable; Defining variable types; Using numeric variables; Strings; String expressions; Concatenation; The MID$ function; The null string; Month names - an example; LEN, LEFT$ and RIGHT$; String insertion; Searching strings - INSTR; Comparing strings; Type conversion functions; The type of a function; Procedures, functions and data types; Prototypes - DECLARE; Constants; Another five easy pieces

Chapter 6   Data Structures   101

Arrays; Two-dimensional arrays; The type of an array; Upper and lower bounds; Index tricks; Scope and existence of arrays; Arrays as parameters; Fixed sized strings; Records; Arrays of records; Records within records; Bubble sort revisited

Chapter 7   Graphics and Sound   119

Graphics modes; Resolution; Using the text screen; Print Using; Text as graphics; Graphics modes; Controlling colour - COLOR and CLS; Drawing points; Drawing lines; Drawing boxes; Dotted lines; Drawing circles and ellipses; Relative co-ordinates; The DRAW command; Painting; GET and PUT; The PALETTE command; Advanced use of GET and PUT; Making patterns; Screen pages; Changing the co-ordinate system; Viewports; Physical and world co-ordinate systems; Text windows; Finding out what's on the screen - POINT; Sound; Music

Chapter 8   Data Files   157

What makes disks different; Files - sequential, random and indexed; Sequential files; A simple example; Records and fields; Fixed and variable length records; File export; Some file practicalities; Direct access files; The old and the new; Opening a direct access file; Reading and writing a record; Using record buffers; Useful commands and functions; Binary files; DOS file commands; Networks

Chapter 9   Advanced Control   183

Multiple selections; Select Case; Logical expressions; Advanced loops; Recursion; Infinite recursion; Conditional recursion; Forward and backward recursion; Local variables and passing by value; When is recursion useful?; Exceptions; Event driven programming; A musical event; Error handling; Interacting with MS-DOS; Low level and BIOS interface; Other I/O devices; Debugging; Testing methods; After testing; Documentation; Standalone programs; Large programs; Beyond QBasic; The final stages

Chapter 10   Applications   219

Dates and Times; Sorting; Quicksort; Using the keyboard; Polling; Key events; Function keys; Keyboard polling; Event handling; Qtress; Creating a database

Index

Preface

I have been using Basic for many years and always found it a suitable language for everything but the largest and most critical of programs. Modern Basic, QBasic in particular, is an ideal language for the beginner to use for learning to program. It is well structured and fully modular so that you learn a good programming style from the outset.

QBasic is included as standard with MS-DOS, starting with version 5. This makes it the natural upgrade for GW-BASIC which for so long was the language that came with MS-DOS. If you want to program in QBasic under earlier versions of MS-DOS then I can recommend the QBasic compiler. This is easy to use and produces fast and efficient programs.

Microsoft seems set to take Basic, in the form of QBasic and Visual Basic, well into the 21st century. Bill Gates (Head of the Microsoft Corporation) has often said that he sees Basic, in one form or another, becoming the main applications programming language of MS-DOS and Windows. What better time could there be to learn QBasic?

Learning to program is like learning any second language - you pick up some bits easily and you struggle over others. It is important to realise that you cannot do it simply by reading a book - you have to write programs of your own and accept that your first efforts will tend to be short and simple. Also, you will find that you cannot just treat this book as a reading book. Some sections will make little sense the first time around and so you will need to return to them - time and time again with some of the most advanced techniques.

Programming is not only a useful skill, it can also be an enjoyable and rewarding activity, so I hope you have some fun along the way.

My thanks to Jane Patience who drew the diagrams throughout this book.

Mike James
March 1992

Preface to 2nd edition

Despite the major changes going on in the PC world, QBasic is still very much with us! It is the only standard programming language included with MS-DOS, PC-DOS and Windows 95. Given the faster machines that are now in common use it also has the speed needed to create ambitious programs that only a few years ago would have demanded a more difficult language such as C. It also forms the core language within Visual Basic for DOS and Visual Basic for Windows. All this makes QBasic a good starting point for anyone wanting to learn to program.

In this revised 2nd edition I have removed some errors and improved both the text and the illustrations.

Mike James
October 1994

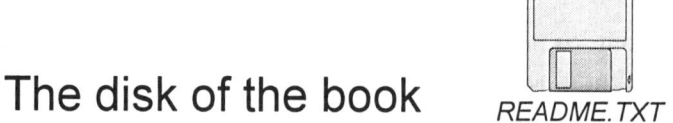

The disk of the book

README.TXT

The 3.5 inch disk included contains all the major programs listed in this book. The name of each program on the disk is indicated by the diskette icon which appears throughout this book. The disk also contains additional example programs, complete with documentation that discusses the techniques used. If this disk is missing contact I/O Press at the address given below.

Bonus disk

Although this book and disk set is completely self-contained you can also buy a bonus companion disk containing additional programs and tutorials in QBasic and useful shareware. The disk costs £3.00, postage and packing free. To place an order or for more information contact:

I/O Press, Freepost, Leyburn, North Yorkshire DL8 5BR
Tel: (01969) 624402 Fax: (01969) 624375
Email: infomax@cix.compulink.co.uk

Please remember to state the size of diskette, 3.5" or 5.25", you require.

Chapter 1

RUN
Getting Started

This chapter introduces the basic ideas of programming and describes how to make a start on using QBasic. It explains how to enter and run a program and discusses the idea of a separate editing and output screen. If you have never programmed before, or if you are completely self-taught, you should read this chapter carefully and try the short examples.

Programming is a practical skill that can only be mastered by doing it but there is some theory that will help you do it correctly. Don't be put off by the word 'theory' - it is neither difficult to understand nor hard work to put into practice. Indeed, without some idea of what programming is all about you will only succeed in making things much more difficult.

If you have programmed in other dialects of Basic, GW-Basic or Basic-A for example, then you will find QBasic very familiar and you should be able to get it started, enter and run a test program in a few minutes without any help. However, there are differences between traditional Basic and modern QBasic that without some help you might misunderstand and even find irritating. You should skim read this chapter to understand why QBasic works in the way it does.

» What is a program?

Although we normally associate programs with computers they are actually an example of a wider idea. A program is nothing more than a list of instructions that can be obeyed to achieve a particular result. The instructions that you get with a kit telling you how to put it together is a program, so is a knitting pattern, the score of a piece of music, a recipe etc.. What is different about a computer program is that the agent that obeys the program isn't at all intelligent. For this reason computer programs cannot contain vague phrases such as "glue part A to part B". What is vague about this instruction? Nothing if you are a reasonably intelligent human because you could be relied upon to orient parts A, B, C and D so that they meet in a natural way and glue them accordingly. A computer, on the other hand, would either complain that it didn't know how to orient the part or would just glue them together randomly.

Clearly computer programs have to be more precise than programs intended for intelligent humans and as a result the commands that are used, and the way in which they are used, have to be tightly controlled. Even so there are only a few QBasic commands that are used frequently. Perhaps one of the most common and useful of commands is PRINT. For example, the command:

```
PRINT "Hello"
```

is an instruction to print (or more descriptively display) the word Hello on the screen. This is your first QBasic program and all that remains is to discover how to enter and run it!

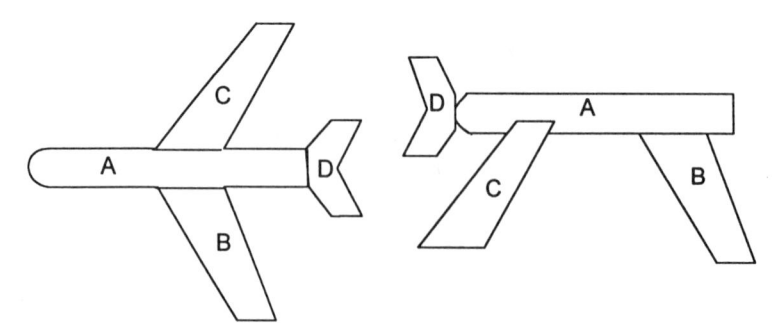

Figure 1.1
The program "Glue parts B, C and D to A"
run on a human and on a computer!

» Starting QBasic

As long as you have installed MS-DOS 5 (or a later version) correctly then starting QBasic is simply a matter of typing:

    QBASIC

at the command prompt. If you are using the DOSSHELL that comes with MS-DOS 5 then you can simply select the program QBASIC.EXE from the DOS program group. You can also run QBasic under Windows - see the box *QBasic with Windows*.

As long as everything is set up correctly you should see the QBasic opening screen as in Figure 1.2. If you are having difficulty running QBasic then the only reasonably likely explanation is that MS-DOS cannot find the program file QBASIC.EXE. You should check the MS-DOS directory, usually called DOS, for the existence of this file. If it isn't present then it is possible that it has been deleted. To restore this file follow the instructions in the box *Installing QBasic*.

Once you see the QBasic opening screen you can either press Enter to read an introductory help screen which contains the very minimum information that you need to use QBasic or you can press Esc to skip this screen and move on to entering and running programs.

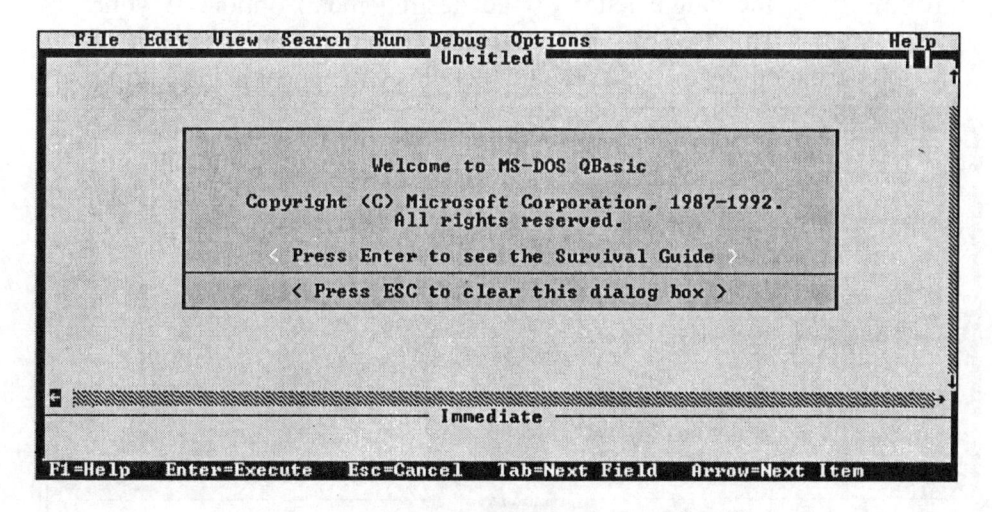

Figure 1.2
The QBasic opening screen

> ## Installing QBasic
>
> If you can't find the file QBASIC.EXE somewhere on your machine's hard disk then the chances are that it has been deleted to save space. You could use the MS-DOS setup program to reinstall it but it is generally quicker and simpler to do the job directly. First find the original MS-DOS diskette which contains the file QBASIC.EX_ - notice that this is the same as QBASIC.EXE but the last letter E is replaced by an underscore. Once you have found this file use the command
>
> ```
> EXPAND A:QBASIC.EX_  C:\DOS\QBASIC.EXE
> ```
>
> This both copies and expands the compressed file to the DOS directory. If you want to install QBasic somewhere else then use an alternative directory name.

In this case you should press Esc to move on to the QBasic editor - see Figure 1.3. The screen is divided into two windows. The larger, top window is used to enter and display any program that you want to work with. There is a menu bar at the top of the window and the commands that this contains can be accessed in the usual way by pressing Alt followed by the single letter of the desired menu option. If your machine has a mouse you can also select menu commands using it. If you type something on the keyboard then this will appear in the editing

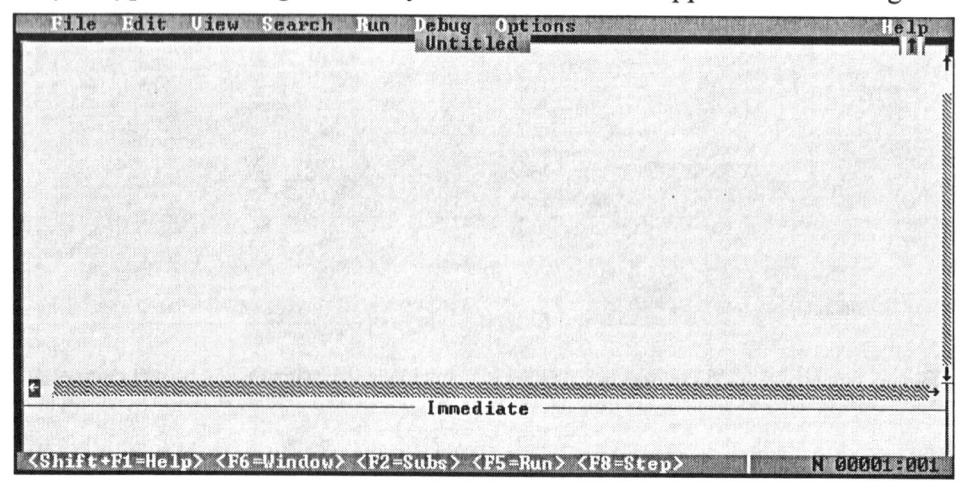

Figure 1.3
The QBasic editor

window which acts like a simple text editor. Indeed the QBasic text editor is the same editor that is used under MS-DOS 5 to prepare and modify simple system files such as Config.sys and Autoexec.bat. Later on it will become important to know how to make use of all of its facilities but for a short program consisting of one line all that you need to know is how to use the backspace key to correct errors. To enter your first program simply type in:

```
PRINT "Hello"
```

as shown in Figure 1.4. Notice that the word Hello has to be enclosed in double quotes (produced by the combination Shift+2).

If you are used to other dialects of Basic you may be wondering where the line numbers are. The answer is that while line numbers can be used in QBasic they are unnecessary, old fashioned and a source of errors. If you don't know anything about line numbers then you can count yourself as lucky!

After entering the program the next step is to run it. Notice that simply entering an instruction isn't enough to make the machine obey it - you actually need to give a special command to make it do so. This means that you can use the program editor to enter longish programs consisting of many lines of instructions and then, when you are ready you can give the Run command to see it all in action. This is an

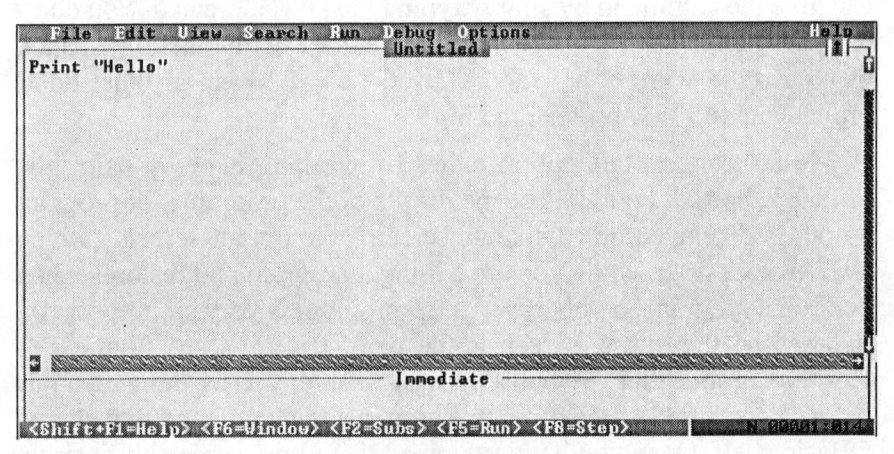

Figure 1.4
Entering the Hello program

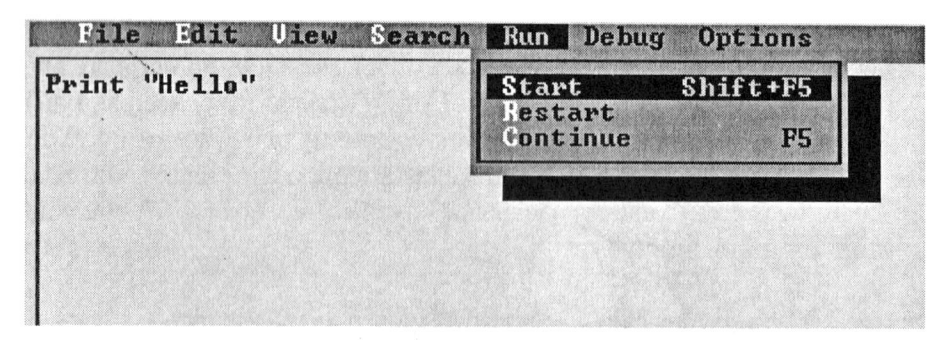

Figure 1.5
The Run menu

important idea and you should be sure that you distinguish clearly between entering the text of a program using the editor and running the program.

The Run command is one of the menu options. To select Run simply hold down the Alt key and press R. This produces the drop down menu as shown in Figure 1.5. Of the three options Start, Restart and Continue, only Start interests us at the moment. This starts the program shown in the editing window running. You can also see that next to the Start option is a shortcut key combination - Shift+F5 in this case. Any time that you see a shortcut key combination listed in a menu option you can give the command by simply typing the keys indicated. You don't have to learn the shortcuts because any that are really useful will stick in your mind without any effort. By the same token any that don't probably aren't worth remembering.

If you select the Start option either by pressing S or by using the Shift-F5 shortcut you will see the results of the program. All program output is displayed on a separate screen - the output screen - which QBasic keeps safe while you are editing a program and restores when you run a program. In this case, as the program is very simple, all you will see on the output screen is the word 'Hello' - see Figure 1.6. However, notice that you will also see whatever was on the screen just before you started QBasic - in this case just the command that started QBasic itself. Once you have examined the output screen sufficiently you can return to the QBasic editing screen by pressing any key - as the message at the bottom of the screen informs you. The output screen

```
C:\DOS>qbasic
Hello




           Press any key to continue
```

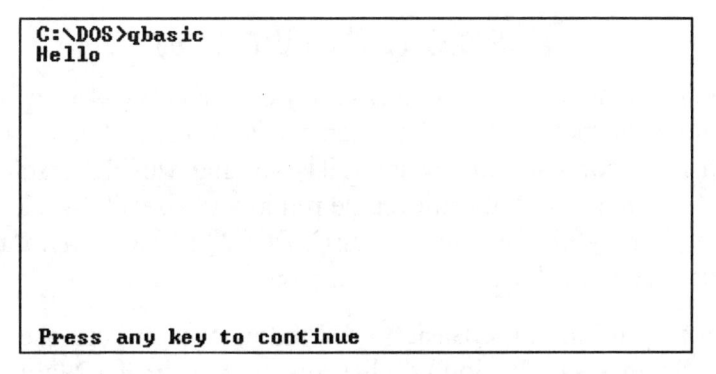

Figure 1.6
The results of running the hello program

also retains whatever is written on it between edits and runs. This means that you will see a line saying 'Hello' for each time you run the program. Methods for controlling the output screen so that it shows exactly what you want it to show are described later. For the moment all that is important is that you know that the output screen exists and is separate from the editing screen.

» Using the editor

Although using the QBasic editor is mainly a matter of common sense, there are a few details worth mentioning. Many of the operations described here are only needed occasionally so you can skip the details and return to them later.

The editor is used to create text files that contain QBasic commands. In principle you can use another editor or a word processor if you want to, but the QBasic editor is very easy to use and very convenient. (If you do want to use an alternative then the files created by it have to be saved in simple ASCII format while the files that the QBasic editor creates can be saved on disk and re-loaded at a later date without any additional steps.) The QBasic main menu is:

```
File Edit View Search Run Debug Options
```

The commands File, Edit and Options are the ones concerned with editing while View, Search, Run and Debug have more to do with

QBasic with Windows

With more and more users are coming to rely on Windows as a way of running all their programs, including DOS programs, it is worth mentioning that QBasic can be run in a re-sizeable window unless it is working with high resolution VGA graphics. (In Windows 95 it can even be run in a re-sizeable window at VGA resolutions.) Simply add the program item C:\DOS\QBASIC.EXE to any suitable group and run it by double clicking on the icon.

A simpler way of adding QBasic to a Windows group is to use Windows Setup - simply double click on its icon in the Main group. This produces this dialog box.

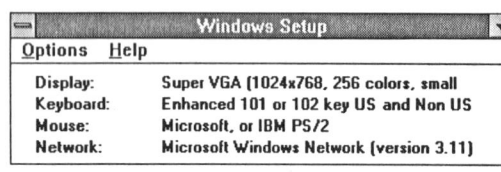

Windows Setup

You can ignore most of the details that it displays unless you actually want to alter your Windows hardware setup. The command Options, Setup Applications can be used to add DOS applications automatically. You next have a choice of letting Windows search for all the .EXE files it can find or you can opt to specify exactly the program you want to add. Specify the program that you want to add as C:\DOS\QBASIC.EXE and QBasic will be added to a program group, normally the Applications group, and it will have an icon and an appropriate PIF file created.

PIF Editor

The PIF file controls how Windows will run a DOS program. To change it use the PIF editor, to be found in the Main group, to edit the file QBASIC.PIF which is usually stored in the \WINDOWS directory. For example, if you select Windowed instead of the default Full Screen and save the PIF file, QBasic will automatically run in a window.

programming and will therefore be described later. You can select any of the main menu commands by pressing Alt plus its first letter which causes a sub-menu to drop down. Selecting from the sub-menu can be done by typing the highlighted letter of the option you want or by using the cursor keys to move the highlight bar. You can also make use of the shortcut key presses listed against each option. The editing shortcuts are:

Shift+Del	Edit,Cut
Ctrl+Del	Edit,Copy
Shift +Ins	Edit,Paste
Del	Edit,Clear
F3	Search,Repeat last find

It is also important to know that items in a dialog box (an on screen form which appears in response to some menu selections) can be selected by pressing Tab, which causes the selection to rotate in a clockwise direction or Shift and Tab which causes the selection to rotate anti-clockwise. If you have a mouse then selection is just a matter of pointing and clicking. If you are going to make a great deal of use of QBasic then a mouse is a good investment.

The text cursor indicates the point where any action, such as new text being inserted into the document, takes place. Use the cursor keys to move it, or if you are using a mouse simply click on the desired new position. You can use the scroll bars or the PgUp/PgDn keys to move so that you can see the portion of the text that you want to edit. If you don't have a mouse then you can use the list of control keys shown in the box *Editing control key*s. As well as its own set of movement and editing keys, Edit also supports a limited subset of the WordStar keys. These are listed in the box but there is little reason to use them unless you are a seasoned WordStar user and they are already second nature. It is also worth knowing that you can enter a control code by typing Ctrl+P followed by Ctrl+*letter*.

As with most word processors, you can cut, copy, and paste blocks of text. A block of text can be highlighted using mouse or keyboard. With a mouse, it's just a matter of finding the starting point, clicking, and then dragging while holding the button down to the end of the block you want to highlight. A block can be de-selected by clicking anywhere

Edit control keys

The basic principle of the movement keys is that the cursor keys move the text cursor by the smallest amount possible in the direction indicated - the left and right arrows move one character to the left or right, the up and down arrows by one line. The Ctrl key, when used in combination with any movement key, makes the move 'bigger'. For example Ctrl+left arrow moves one word to the left. This pattern isn't perfect and you should notice, for example, Ctrl+ PgUp/PgDn, which moves left/right one whole screen!

Simple movement keys

Left/right arrow	moves one character left/right
Up/down arrow	moves up/down one line
PgUp/PgDn	moves up/down one screen
Home	moves to start of current line
End	moves to end of the current line

Keys in combination with Ctrl

Left/right arrow	moves one word left or right
Up/down arrow	scrolls the whole screen one line up or down
PgUp/PgDn	moves left/right one screen
Home	moves to start of document
End	moves to end of document
Enter	moves to the start of the next line

The following keys are used for editing

Delete	deletes the character under the cursor
Backspace	deletes the character to the left of the cursor
Insert	turns insert mode on/off

The following WordStar control keypresses are also supported

Ctrl QE	moves to the top of the screen
Ctrl QX	moves to the end of the screen
Ctrl QR	moves back to the top of the text
Ctrl QC	moves forwards to the end of the text
Ctrl W	scrolls the screen up one line
Ctrl Z	scrolls the screen down one line
Ctrl R	scrolls up one screen
Ctrl C	scrolls down one screen
Ctrl T	deletes the current word
Ctrl Y	deletes the current line
Ctrl N	inserts a new line

Keywords and syntax checking

A QBasic command such as PRINT is usually called a *keyword* or *reserved word*. You can type keywords in upper or lower case or a mixture of the two but there are advantages to using nothing but lower case. QBasic uses a clever method of checking what you type as you type it in and when it recognises a keyword it will automatically convert it to upper case, so showing you that it recognises it. For example, if you type in

        print "HELLO"

then when you move the cursor to a new line (either by pressing Enter or using the cursor arrow keys) the line is checked and print is converted to PRINT. Of course, if you haven't typed the word print correctly it will not be converted to upper case. This immediate checking of each line extends to details other than keyword recognition and if any errors are detected you will see an error message displayed. You can turn the checking on and off using the menu command Options,Syntax checking.

on the Edit screen. With the keyboard, a block can be highlighted by moving the cursor to the start of the block, holding down one of the Shift keys and moving it to the end of the block. A block can be de-selected by pressing a cursor key without holding down the Shift key.

Once you have a highlighted block of text there are a number of operations that can be performed, most of which use the Clipboard. The Clipboard is an area of memory to which you can copy a block of text for later use. A block can be removed or cut from the text and copied to the Clipboard by selecting the Cut option from the Edit menu or by pressing Shift and Del. If you don't want to remove a block from the text you can just copy it to the Clipboard by selecting Copy from the Edit menu or by pressing Ctrl+Ins. Once a block of text has been transferred to the Clipboard it can be inserted or pasted back into the text in a new position. All that you have to do is position the cursor where you would like the Clipboard text inserted, and select Paste from the Edit menu or press Shift+Ins. Pasting text does not clear the Clipboard which means that you can paste the same block of text as many times as you want to.

Notice that the Clipboard can only hold one block of text at a time. If you copy or cut a subsequent block of text it overwrites what is currently on the Clipboard. If you want to delete a block without transferring it to the Clipboard then select the Clear option from the Edit menu or press Del, the delete key. A trick worth knowing is that you can replace a block of text with the current contents of the Clipboard by selecting it and then pasting the new text. The paste operation automatically deletes the selected block.

It is also important to realise that the Clipboard used by QBasic and any other DOS program is not the same as the Windows Clipboard and cannot be used for transferring data between QBasic and Windows programs.

You can also make regular changes to a program via the find and replace operations in the Search menu - Search,Find and Search,Change. In each case a dialog box appears and all you have to do is fill in the text that you are searching for and, in the case of the Change operation, the text that you want to replace it, see Figure 1.7. If you want to be prompted to supply a Y/N answer before each

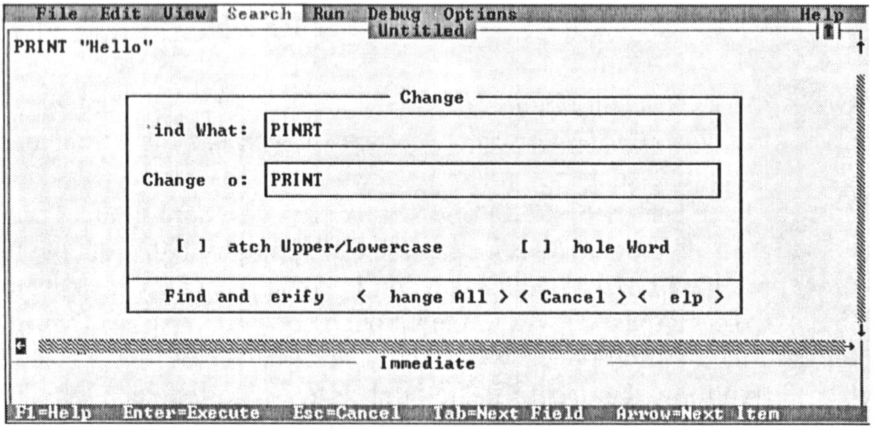

Figure 1.7
The Change dialog box

occurrence is replaced then you should click on the Find and Verify button. Selecting the Change All option will mean that every occurrence of the text will automatically be changed.

The File menu contains options for saving and printing the current file, as well as for creating a new file, opening a new document, and exiting Edit. If the New, Open or Exit options are selected before a file has been saved, a prompt will appear asking if you want to save the current file. Notice that you have to save a program if you want to use it again.

The Print option is useful if you need a paper copy of a file, but notice that only standard ASCII printers are supported and the printer has to be connected to LPT1. In practice this restriction debars only PostScript printers.

There are a small number of changes that you can make to the way that the editor works. You can change the display colours using Display in the Options menu and you can switch the scroll bars off. The only advantage of not having scroll bars is that you can display a slightly longer line. On the other hand, if you aren't using a mouse then the scroll bars are more trouble than they are worth. You can also set the size of the regular tab - i.e. the number of characters that the cursor moves when you press the Tab key.

The only other customisation option allows you to set the directory where the help files are stored - Help Path in the Options menu. If the directory in which the help files are stored in is already included in a Path command there is no need to worry about this option.

Key points

» A program is a list of instructions that can be obeyed.

» QBasic has a special set of commands that can be used to form a QBasic program.

» A program has to be entered, i.e. each instruction has to be typed in. Entering a program is not the same as running it, i.e. obeying it.

» You can enter a program using the QBasic editor which behaves much like a simple text editor. The commands in the menu bar can be accessed by holding down the Alt key while typing the highlighted letter.

» QBasic commands are entered one-per-line without the need for line numbers.

» You can run a program using the menu selection Run,Start i.e. Alt+R followed by S or by using the shortcut Shift-F5.

» While a program is running you see the output screen which is separate from the editing screen. All program output is displayed on the output screen.

» The output screen is saved while you are editing a program and restored each time you run a program.

» The QBasic editor has an extensive range of text manipulation commands including cut, copy, paste and search and replace.

» The text of a program has to saved to disk, using the menu option File,Save if you want to make use of the program at a later date. Existing programs can be loaded using File,Open.

Chapter 2
Multi-line programs

In this chapter the idea of a program is extended by increasing the number of instructions used. The important idea of a variable is also introduced.

The idea of a *variable* is the most important single idea in programming and is important that you meet and master it as soon as possible. It isn't a difficult idea and indeed after you have grown accustomed to it you will hardly notice it. So much so that many programmers are only just aware that it is an independent idea separate from other aspects of programming! If you already know about variables then spare a moment to reflect on just how important and central a concept they represent.

» What is a variable?

A variable is just a named area of memory that you can use to store data. This idea of 'named storage' isn't so unusual and it occurs in other areas of everyday life. For example, the files in a filing cabinet each have a name that indicates what is stored inside. There are a few simple and fairly obvious rules governing the names that you can give to a variable. After all, if there are two files in a filing cabinet with the same name then how can you specify exactly which one you mean? Clearly there can only be one variable with a given name in a program.

Equally obviously you cannot use names that would confuse QBasic. For example, a variable called 1 could be confused with the number 1. To avoid this problem a variable name must start with a character but after that you can use a mixture of characters and digits. Also you cannot give variables names that mean something to QBasic. For example, a variable called PRINT isn't legal. You can tell that QBASIC has recognised a variable as a keyword because the editor automatically converts it to upper case. Another way of checking is to place the cursor on the variable name and press F1. If the variable is a keyword then you will see a help screen describing it. Of course this same procedure is a good way to find out about any keywords that you are unsure of as well as checking variables.

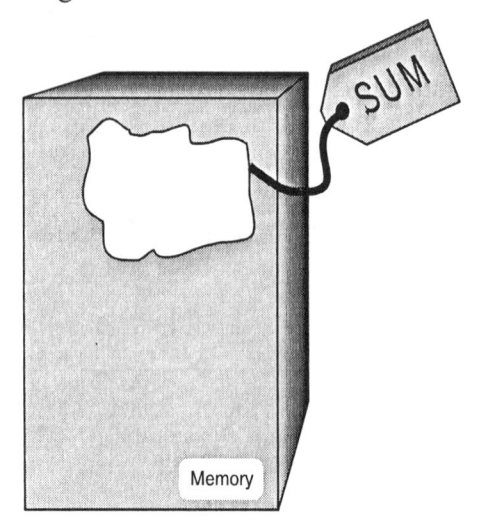

Figure 2.1
A variable is a named area of memory

In short, a QBasic variable name must start with a character, can be up to 40 characters/digits long and cannot be one of QBasic's reserved command words. You cannot include spaces in a variable name but you can use upper case characters to create names that look as if they are made up of separate words such as CostOfParts. QBasic is case insensitive, that is it treats upper and lower case characters as being the same, so you can place upper case characters where you want within a name. For example, the variable names SUM and sum; costofparts and CostOfParts are the same - as far as QBasic is concerned. If these rules for naming variables seem complicated, don't worry too much because variable naming soon becomes second nature.

» Using variables

Now that we know a little about variables and how to give them names it is time to discover how to store information in them. This can be done using the *assignment statement*. For example, the assignment:

```
SUM=56
```

will store the number 56 in an area of memory called 'SUM'. Or put another way it will assign the value 56 to the variable SUM.

If you enter this command using the editor as described in Chapter 1 then you will find that nothing happens until you give the Run,Start command. Following this the program is obeyed but there still isn't

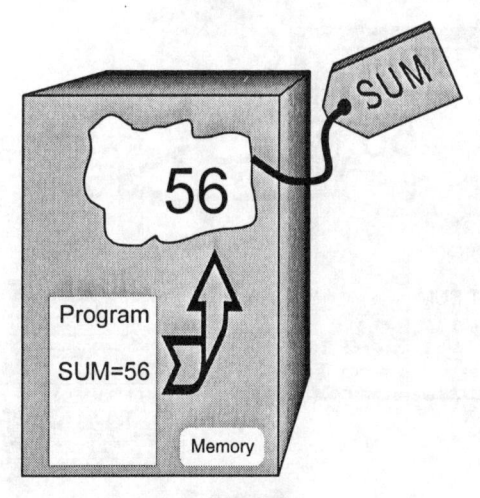

Figure 2.2
Storing 56 in SUM

much to see! As long as you enter the line correctly QBasic really will store 56 in a variable called SUM but there is no outward sign that this has occurred or worked.

Notice that for the moment it is assumed that the only type of data that a variable will store is a numeric value. Later the idea of storing different types of data in different types of variable will be introduced.

» Finding out what's in a variable - PRINT

What is needed next is some way of displaying what is stored in a variable. The PRINT command introduced in Chapter 1 will do exactly this. The instruction:

```
PRINT variablename
```

will display the current contents of the specified variable on the output screen. If you add a new line to the previous example you will have the following two line program:

```
SUM=56
PRINT SUM
```

If you enter this program and run it you will see the number 56 printed on your screen on the next free line. This should give you a little more confidence that the variable SUM really does exist and really does hold the value that you assigned to it.

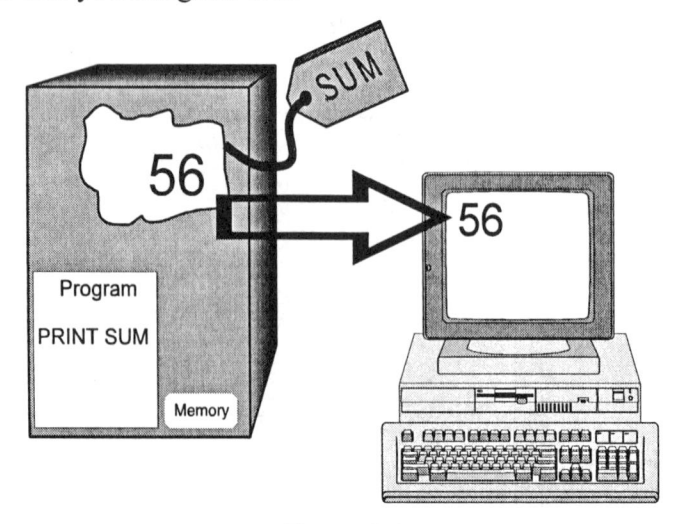

Figure 2.3
Printing SUM

» Arithmetic

Our programs are slowly becoming more interesting but they are still a long way from being useful. We can now store numbers in variables and print out what we stored in any variable but this isn't very useful. To be of any use we have to be able to change what is stored in a variable and print out something that we regard as an answer. The key to doing this lies in the idea of an *arithmetic expression*. An arithmetic expression is nothing more than a piece of arithmetic that you would like the machine to work out for you. For example, 3+6 is an arithmetic expression that works out, or evaluates, to 9. You can write an arithmetic expression on the right-hand side of the equals sign in an assignment statement with the effect that the expression will be evaluated and the result stored in the variable. For example try entering and running:

```
SUM=3+6
PRINT SUM
```

and you should see 9 printed on the screen. In this case QBasic evaluates the expression 3+6 and stores the result in SUM. The PRINT statement does what it always has and simply displays on the screen what is stored in SUM.

As with most things to do with computers, there are rules governing what makes a correct expression. You can use the four operations that you should be familiar with from simple arithmetic. Addition and subtraction are indicated by the usual symbols + and - but multiplication and division use the symbols * and /. The reason for using * to mean multiply instead of a cross is that the traditional symbol is too easy to confuse with the letter x. Some examples of correct arithmetic expressions are:

Expression	Evaluates to
3+2	5
4-3	1
3*2	6
6/2	3
2.1+3.3	5.4

Why arithmetic goes wrong - the order of evaluation

Although the idea of an arithmetic expression seems straightforward, there is a hidden complication. For example, if you write the innocent looking expression 3+2*4 does it mean "three plus two (i.e. five) times four", answer twenty, or does it mean "three plus the answer to two times four", answer eleven. It may seem strange to you that there are two possible ways to work out this expression because you may feel that one of the two methods is obviously correct and the other is equally obviously incorrect. However, the correct interpretation is a matter of convention. The question of whether we do the "+" or the "*" first in an expression like 3+2*4 is settled by a general agreement that multiplication is more important than addition and so it should be done first, making the correct answer eleven. This agreement that multiplication is more important than addition can be formalised in terms of assigning priorities to each operation and carrying out the operation with the highest priority first. The assignment of priorities can be extended to every operation that can be used in an expression (even some that we haven't met as yet). The priorities that QBasic uses to sort out the order in which arithmetic should be carried out are:

	Priority	**Examples**
- (negative)	highest	-4
^		2^3
*,/		2*3/4
+,-	lowest	3+4-2

When evaluating an expression you should always work out the operators with the highest priority first. If two operators in an expression have the same priority then you should do the one furthest to the left first (i.e. in the absence of any other preference, you work from left to right).

Another way of specifying the order of evaluation, enabling you to override the usual priorities, is to use brackets (). It is a long-standing convention that any parts of an expression enclosed in brackets are carried out first. For example, although 3+2*4 is 11, (3+2)*4 is 20. If you are in any doubt about how to evaluate an expression then put brackets around the parts that you want worked out first. Brackets sometimes waste time and effort but they can never cause trouble!

» Variables and constants

So far we have looked at arithmetic expressions involving only numbers but there is no reason why we cannot use variables and the values stored in them within expressions. If you write an expression such as:

```
SUM+3
```

QBasic will find the variable called SUM and retrieve the number stored in it. It will then add three to this number to give the result of the expression. For example, if SUM had 32 stored in it, the expression SUM+3 would evaluate to 35. Notice that there is no suggestion that what is stored in the variable SUM is in any way altered. Its contents are simply used in the evaluation of the expression. A number such as 32 is known as a *constant* (because its value never changes) and now we can see that an expression can be made up of variables and constants with the arithmetic operators + - / *. An expression always evaluates to a constant and it is this constant that is stored in a variable by an assignment statement.

To store the results of the expression SUM+3 in a variable called answer, we would write

```
ANSWER=SUM+3
```

» A short program

Using all that we have found out so far about constants, variables and expressions we can now write a short program that adds two numbers together:

```
N1 =23.34
N2 =44.32
ANSWER=N1+N2
PRINT ANSWER
```

FIRST.BAS

If you enter and run this program you will see that the sum of the two numbers in the first two lines is printed by the last line.

» The INPUT statement

In the previous example the two variables N1 and N2 had numbers stored in them by use of the assignment statement. This is convenient unless we want to use the program many times with different values. With the program as it stands the only way that it is possible to change the values stored in the variables is to edit the first two lines before running the program. Obviously, what we need is a statement that will allow us to enter any value into the variable (while the program is running). This is what the BASIC statement INPUT is for. For example, try the following program:

```
N1=5
INPUT N2
ANSWER=N1+N2
PRINT ANSWER
```

SECOND.BAS

If you enter and run this program you might be surprised by its behaviour - instead of printing out a result it prints a question mark on the screen and waits. What has happened is that the first line was carried out and 5 was stored in the variable N1 as you would expect. Then QBasic moves on to the next line where it obeys the INPUT command by waiting for you to type a number, and this is why the question mark is displayed. QBasic is waits for you to press Enter (the key marked ↵) to signal that you have finished typing the number. It then stores the number that you have typed in the variable N2 and proceeds to the next instruction. So if you haven't already done so, run the program and type a number of your choice. You will see your number plus 5 printed in the usual way.

» Input prompting

Although we can now use INPUT to store information in variables, the way that this just stops and waits for someone to type in a number is a little unsatisfactory, even allowing for the ? prompt that appears on the screen. What is required is the ability to print a message on the screen saying something like - "TYPE IN A NUMBER NOW" or "WHAT IS YOUR NUMBER". Such a message is often called an *input prompt* and QBasic provides two ways to print such messages. Try the following short program:

```
PRINT "THIS IS A PROMPT"
INPUT "WHAT IS YOUR NUMBER?",N1
```

The first line will display "THIS IS A PROMPT" on the screen, the second displays "WHAT IS YOUR NUMBER?" just below it and then waits for you to type a number. In both cases the characters printed on the screen are the ones inside the double quotation marks. A set of characters in double quotes is known as a *literal string* or simply as a *string*. You can use either PRINT or INPUT to produce prompt messages on the screen depending on which is more convenient. As an example of the use of both, consider the following version of the number addition program given earlier:

```
PRINT "WHAT IS YOUR FIRST NUMBER "
INPUT N1
INPUT "WHAT IS YOUR SECOND NUMBER?", N2
ANSWER=N1+N2
PRINT ANSWER
```

THIRD.BAS

The ability to print messages on the screen is clearly a very useful facility for other things than just printing prompts. For example, in the last program it would have been better to print a message saying that the number about to be printed was the sum of the two numbers.

Which of the two methods that you use to print prompts on the screen is a matter of choice and style. The PRINT statement is a more sophisticated way of displaying values and prompts on the screen. You can in fact use a single PRINT statement to print more than one thing at a time. For example, change the last line in the previous program to:

```
PRINT N1;" + ";N2;" = ";ANSWER
```

and you will see that the contents of N1 are printed, then a space and a plus sign, followed by another space, then the contents of N2 followed by an equals sign with a space on either side of it and the answer. You can consider this PRINT statement as a list of items to be printed, each item in the list being separated by a semi-colon and printed in the next free printing position.

> ## Print Hello and Print "Hello" a warning!
>
> Before reading on ask yourself what is the difference between
> ```
> PRINT Hello
> ```
> and
> ```
> PRINT "Hello"
> ```
> They may look similar but they have very different effects within a program, and the difference is all down to the double quotes that surround the second Hello. The double quotes make the second Hello a literal string and so PRINT "Hello" prints the word Hello on the screen exactly as it appears between the quotes. The first PRINT statement doesn't have the quotes around the Hello and so this is an instruction to print the variable called Hello. In this case what you will see displayed on the screen is a numeric value corresponding to the value currently stored in the variable Hello.
>
> You may think that this distinction is obvious - if so, all well and good because recognising the difference is second nature to a programmer. If you are in the least bit doubtful about the difference re-read this chapter, try out the programs and experiment until you are sure that the difference really is obvious.

The general definition of PRINT can now be updated to read:
```
PRINT print list
```
where *print list* is a list of items, variable names or literal strings, separated by semi-colons.

It is also worth knowing that each PRINT statement starts printing on a new line. So the difference between:
```
PRINT A;B
```
and:
```
PRINT A
PRINT B
```
is that the first prints both values on one line and the second prints each value on a new line. How to control output more accurately will be described in later chapters.

» The estate agent's problem

Even with just the three QBasic statements that you already know you can start to tackle some simple problems. Consider, for example, the estate agent's problem of working out the size of a room in square feet and, for the sake of EEC harmonisation, in square metres. If the estate agent has only a tape measuring feet and inches then working out the area in square feet is simply a matter of multiplying the width of the room by its length. Converting from square feet to square metres is simply a matter of using the appropriate conversion factor.

At this point it is worth making the point that programming is just a matter of writing down in an exact form what you already know how to do. It certainly cannot solve any problem that you yourself cannot solve. In this case if you do not know how to work out the area of a room in square feet or have no idea what the conversion factor from square feet to square metres is then you cannot write the program - no matter how good a programmer you are! To save you looking up the conversion factor in a book, .092903 square metre equals 1 square foot.

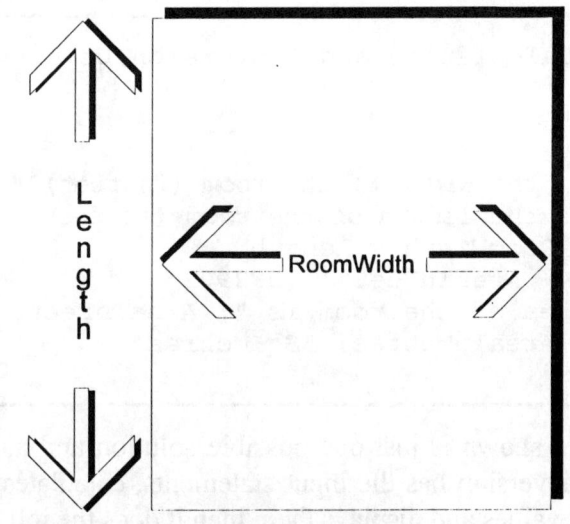

Area in feet= RoomWidth * Length
Area in metres = RoomWidth * Length * 0.092903

Figure 2.4
The estate agent's program

In tackling real problems you very quickly discover that much of the art of programming is being able to look things up in books!

At this point you should have a reasonably clear idea in your mind what the program has to do. It has to get two values, the room width and the room length, multiply these together to get the area in square feet and then multiply this by the conversion factor of .092903. You should now try to write this program before looking at the solution supplied below. One word of warning - don't use a variable called WIDTH, the reason is explained after we have looked at the program.

The program is fairly easy but notice that there is plenty of opportunity for elaboration. For example, the first four PRINT statements do nothing but print a totally unnecessary title. The real work of the program is done by the two input statements which prompt the user for the values needed and the two assignment statements which work out the results. At the end of the program all that is necessary is to print the answer. If your program doesn't look like the following example then don't worry because the chances are that it is still correct. There are as many ways to write a program as there are programmers willing to try.

```
PRINT "Area Calculation and Conversion Utility Program"
PRINT
PRINT "ACCUP"
PRINT "*****"
INPUT "What is the width of the room (in feet)?", RoomWidth
INPUT "What is the length of the room (in feet)?", Length
AreaInFeet = RoomWidth * Length
AreaInMetres = AreaInFeet * .092903
PRINT "The area of the room is "; AreaInFeet; "Sq Ft"
PRINT "or "; AreaInMetres; "Sq Metres"
```

The example shown is just one possible solution and as long as your version has the input statements, calculates the required values and displays them then it does the job. You can add the embellishments later!

ESTATE.BAS

The estate agent's problem

There are two points worth making about the example. The first is what does the second PRINT statement do - the one without anything to print? An empty PRINT statement simply leaves a blank line and this is very useful when you are trying to format a screen display.

The second is why are the two variables used called RoomWidth and Length and not just Width and Length? The reason is that Width is a QBasic reserved word. The main problem with this is that if you do use Width as a variable name the error message that you get isn't particularly informative - "Expected: # or LPRINT or expression or ,". The reason why this message seems cryptic in the extreme is that it is giving you information about how you have misused the WIDTH command rather than telling you that you have accidentally used a reserved word as a variable name! Error messages usually tell you about the nature of the error, it's just that it is not always the error that you have actually made!

The solution in this case is to find another name for the variable and RoomWidth (as a single word) will do very nicely.

Finally, you might like to notice how the final pair of PRINT statements produce a nicely formatted display on the screen with the numeric results embedded in the messages. Even simple programs can be polished.

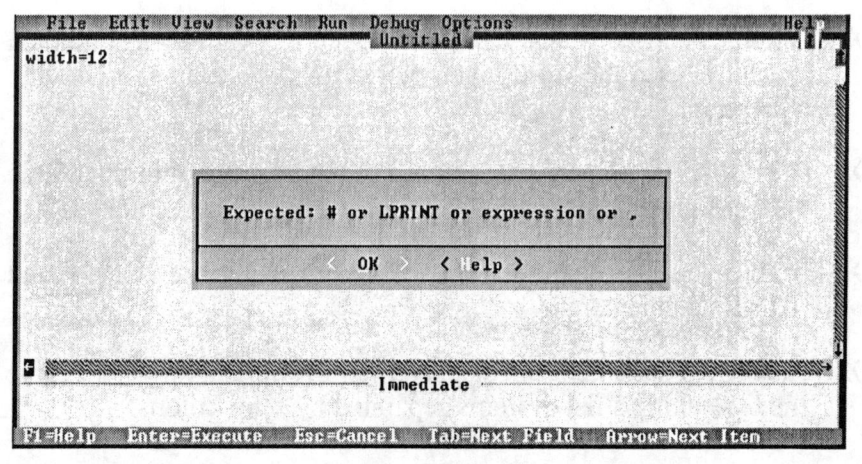

Figure 2.5
How to misuse the Width statement without even trying!

Key points

» A variable is a named area of memory that can be used to store and retrieve an item of data.

» A variable name has to start with a character and have no more than 40 characters or digits in total. Upper and lower case letters may be used to improve readability but otherwise have no effect on the meaning of a name. A variable name cannot be any of the QBasic reserved words such as PRINT or INPUT.

» Data can be stored in a variable using the assignment statement.

» The value stored in a variable can be displayed on the screen using the PRINT statement.

» Results can be worked out using arithmetic expressions consisting of values, variables and arithmetic operators.

» Expressions are evaluated by working out operations in order of their priority. Priorities can be overridden by using brackets to enclose sections of the expression that should be evaluated first.

» The result of an expression can be assigned to a variable using the assignment statement.

» Variables and constants can be included in expressions. When a variable is used the value that is stored in it is used to work out the expression.

» The INPUT statement can be used to read a value into a variable when the program is running.

» Prompts can be displayed on the screen using the INPUT and PRINT statements.

» The PRINT statement can display a number of items all on the same line by making a list of items separated by semi-colons.

Chapter 3

The Flow of Control

Repeating actions and making choices based on input are the basic building blocks of any program. In this chapter the idea of the flow of control is introduced, along with the commands needed to change it.

Programming is the creation of lists of instructions that are precise enough for even the most dimwitted of computers to obey without mishap. Although we are all used to reading and creating lists of instructions these lists generally lack the character of a program. The reason is simply that they are usually "start at the top and work your way to the end" lists of instructions. Programs, and lists of instructions in general, can be more sophisticated than this in that they can include instructions like "only do this part if..." or "repeat steps 2,3 and 4 until..." which tell you how to use or implement other instructions in the list. This is much more like programming and the ability to create such sophisticated lists of instructions is the hallmark of a programmer.

» The flow of control

At any given moment while a program is running the computer will be obeying a particular instruction. There is a sense in which this instruction is controlling the computer and you can think of this 'control' being passed from instruction to instruction as the program progresses. The way in which control moves through a program is called the *flow of control*. The simplest programs that you can write only use the default flow of control which follows a top to bottom order in the same way that you might read a shopping list. Such programs are very limited and most programmers quickly move on to more complicated flows of control.

Within a program there are only two types of change that can be made to the default flow of control:

» You can repeat a group of instructions, so forming a loop

» You can select between a number of alternative groups of instructions

The important point is that -

» all programs are made up of the default flow of control combined with repetition and selection and there are no other possibilities.

» The infinite loop - DO and LOOP

If you were asked to write a program that printed the word Hello on the screen over and over again then you would find this difficult using only the commands introduced in Chapters 1 and 2. The best you could do would be to write a long list of PRINT "Hello" commands. For example, the program:

```
PRINT "Hello"
PRINT "Hello"
PRINT "Hello"
```

will print Hello on the screen three times and you can carry on adding PRINT "Hello" commands in this way. However, this program doesn't really embody the idea of repeating the same instruction over and over again. What we need is some way of being able to write "repeat this section of program".

The simplest way of repeating a section of program is to place it between a pair of DO and LOOP commands. For example:

```
DO
   PRINT "Hello"
LOOP
```

will repeat the PRINT "Hello" instruction over and over again. You can halt it by pressing Ctrl-Break - otherwise it will repeat forever, or until you restart your PC whichever is sooner.

This sort of repetition is generally referred to as an *infinite loop*. You can place any list of QBasic instructions between DO and LOOP and they will be repeated over and over again. In this sense the DO and LOOP commands can be thought of as brackets which enclose the section of program to be repeated. The DO is like an opening bracket which marks the start of the program section to be repeated and the LOOP is like the closing bracket.

» Indenting

To make the part of the program within the loop stand out clearly it is worthwhile following the convention of *indenting*. Program indents are used rather like paragraphs in ordinary text to show which instructions form a natural group. If you indent, by pressing the Tab key, when you start a loop, i.e. following a DO command, and then take the indent off when you finish a loop, i.e. just before the LOOP command, you will be able to see at a glance the instructions that are repeated.

The QBasic editor makes indenting easy because, once you have moved to a starting point on a line, subsequent lines start at the same point, i.e. they have the same indent. To clear the indent all you have to do is move the cursor, use the backspace key or press Shift+Tab which removes all of the spaces at the start of the current line. You may also find it useful to alter the default tab settings from 8 to 5 or fewer

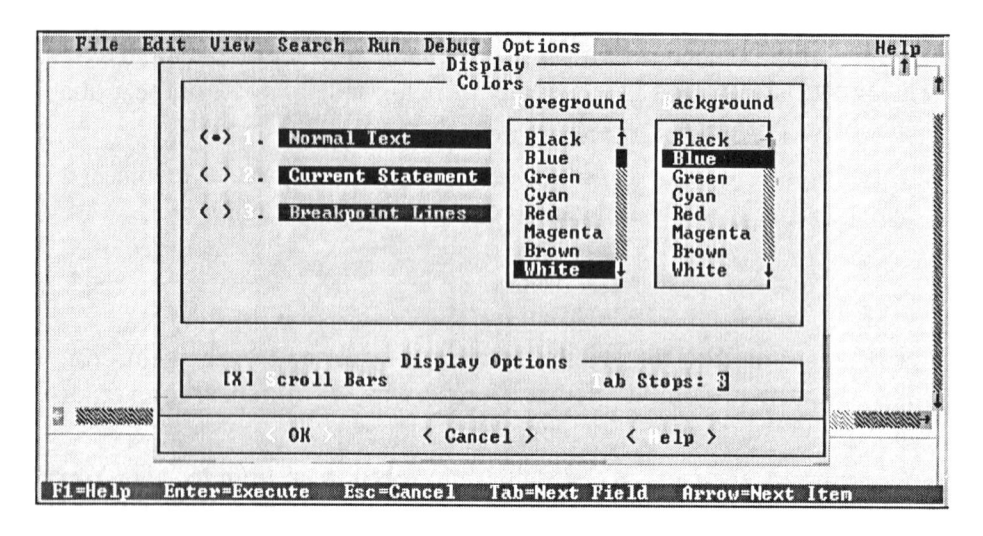

Figure 3.1
Changing the tab settings

characters. To do this use the menu command Options,Display and then fill in the desired tab value in the Display Options dialog box - see Figure 3.1.

» Getting out of a loop - EXIT

The infinite loop is certainly the fundamental form of loop but it is clearly of very limited practical use! Rather than repeating some set of actions forever, what is normally required is a controlled repetition that stops when some condition is satisfied. For example, if you are painting a room you might repeat the application of a complete coat of paint until you decide that the old colour has been covered. Such a repetition is called a *conditional loop* and it is typical of the "repeat until some condition is satisfied" type of loop. The QBasic instruction for leaving a loop when some condition is satisfied is:

```
IF condition THEN EXIT DO
```

where *condition* is a logical condition that can be evaluated to TRUE or FALSE.

Using this command the room painting example could be written:
```
DO
   paint room
IF old colour is covered THEN EXIT DO
LOOP
```
Each time through the loop the room would be painted and the test for covering the old paint would be made. If the old colour has been covered the condition is true and the repetition ends. If the old colour hasn't been covered the condition is false and the loop repeats again. Of course this conditional loop isn't QBasic because the instruction "paint room" and the condition "old colour is covered" aren't valid QBasic commands but the idea is correct.

In the case of QBasic, the condition has to be something that can be easily evaluated involving comparisons between values such as A=10 or PAY>LIMIT. If the condition is TRUE then the loop is terminated and execution of the program continues with the instruction that follows the LOOP command - i.e. the first instruction outside the loop. For example, the following program will print out the greeting "Hello" until the user responds with a 0 to the question "Again?"
```
DO
   PRINT "Hello"
   INPUT "Again (Yes=1/No=0)",A
IF A=0 THEN EXIT DO
LOOP
   PRINT "Program over!"
```
LOOP1.BAS

The important point about this program is that the instructions within the loop - PRINT and INPUT - are repeated until the condition A=0 is true and then control passes out of the loop to the final PRINT statement.

» Thinking about loops

If you are just starting to program then it is worth knowing how most programmers think about loops. If you follow the flow of control through a program with your finger, as you once did when you were learning to read, then you will see drawn out the basic shapes that every programmer uses to build programs. For a section of program that contains no loops the flow of control passes from each instruction down the list and the shape of the default flow of control is a straight line. If you trace through a section of code containing an infinite loop then the path that your finger follows is a continuous looping motion. A conditional loop is the same but when the condition is true the flow of control jumps out of the loop and passes on to the rest of the program. You can think of each of these paths through the program as a sort of software equivalent of railway lines and even draw them as railway line diagrams - see Figure 3.2.

Default flow of control

Infinite loop

Conditional loop

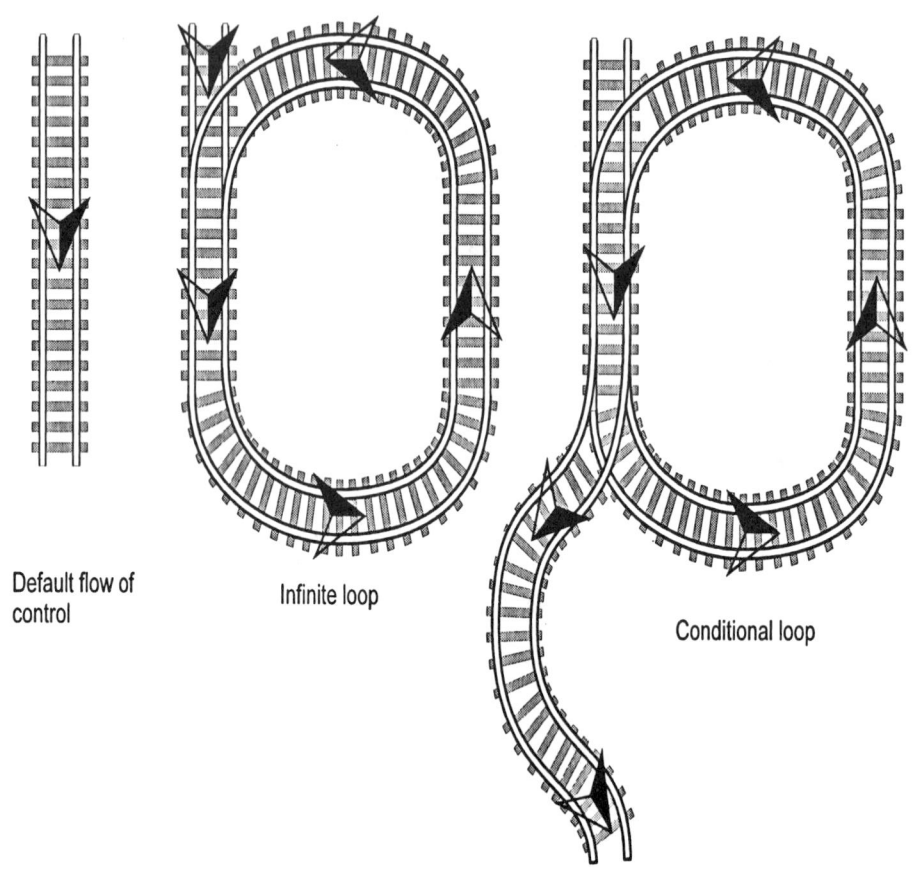

Figure 3.2
Railway diagrams

The WHILE-WEND loop
(and a note for users of other languages)

Other languages, including other dialects of Basic, offer a slightly different range of facilities for forming loops from that in QBasic. Languages such as Pascal offer the programmer two type of loop; the REPEAT - UNTIL loop and the WHILE - WEND loop. These essentially confuse the two aspects of loop specification - where the exit point is and the sense of the exit point, i.e. exit if true or exit if false. The REPEAT - UNTIL condition loop has its exit point at the end of the loop and the condition has to be true for the loop to end. The WHILE condition - WEND loop has its exit point at the start and the condition has to be true for the loop to continue. Thus older languages do not give you the freedom to choose between specifying a termination condition or a continuation condition for both types of loop. QBasic, for compatibility, allows you to use:

```
WHILE condition
    statements
WEND
```

to mean the same thing as:

```
DO WHILE condition
   statements
LOOP
```

If you need to be compatible with other dialects of Basic then use only WHILE and WEND to form loops. On the other hand, if compatibility isn't something you are interested in, there seems to be no good reason to use WHILE-WEND as opposed to the more general and more powerful DO-LOOP command.

Notice that QBasic doesn't support an explicit REPEAT-UNTIL loop but:

```
DO
    statements
LOOP UNTIL condition
```

does exactly the same job.

» UNTIL and WHILE

You can place the exit point from a loop at any position within the loop using the EXIT statement. However, you will often find that the natural place to leave a loop is either just at the start or just at the end of the block of code to be repeated. Such loops are simple because all of the instructions that make up the body of the loop are executed the same number of times. (This should be contrasted to a loop with an exit point somewhere in the middle where the instructions before the exit point will be carried out once more than the instructions following the exit point.) As leaving a loop at the beginning or at the end is such a common requirement, QBasic allows exit conditions to be written as part of the DO and the LOOP statements. It also gives you a choice of specifying whether the condition has to be true for the loop to stop or true for the loop to continue. If you want the loop to continue as long as the condition is true then use:

```
WHILE condition
```

If you want the loop to stop as soon as the condition is true then use:

```
UNTIL condition
```

That is, the WHILE condition is a continuation condition and the UNTIL condition is a termination condition. For example, the previous loop can be written:

```
DO
   PRINT "Hello"
   INPUT "Again (Yes=1 No=0)",A
LOOP UNTIL A=0
PRINT "Program over!"
```

LOOP2.BAS

The only difference between WHILE and UNTIL is that the first type of loop continues WHILE the condition is true and in the other type it continues UNTIL the condition is true. So, you could write the above loop as:

```
DO
   PRINT "Hello"
   INPUT "Again (Yes=1 No=0)",A
LOOP WHILE A=1
PRINT "Program over!"
```

LOOP3.BAS

This is a very convenient method of forming loops and it is a great improvement over traditional Basic and most other languages.

Remember:

》 a WHILE condition has to be TRUE for the loop to CONTINUE

》 and an UNTIL condition has to be TRUE for the loop to END.

» Exit points

Although the use of WHILE and UNTIL are easy enough to use to control the way a loop stops, the effect of their positioning either at the start or the end of the loop is slightly more subtle. If you place an exit point at the start of a loop then it is possible that the exit condition could be true before any instructions in the body of the loop are executed. In other words an exit point at the start of the loop means that it is possible that the loop may never be executed at all. In contrast a loop with an exit point at the end has to carry out the instructions in the body of the loop at least once. For example compare the two loops given below:

```
Loop 1              Loop 2
I=0                 I=0
DO UNTIL I=0        DO
   PRINT I             PRINT I
LOOP                LOOP UNTIL I=0
```

in both cases the condition for the loop to terminate is I=0 but Loop 1 terminates at once and you never see I printed out, while Loop 2 terminates after the instructions in the loop have been obeyed once, and so you do see the value of I printed out.

In practice it is not too difficult to decide whether a loop should have its exit point at the start or the finish. Just ask yourself what should happen if the exit condition is satisfied before the loop is even started - if the loop should still be obeyed once then place the exit condition at the end, otherwise place it at the start. Loop construction soon becomes second nature and you don't have to think about it too hard.

» Counting - the simple FOR loop

The DO - LOOP command is a universal form of loop in the sense that you can build any and every type of loop using it. However, there is one type of loop that is so common that nearly all computer languages make special provision for it - the counting or *enumeration* loop. The types of loop that we have been looking at so far are general conditional loops - they repeat until a condition is satisfied. An enumeration loop is a little more specialised in that it repeats a fixed number of times. An enumeration loop is clearly a special case of a conditional loop in that the condition is simply 'exit when the loop has been done *n* times'. To write this in QBasic all you need to do is to use a variable that counts the number of times the loop has been executed. For example, to print the word Hello five times on the screen use:

```
C=0
DO UNTIL C=5
   C=C+1
   PRINT "Hello"
LOOP
```

LOOP4.BAS

Each time through this loop one is added to C and so the condition C=5 is met when the loop has repeated five times.

As has already been mentioned, this sort of loop is so common that most programming languages provide a special way of writing it, the FOR-NEXT, or just FOR loop. A FOR loop still uses a counter but incrementing it each time round the loop and testing for the final value is done automatically. The general form of the simplest type of FOR loop is:

```
FOR index=start TO finish
   statements
NEXT index
```

where *index* is the variable used to count each time round the loop. For example, to print Hello five times you would use:

```
FOR C=1 TO 5
   PRINT "HELLO"
NEXT C
```

FOR.BAS

C=C+1

If you are new to programming then you might be a little worried by the assignment C=C+1 because the variable C occurs on both sides. How can C be both C and one more than itself!?

As long as you have the idea of a variable and the way that assignment works then you should have no problems understanding this. It is an instruction to retrieve the contents of the variable C, add one to it and then store this result back in C. That is, each time the assignment is executed the value stored in C is increased by one. From this point you should be able to see how this results in C 'counting' the number of times a loop has been executed.

Always remember that an assignment works out the value on the right-hand side and then stores this value in the variable specified on the left-hand side.

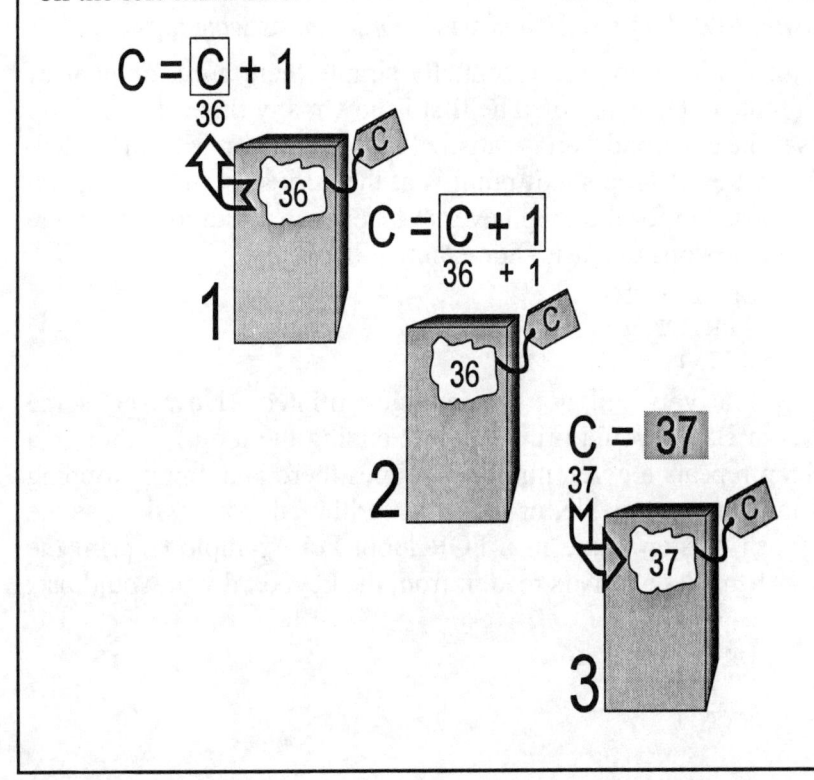

The meaning of this loop is clear from its English reading - that is, the loop is performed for values of C from 1 to 5. This is entirely equivalent to the previous DO - LOOP which printed HELLO five times but it is simpler. The value of C really does vary from 1 to 5 as you can see if you change the PRINT statement to PRINT C. In most cases the value of the index variable is actually used during a loop to perform some calculation or other as, for example, in the following routine to print a table of squares:

```
FOR I=1 TO 10
   PRINT I*I
NEXT I
```

» Finer details of FOR loops

This section tells you about some of the subtler points of using a FOR loop that often lead to mistakes - come back to it again when you have been using FOR loops sufficiently to appreciate its warnings.

Although the FOR loop is essentially simple there are a number of subtle points to be aware of. The first is how many times a FOR loop repeats if the exit condition is satisfied before the loop is even started. In QBasic a FOR loop's exit point is at the very start of the loop, so that it is possible for the loop never to be executed, but this is not the case in all versions of Basic. For example if you try:

```
FOR I=1 TO 0
   PRINT I
NEXT I
```

using QBasic you will not see anything printed. (However, some versions of Basic would print 1 before ending the loop.) Although a FOR loop repeats a given number of times there is nothing stopping you from using a variable, or indeed an arithmetic expression, as the start, finish or step value in a FOR loop. For example to print the numbers 1 to N where N is read in from the keyboard you would use:

```
INPUT N
FOR I=1 TO N
   PRINT I
NEXT I
```

This is easy enough and doesn't go against the basic idea of the FOR loop because the number of times that the loop is to repeat is still known before the loop actually begins. However, sooner or later, by accident or design, you are likely to write something like:

```
INPUT N
FOR N=1 TO N
   PRINT N
NEXT N
```

Does this work in the same way as the first example?. The answer is yes, because all of the values that control the loop are stored away somewhere safe when the loop starts, with the result that you can use or alter the value of variables such as N without altering the way the loop behaves. However, even though this sort of thing works it can hardly be said to be clear and it is best avoided.

Of course the one loop variable that you cannot change during a loop is the index variable itself. In other words, in a loop like:

```
FOR I=1 TO 10
   . . .
NEXT I
```

It is always wrong to make any changes to the the variable I inside the loop. Putting this another way - you can use I on the right-hand side of an assignment but never on the left. If you change the value of the index variable then the loop will loose track of how many times it has been around!

» Step

Although the simple FOR loop suits most situations there are times when it would be nice if the index variable counted the loop execution in some other way then 1,2, 3 or whatever. Sometimes it would be nice if the index variable counted down - e.g. 10, 9, 8 ... and so on - instead of up. Notice that this doesn't alter the role of the index variable, it still counts the number of times the loop is carried out, it just alters the way the loop is counted.

What all this means is that it would be an advantage to be able to set the amount added to the index variable each time through the loop from the default of one to some other value - and this exactly what STEP allows you to do.

To set the amount added to the index variable each time through the loop to x use:

```
FOR index=start TO finish STEP x
```

For example,

```
FOR I=2 TO 8 STEP 2
    PRINT I
NEXT I
```

will print out 2, 4, 6, 8 because I starts with an initial value of 2 and goes up in steps of 2 until it reaches the final value 8. You can create FOR loops in which the amount added each time through the loop is anything you want it to be - just set the increment using STEP.

» When does a loop finish?

The STEP command introduces a new problem in that it is now possible that the values of the index variable will not include the final value. For example, when does the FOR loop below end?

```
FOR I=2 TO 7 STEP 2
    PRINT I
NEXT I
```

It can't be when I equals 7 because the index variable can only be an even value (starting at 2 and going up in steps of 2 implies that the index is always even!) The answer to this problem is that the index value never becomes bigger than the specified final value. That is, the values printed by the loop in question are 2, 4, 6 but not 8 because that is bigger than 7. Thus a FOR loop with STEP is exactly the same as:

```
DO UNTIL index>final value
    statements
    index=index+step
LOOP
```

In other words, a FOR loop will repeat for values of the index that are smaller than or equal to the specified final value - but never for those that are bigger than it.

» Negative steps

Now consider this rule applied to a loop with a negative step, which is perfectly reasonable:

```
FOR I=10 TO 1 STEP -1
    PRINT I
NEXT I
```

This prints 10,9,8...1. Notice, however, that it breaks the ending condition because the first value that the index I is set to, 10, is already larger than the final value of 1 and so the loop should end immediately!

To make negative steps useful the rule is extended to be that the index in a loop with a negative step never gets smaller than the final value. This change in the exit condition depending on whether the step is positive or negative may seem complicated, but in practice it corresponds to what you would expect the loop to do. If you consider the index variable starting with the initial value and approaching the final value every time that the step size is added to it then the general loop ending rule is that the index value never 'passes' the final value.

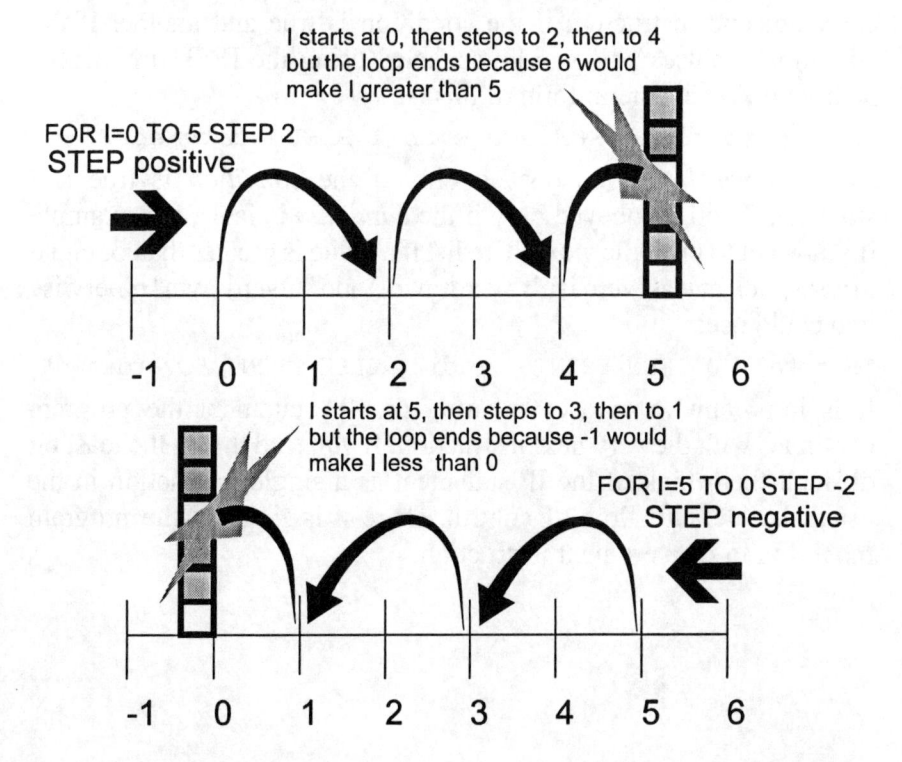

I starts at 0, then steps to 2, then to 4 but the loop ends because 6 would make I greater than 5

FOR I=0 TO 5 STEP 2
STEP positive

-1 0 1 2 3 4 5 6

I starts at 5, then steps to 3, then to 1 but the loop ends because -1 would make I less than 0

FOR I=5 TO 0 STEP -2
STEP negative

-1 0 1 2 3 4 5 6

» Making choices - simple IF

There are many occasions during a program when you want to do different things depending on a condition. For example, if you want to print out the word "Overdrawn" if a value is less than zero then you would use:

```
IF total<0 THEN PRINT "Overdrawn"
```

This IF statement is so close to the English that its meaning is clear. You can use a range of conditions based on comparing values using the following symbols:

```
=    equal to
>    greater than
>=   greater than or equal to
<    less than
<=   less than or equal to
<>   not equal to
```

If the condition is true then the instruction following the THEN will be obeyed and control will be passed on to the next instruction. Sometimes this simple IF statement is not enough because we want to carry out one instruction if the condition is true and another if the condition is false. This can be achieved using the IF..THEN..ELSE instruction. The general form of this is:

```
IF condition THEN statement1 ELSE statement2
```

and *statement1* will be obeyed only if the *condition* is true and *statement2* will be obeyed only if the *condition* is false. For example if you want to print the word "Credit" if a value is greater than or equal to zero (well at least zero isn't overdrawn!) and "Overdrawn" otherwise you could use:

```
IF total>=0 THEN PRINT "Credit" ELSE PRINT "Overdrawn"
```

It is important to realise that after the IF statement the program continues with the very next instruction. If you find this in the least bit difficult then think of the IF statement as a single instruction in the usual, i.e. default, flow of control. Once it is finished the program moves on to the very next instruction.

» The block IF

The only trouble with the IF..THEN and IF..THEN..ELSE statements described above is that you can only put one instruction after either THEN or ELSE. In traditional Basic the solution to this problem is to put commands together on one line using a colon to separate them. For example:

```
IF total>=0 THEN PRINT "Credit":C=1 ELSE PRINT "Overdrawn":C=-1
```

will print Credit and set C to one if the condition is true and print Overdrawn and set C to minus 1 is the condition is false. This grouping of instructions using the colon isn't very practical because the line soon gets too long to read easily.

Fortunately QBasic introduces an extended form of the IF command called a block IF. The general form of the block IF is:

```
IF condition THEN
   statement1
   statement2
      . . .
ELSE
   statementA
   statementB
      . . .
END IF
```

The group of statements following the THEN are obeyed only if the *condition* is true, and the group of statements following the ELSE are obeyed only if the *condition* is false. Notice that a statement must not be on the same line as THEN, that the list of statements following the THEN is terminated by ELSE, and that the list of statements following the ELSE is terminated by END IF. Using the block IF the previous example can be written as:

```
INPUT total
IF total>=0 THEN
  PRINT "Credit"
  C=1
ELSE
  PRINT "Overdrawn"
  C=-1
END IF
```

There is an IF..THEN form of the block IF that can be used whenever you need to carry out a list of instructions when a condition is true but just go on with the rest of the program if it is false. i.e. you don't actually need an ELSE part.

For example:

```
IF total>0 THEN
   PRINT "Credit"
   C=1
END IF
```

Notice that you still need to use END IF to mark the end of the block IF. This is completely equivalent to:

```
IF total>0 THEN
   PRINT "Credit"
   C=1
ELSE
END IF
```

Where nothing following the ELSE is taken to mean "do nothing" if the condition is false.

As in the case of the simple IF and the IF..THEN..ELSE it is very important that you are entirely clear about when each block of instructions is actually carried out. The IF and END IF mark out the start and end of a region of your program which will be obeyed according to the state of the condition that you specify. Once the block IF is completed your program carries on with the instruction following the END IF as normal. If it helps, think of the everything from the IF to the END IF as a single instruction in the default flow of control.

The block IF is a much more powerful and a much clearer way of expressing a program than the traditional Basic IF statement and unless you need to be compatible with these older forms, it is strongly recommended that you use this form of the IF statement as standard. Notice the use of indenting of the statements between THEN and ELSE and ELSE and END IF. This is entirely optional but it does help to mark out the different parts of the IF statement within a program and so makes it even easier to understand.

There are more advanced versions of the IF statement but these aren't commonly used and are described in Chapter 9.

» The shape of an IF

Just as the default flow of control is a straight line and a LOOP is a loop, so the IF statement has a characteristic shape associated with it. If you follow the flow of control through an IF..THEN..ELSE statement then the condition controls which of two possible routes through the program is taken. This is very much like a railway diagram with a set of points selecting which of two branch lines are used - see Figure 3.3.

This two-way split is typical of commands that make selections. It doesn't take much imagination to see that the same sort of diagram results from three-, four- and multi-way splits.

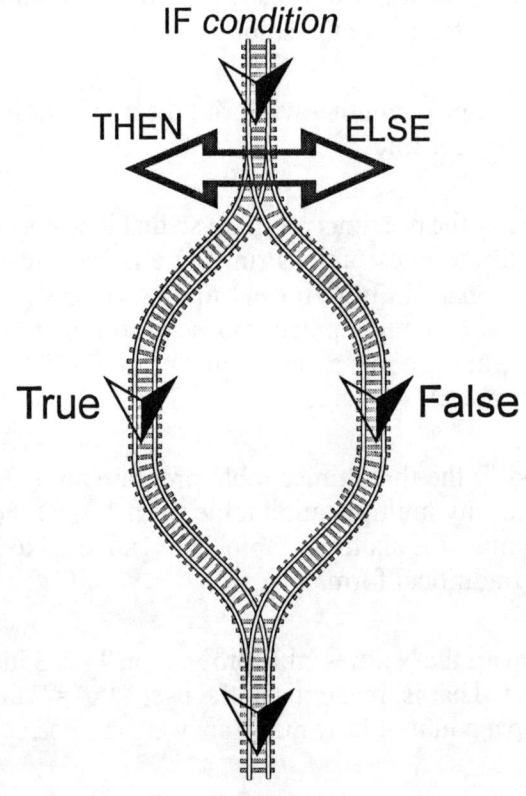

Figure 3.3
Railway diagram for IF..THEN..ELSE

» Five easy pieces

To help you come to terms with the ideas expressed in this and previous chapters you might like to try the following five practice pieces. Just like piano practice pieces they don't really do anything exciting but they are still worth having a go at. Look back at the earlier examples if you need some ideas and then compare your results with the suggested solutions.

Don't worry if your solutions aren't exactly the same as those presented here - there are many ways to write the same program. Try to compare your solutions with the suggested ones and to see how they differ. You may discover that your way was better. The important thing is to make sure that you understand why the solution works.

1. Write a program that will print the numbers 1 to 12, one per line.

2. Modify the previous program so that it prints out the three times table. Print the answers in the traditional "1x3=3" format in a table down the screen. (For this piece you need to remember the purpose of a semi-colon in a PRINT statement.)

3. Modify the three times table program so that it prints any multiplication table from 1 to M. For example, the six times table from 1x6 to 15x6 in the traditional format.

4. Convert the N times table program in Task 3 into a test. That is, make it ask the user "1x4=?" and keep a count of how many answers are correct.

5. Write a short program that counts down, 10, 9, 8... and when it reaches 0 prints "BANG!"

» Suggested solution 1

Doing anything 12 times should immediately suggest the use of a FOR loop. After you have worked that out the rest is easy:

```
FOR i=1 TO 12
   PRINT i
NEXT i
```

EASY1.BAS

» Suggested solution 2

To print the three times table all we need is the result of i*3 suitably formatted:

```
FOR i=1 TO 12
   ans=3*i
   PRINT i;"x 3 =";ans
NEXT i
```

EASY2.BAS

The only tricky part is the PRINT statement which should make sense if you study it.

» Suggested solution 3

In this case you have to get two pieces of information from the user, which table and where it should finish:

```
INPUT "Which table ",N
INPUT "Last value ",M
FOR i=1 TO M
   ans=N*i
   PRINT i;"x ";N;" =";ans
NEXT i
```

EASY3.BAS

Notice the way that the variable M now controls the end value of the loop and the way the variable N has replaced the constant 3. If you want to make a program more flexible you should use variables instead of constants. Also notice the way that the PRINT statement has changed to accommodate printing the value of N.

» Suggested solution 4

This is the most difficult of the problems in that it involves input, loops and IF statements. The FOR loop of the earlier example is clearly sufficient to generate each question and all we need to do is get the answer and count the number which are correct.

```
INPUT "Which table",N
INPUT "Last value",M
correct=0
FOR i=1 TO M
   ans=N*i
   PRINT i;"x ";N;" =?"
   INPUT answer
   IF ans=answer THEN correct=correct+1
NEXT i
PRINT "You got ";correct;" right out of ";M
```

EASY4.BAS

Notice the use of the variable correct to count the number of correct answers. It is set to zero in the third line and then has one added to it by the IF statement whenever the user-supplied answer is equal to ans, the calculated answer. Notice also the change to the PRINT statement to make it ask a question. If you are a beginner you may have been slightly confused by the idea of including the IF statement within the loop, but why not as it has to be repeated for each question? If you would like to improve on this example try changing it so that it tells the user when the answer is incorrect and supplies the correct answer.

» Suggested solution 5

Once again the fact that you have to do something a given number of times suggests a FOR loop but this time with a negative increment, i.e. a decrement! The program is simply:

```
FOR i=10 TO 0 STEP -1
   PRINT i
NEXT i
PRINT "Bang"
```

EASY5.BAS

The only possibility for confusion here is that you might have thought that some kind of IF statement was necessary to detect when to print Bang. It isn't, because when the loop reaches 0 it ends anyway!

» An example - The bubble sort

The program given below sorts a list of numbers into order using a method known as a *bubble sort*. It illustrates all the types of control described in this chapter - conditional loop, FOR loop and block IF - but it also uses some ideas - arrays and random numbers - that are not discussed until later chapters. This is unavoidable because it is next to impossible to come up with a convincing example using just the statements introduced so far. Therefore the best approach to understanding this example is to read it through and try to follow it at a reasonably superficial level and then return to it later. Indeed this is good advice that applies to the reading of any book on computing!

Sorting is one of the most interesting and important topics in computing and there are a wide variety of methods that you can use. Bubble sort has the advantage of being easy to understand, quick to program but it is not particularly quick in its operation. That is, there are better methods of sorting but none simpler!

The basic principle of a bubble sort is to perform a scan of the list of numbers comparing adjacent values and swapping them over if they are in the wrong order. For example, a scan of the list 3,1,4,2 can be seen in Figure 3.4. The result of a single scan is 1,3,2,4 - not a completely sorted list but more in order than it was. The idea of a bubble sort is to repeat this scan on the list until it is completely sorted into order. In the case of our example a second scan - see Figure 3.4 - produces a sorted list but in a more general example additional scans may be necessary before the list is sorted.

You should be able to see that our program is going to be along the following lines (expressed in a cross between Basic and English):

```
DO
  scan list   IF adjacent numbers are in the wrong order THEN
              swap positions
              END IF
LOOP UNTIL the list is sorted
```

The only problem is how do you know when the list is sorted? The answer is that if the list is sorted you can make a complete scan through the list without making a single swap.

First scan

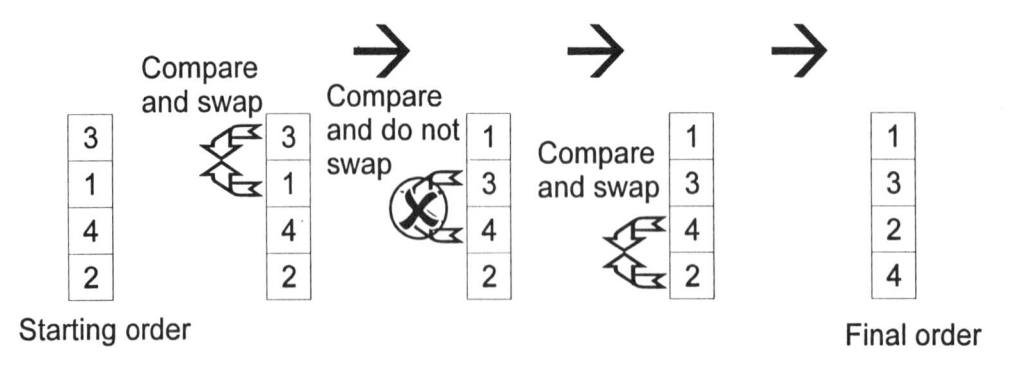

[Starting order: 3,1,4,2] → Compare and swap → [3,1,4,2 with 3,1 swapping to 1,3] → Compare and do not swap → [1,3,4,2] → Compare and swap → [1,3,4,2 with 4,2 swapping] → [Final order: 1,3,2,4]

Second and final scan

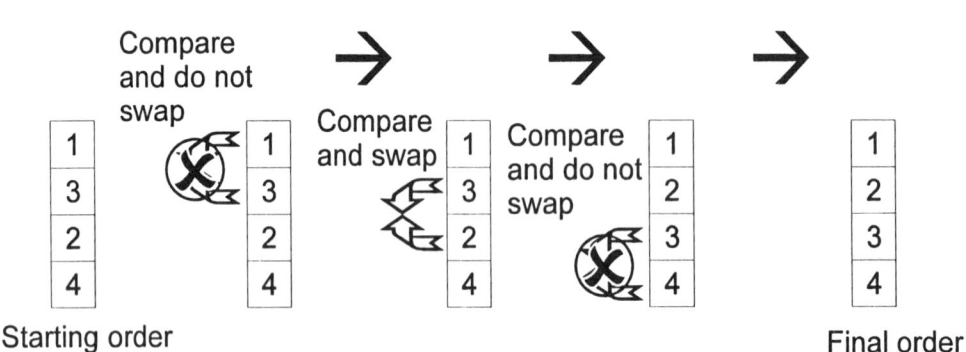

[Starting order: 1,3,2,4] → Compare and do not swap → [1,3,2,4] → Compare and swap → [1,3,2,4 with 3,2 swapping] → Compare and do not swap → [1,2,3,4] → [Final order: 1,2,3,4]

Figure 3.4
Sorting by swapping

If we use a variable - notsort say - and set it to 0 before the scan and to 1 if a swap occurs then notsort will equal 0 if list is sorted and 1 if it isn't. The use of a variable in this way is called a *flag* and it is one of the tricks of the trade that all programmers use. We can now write our program as:

```
DO
notsort=0
scan list   IF adjacent numbers are in the wrong
order THEN
            swap portions
            notsort=1
         END IF
LOOP UNTIL notsort=1
```

An example - The bubble sort

The next step in completing the program is to change 'scan list' and the IF statement into correct QBasic. It is not difficult to see that the instruction 'scan list' is itself a loop that looks at each value in the list and compares it to its neighbour. If the list has *n* values then you need to compare all values from value 1 to value *n*-1 with the value above it. (You only compare 1 to *n*-1 with its neighbour because the *n*th value in the list does not have a value just above it - it's the last value!) This is clearly a FOR loop from 1 to *n*-1 and so our program now reads:

```
DO
 notsort=0
 FOR i=1 to n-1
  IF value i and the value just below
                       are in the wrong order THEN
   swap positions
   notsort=1
  END IF
 NEXT i
LOOP UNTIL notsort=1
```

From here on in we need to use an idea that is discussed in Chapter 6 - the array - and if you don't follow the next part of the explanation then return to it after reading Chapter 6. However, the main part of our example as it relates to loops and IF statements is now complete. Our program consists of a conditional loop DO-LOOP UNTIL and a FOR loop with a single IF..THEN statement.

The final details are based on the fact that if a(i) is value number i in the list, e.g. if i=2 then a(2) is the second value, then to the value above it is a(i+1), e.g. the value just above a(2) is a(3). So adjacent values are in the wrong order if a(i)>a(i+1) is true. To swap adjacent items you have to perform three steps:

```
temp=a(i)
a(i)=a(i+1)
a(i+1)=temp
```

To understand why another variable - temp - is needed to swap the contents of two variables then try to work out the identical problem of swapping the contents of two bowls full of breakfast cereal - it doesn't take long to see that you need an additional empty bowl - see Figure 3.5.

54 *The Flow of Control*   *Chapter 3*

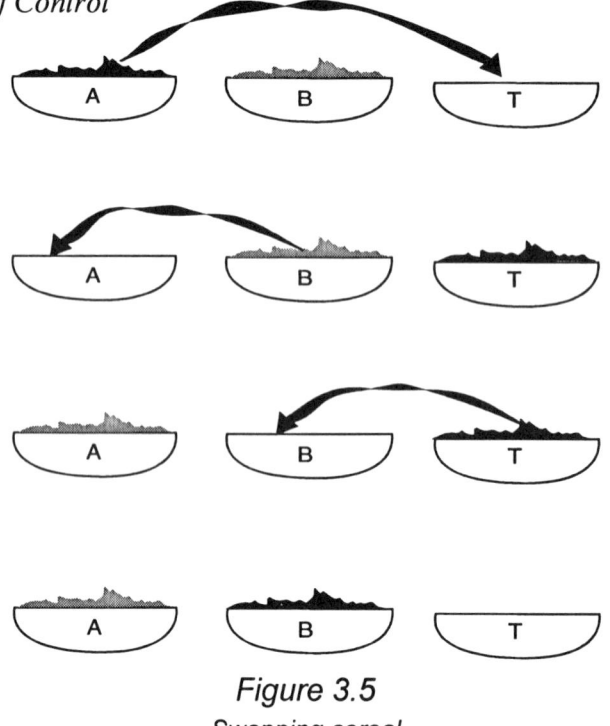

Figure 3.5
Swapping cereal

Swapping the contents of a pair of variables is so common an operation that QBasic has a special command

```
SWAP A,B
```

which will transfer the contents of A into B and B into A without the need for a temporary variable. In practice the SWAP command is a faster and more convenient way of swapping variables but you still need to know about the general principle of using temporary variables.

Thus the final version of our program is:

```
DO
   notsort=0
   FOR i=1 to n-1
      IF a(i)>a(i+1) THEN
         temp=a(i)
         a(i)=a(i+1)
         a(i+1)=temp
         notsort=1
      END IF
   NEXT i
LOOP UNTIL notsort=0
```

An example - The bubble sort

This is a complicated example and it is worth remembering the initial advice about returning to it after reading later chapters. However you should be able to see the way that the two loops are combined together - the inner loop performing the basic scan and the outer loop repeating that scan until the list is completely sorted. Also notice the way the practice of indenting each time you start a loop or an IF statement makes it much easier to see where each block or instructions starts and ends.

A complete listing of the bubble sort program, together with short sections that generate some random data and print the initial list and the final list, can be seen in Listing 3.1. Type it in (or load it from disk) and try it. If you are interested in such things you might like to see how good it is by timing it for different sizes of list. We return to the subject of sorting in Chapter 10.

Listing 3.1

```
REM bubble sort
REM dimension the array and generate the data
CLS
INPUT "how many numbers ?", n
DIM a(n)
FOR i = 1 TO n
   a(i) = INT(RND(3) * n)
NEXT i
REM print the unsorted array
PRINT "This is the Unsorted array"
PRINT
PRINT
FOR i = 1 TO n
   PRINT a(i)
NEXT i
REM sort the array
DO
   notsort = 0
   FOR i = 1 TO n - 1
      IF a(i) > a(i + 1) THEN
         temp = a(i)
         a(i) = a(i + 1)
         a(i + 1) = temp
         notsort = 1
      END IF
   NEXT i
LOOP UNTIL notsort = 0
REM prints the sorted array
PRINT
PRINT "This is the sorted array"
PRINT
FOR i = 1 TO n
   PRINT a(i)
NEXT i
END
```

BUBBLE1.BAS

Relics of the past - GOTO

The early version of Basic handled the flow of control in a very different way from QBasic and other modern languages. Each line had to have a line number which governed its position in the program and provided a label that could be used to identify the command. The default flow of control was simply from lower to higher line numbers and corresponded to the QBasic top-to-bottom flow.

To alter the default flow of control to form loops and selects you had to use the GOTO instruction. The instruction:

```
GOTO x
```

meant "execute line x next". For example GOTO 50 would make line 50 the next instruction to be obeyed. You could use GOTO, with the help of the IF statement, to construct loops and make selections. Unfortunately GOTO also gave you the possibility of making a complete mess of such constructions. The trouble is that most programmers were not taught explicitly the ways in which the GOTO should be used - they were simply expected to discover them by use. As a result some did but most didn't. For this reason Basic and the GOTO statement have often been criticised as being the cause of bad programming habits - in all cases the blame should have been placed on poor teaching!

If a program is to be easy to understand (and hence easy to write, debug and modify) it should use the simplest and clearest flow of control possible. The programming method that concentrates on simplifying and clarifying the flow of control in programs is known as *structured programming* and this is the method used throughout this book. QBasic supports the use of GOTO and line numbers and even extends the principle to the use of line labels, allowing you to write instructions such as GOTO SECTION3. You can use these facilities if you want to, and they are handy if you want to run an program written in old fashioned Basic, but you are more likely to produce good programs using DO-LOOP and IF..THEN..ELSE. If you feel the need to use a line label when writing a new program then the chances are that you haven't really understood the basic ideas of loops and selects:

» When you want to repeat something use a DO-LOOP or FOR loop

» When you want to make a choice use an IF

» It is never necessary to use a GOTO

Key points

» The order in which instructions are obeyed in a program is known as the flow of control. Part of the art of programming is learning how to modify the flow of control.

» There are only three basic forms of the flow of control - the default top-to-bottom flow, the loop and the select. Each of these can be visualised via a railway diagram.

» In QBasic loops can be formed using the instructions DO-LOOP to bracket the group of statements to be repeated.

» A loop can be terminated either by using an IF..THEN EXIT DO statement within the loop or by adding a WHILE condition or an UNTIL condition to the DO or LOOP instruction.

» Conditional loops differ in the placement of the exit point and the sense of the exit condition.

» The FOR loop is a special type of conditional loop that executes a given number of times. To allow for all of the needs of practical use the FOR loop has many different options governing the range of values of the index.

» Selections are made using IF... THEN...ELSE...END IF

» Because of QBasic's modern command set you never need to use line numbers, line labels or the GOTO command and it is better not to.

Chapter 4
Modular Programs

Subroutines and functions are an essential component of modern programming methods. In this chapter QBasic's approach to modular programming is described along with the basics of subroutine construction. Some of the ideas introduced are rather difficult and so will be worth returning to more than once.

The key to the easy and successful writing of large programs is not to write them at all! All large programs are in fact made up of a collection of smaller functional units each dealing with a particular task. Rather than write a single large program it is much easier to write a number of smaller units or modules, each one small enough to hold in your memory, and then use these to construct the complete program. This programming method is usually known as *modular programming* and the most successful programming method in use today is known as *modular structured programming* indicating the combined use of modular construction and well structured code (i.e. simple flow of control) within each module. If you use the DO-LOOP, FOR-NEXT and block IF instructions introduced in the previous chapter then it is very likely that your programs will have a good structure and so all that remains is to explain how to build modules.

» Windows of the mind

Most programmers start out by writing short, 10-20 line, exercises. When you are first learning to program such tiny programs are hard enough because you have to think about the details of the language as well as the correct algorithm or method. After a little practice such short programs become easy and the time has come to tackle something larger. The only trouble is that there is no general recognition of the fact that large programs need a completely different technique from small programs. Indeed large programs present a whole new type of problem - they are not just small programs writ large. The reason for this is the limitation of human memory. When writing a short program you can usually keep it all - program structure, variable names, etc. - in your head. When writing a large program you can at first keep it all in your head but eventually there comes a time when you have written more lines than your memory span can encompass and from then on it's all downhill. You can write large programs by a superhuman effort to remember everything, but the alternative, rather more intelligent, method is much less effort.

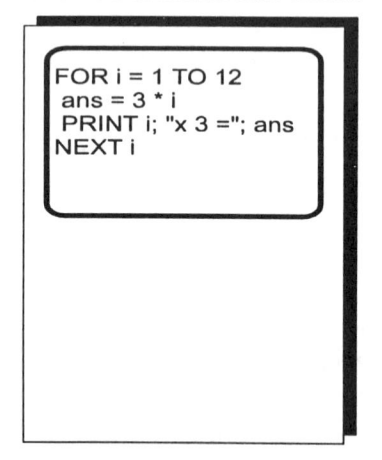

```
FOR i = 1 TO 12
ans = 3 * i
PRINT i; "x 3 ="; ans
NEXT i
```

```
CLS
INPUT "how many numbers ?", n
DIM a(n)
FOR i = 1 TO n
    a(i) = INT(RND(3) * n)
NEXT i
REM print the unsorted array
PRINT "This is the Unsorted array"
PRINT : PRINT
FOR i = 1 TO n
    PRINT a(i)
NEXT i
REM sort the array
DO
    notsort = 0
    FOR i = 1 TO n - 1
        IF a(i) > a(i + 1) THEN
            temp = a(i)
            a(i) = a(i + 1)
            a(i + 1) = temp
            notsort = 1
```

Figure 4.1
The memory limit - a small program fits into the window of the mind, but how much can you remember of a large program?

When you examine any list of instructions you will usually discover that various parts of it are dedicated to performing particular identifiable jobs. In other words, even if a program has been written as one long list of instructions it still has a 'granular' structure composed of a number of sub-lists each of which deals with a particular task. If you look more closely at the program you will see that each of the sub-lists is composed of a number of sub-lists and so on. That is, the granular structure of a program is *hierarchical*. The program performs a particular task as a number of distinct sub-tasks, which are themselves in turn composed of a number of sub-tasks and so on. The important thing to notice is that this hierarchical granular structure is a natural property of programs rather like the atomic nature of matter. It is possible to make use of this granular structure to break a program down into a collection of smaller programs or *module*s. By reducing these smaller programs into collections of even smaller programs and so on until we arrive at something that can be written as a 'mind size' piece of QBasic. In this way you can avoid ever having to write a large program.

» The subroutine

Most versions of Basic only have a very limited method (GOSUB and RETURN) of grouping instructions together to form modules. Rather than dwell on past history it makes more sense to make use of QBasic's more sophisticated and easier to use SUB and END SUB commands to create subroutines. This allows you give a group of instructions a name and use them whenever you need, just by quoting the name. To define a subroutine you would use:

```
SUB name
    list of instructions
END SUB
```

Once defined you can use the subroutine by simply typing:

```
CALL name
```

If you want to you can leave out the keyword CALL and just write the name of the subroutine. This is convenient but using CALL does have the advantage of making it clear that a subroutine is being used. For example, a common requirement within a program is to print a couple of blank lines to leave a little space between items. This can be achieved by defining a subroutine called blank:

```
SUB blank
    PRINT
    PRINT
END SUB
```

Following this anywhere within another part of the program that you want to print two blank lines you can write:

```
CALL blank
```

or just

```
blank
```

» Subroutine structure and the editor

The use of SUB and END SUB to define a procedure is not a difficult idea but QBasic goes a step further in enforcing and facilitating the use of subroutines. You can see from the previous example that subroutine blank is very much a new command that has been added to the language. You don't need to trouble yourself about how blank is implemented while you are using it and as a result you don't need to see the lines of instructions that make up the definition of blank. In most other programming languages you have to prepare a program as a single list of instructions that includes subroutine definitions and the parts of the program that make use of them. They are not 'mixed up' in the sense that each subroutine occupies a clearly defined area of the text - i.e. between a pair of SUB and END SUB statements - but you can still be confused by seeing details of subroutines that do not concern you at that moment.

The QBasic editor helps with the task of organising subroutines by only allowing you to see one subroutine at a time. The editing screen that we have been using is in fact a window onto the text file that makes up the program and it can only be positioned on a single subroutine at a time. To select which subroutine you are viewing you have to use the View,SUBs command or its shortcut key F2. This produces a list of all of the subroutines defined so far and the subroutine that you pick from

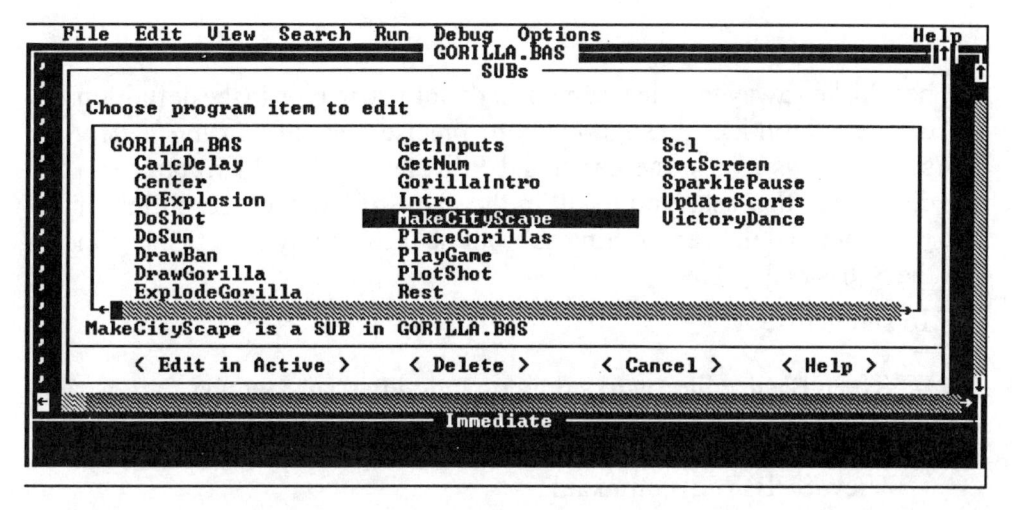

Figure 4.2
Selecting a subroutine to view (the program is Gorilla)

this list is the one that you will see in the editing window - see Figure 4.2. Notice that all of the subroutines are stored in the same file when you use the File,Save command and they are all loaded when you use the File,Open command. The text of a program is a single entity as you will discover if you use another editor or word processor to examine it but the QBasic editor recognises the divisions of the text into subroutines and will only show you one subroutine at a time.

You can in fact view two subroutines at a time using the command View,Split which produces two editing windows. This doesn't break the rule of one subroutine per window and is useful if you want to compare the definition of two subroutines or if you want to copy and paste sections of program between them.

Many users find this restriction to one subroutine at a time inexplicable and irritating. If you subscribe to this viewpoint then it is very important that you give time for the modular method of programming time to sink in. QBasic's approach is not only in accord with good programming methods, it is actually far superior in terms of productivity, easy of use, reduction of errors and so on.

If you can only view one subroutine at a time, how do you start a new subroutine? There are two ways. The first is simply to type the command SUB followed by a name at which point you will instantly be whisked away to a clear screen ready for you to type in the definition of the subroutine. A slightly more precise way of starting a new subroutine is to use the command Edit,New SUB. This produces a dialog box that asks you to fill in the name of the new subroutine. If you want to delete an existing subroutine then simply select Delete in the SUBs dialog box.

To summarise:

» The QBasic editor works only on individual subroutines.

» You can select which subroutine you are editing using the View,SUBs (F2) command.

» You can create a new subroutine by simply typing SUB *name* within an existing section of the program or you can use the Edit,New Sub command.

» You can delete an existing subroutine using the Delete button in the dialog box of the View,SUBs (F2) command.

» Step by step programming

You can use procedures to slice up a large program into a collection of smaller programs and then repeat the process of division until you have something small enough to write easily, i.e. no more than 10 or 20 lines of QBasic. The problem that remains is to determine how this division into smaller modules is to be achieved. After all, if it is as difficult as the original task then we have not succeeded in making anything easier.

There is a programming method called *stepwise refinement* that is particularly good at exploiting the modular nature of a program. In stepwise refinement you first concentrate on defining the topmost level in terms of calls to procedures that are to be fully implemented at a later date.

For example, if you want to implement a program to play a game of noughts and crosses, a very major program, the usual problem is getting started. But using stepwise refinement the program can be written almost at once:

```
CALL setup
DO
   CALL playX
   CALL playO
LOOP UNTIL Win
CALL endgame
```

You might think that writing the program in this way has not made much progress but you would be wrong! The problem is now broken down into a number of sub-problems each of which can be tackled independently and can be further split down into sub-sub-problems. A more important gain is that now the overall structure of the program is revealed to be a conditional loop - in effect this part of the program gives you an overview that says "keep playing until somebody wins and then report who won". This is the top-most view of your program and it is generally referred to as the *main program*.

The next stage of the refinement is to fill in the details of the procedures used by the main program. For example, you might write the setup procedure next. This is a complex procedure because it has to do things like draw the playing board and initialise any variables that have to be used. How should setup be written? Using stepwise refinement of course!

```
SUB setup
CALL initialise
CALL DrawBoard
END SUB
```

You would carry on in this way working your way down a hierarchy of procedures until the evil day can no longer be put off and you reach a procedure so small that you really do have to write some QBasic! (There is a tendency for all programmers to be enthusiastic about what they are doing but a good programmer is inherently lazy and will put off writing any serious QBasic for as long as possible.) You can even start to test your program by creating empty subroutine definitions - i.e. nothing more than SUB *name*..END SUB. Thus programming becomes a gradual process of refinement of what already exists.

» Interaction

If dividing a large program up into smaller pieces is going to make it easier to write then it is essential that each small piece can be written without reference to the rest. If this is not the case then you cannot concentrate on a section of program small enough to hold in your head because you have to keep track of the rest of the program, even though you are only working on one small procedure.

This is the principle of *non-interaction* and QBasic procedures obey it! When you begin a procedure, QBasic wipes the slate clean and starts as if this was the first and only program you had written. The most immediate effect of this is that any variable that you use within a procedure has nothing to do with any variable of the same name that you might use in another procedure. That is, all variables within a procedure are *local* to that procedure. If you have two subroutines with variables called Count defined and used in each then they are different variables and each one has the value assigned to it within its respective subroutine.

This makes life easy because you don't have to remember the variables that have already been used for some purpose in all the other procedures. This is not the case in traditional Basic where all variables are *global*, that is shared by all parts of a program. Here the main problem is avoiding using the same variable name for two different purposes at the same time. Of course, there is an alternative argument that says if you use a variable called GrossPay in one part of a program you want to mean the same thing if you use it in other parts of a program. Indeed the idea of GrossPay being used for different purposes in different parts of the program is clearly an error waiting to happen! In this case, though, the variable is likely to be used to transfer data between subroutines and this is different from variables that have meaning only within a particular subroutine.

Of course a complete application of the principle of independence is equally undesirable. The reason for this is that to make a program work as a whole procedures have to interact. They have to receive data from other procedures, process it and then pass the results on. This means they affect each other and, even in an ideal world, procedures cannot be written without reference to one another. The point is that there are wanted and unwanted interactions between subroutines. Unwanted interactions are often called *side effects* and QBasic makes it possible to write subroutines without having to worry about the chance of side effects by using parameters.

» Parameters

Parameters are the ultimate way of restricting the way that procedures can interact. In essence they are just a way of establishing contact between particular variables in different procedures.

For example, if you have written a procedure that will print a number of blank lines,

```
SUB blank
FOR I=1 TO N
   PRINT
NEXT I
END SUB
```

then clearly N is a variable that determines the number of blank lines printed. However, it is impossible for another part of the program to give a value to N because it is local to procedure blank and has absolutely nothing to do with any other variable called N in any other part of the program.

What we need is some way of making a connection between N and a variable in another part of the program. This can be done by defining N to be a parameter of the procedure. This is written:

```
SUB blank(N)
FOR I=1 TO N
   PRINT
NEXT I
END SUB
```

Now when blank is called the variable with which N has to 'connect' has to be specified. For example,

```
count=10
CALL blank(count)
```

will result in ten blank lines being printed. The connection between N in procedure blank and count in the calling program remains for the duration of the procedure. When the procedure ends they go their separate ways again! At some other point in the program you could make a call to blank using a different variable, for example,

```
CALL blank(Z)
```

In this case a connection would be made between Z and N.

In general a procedure can have more than one parameter - up to a maximum of 60. When you call a procedure you have to name a variable in the calling program to be connected with each parameter. For example,

```
SUB sum(a,b,c)
d=a+b+c
PRINT d
END SUB
```

will add together the three parameters a, b and c and print the result. Notice that d is a local variable and not a parameter. To use sum all you have to do is call it with suitable variables named in the call. For example,

```
CALL sum(price,delivery,vat)
```

makes connections between price and a, delivery and b, and vat and c. The result of course is that the procedure prints the sum of price, delivery and vat.

CALL blank(count)
↓
SUB blank(N)
↓
FOR I=1 TO N
PRINT
NEXT I
END SUB

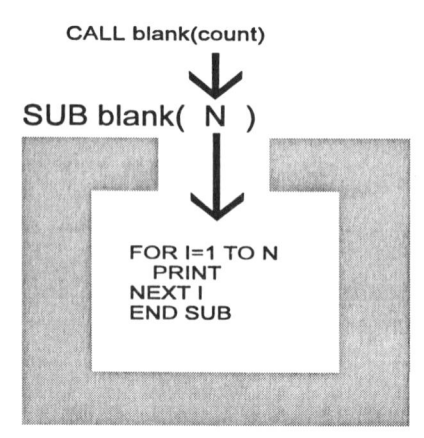

Figure 4.3
A parameter allows a value to be passed into a subroutine.

» Value and reference - out and in

The parameters that we have used so far are called *variable parameters* because they really do work by making a connection between the variable within the procedure and the variable within the calling program. In a sense the two variables become one for the duration of the procedure and any value stored in one is also stored in the other. Although in the examples given in the previous section parameters were only used to pass data into procedures they can also be used to transfer information out.

For example, the sum procedure in the previous section could be written:

```
SUB sum(a,b,c,d)
d=a+b+c
END SUB
```

Now when you call the procedure the fourth parameter will be used to return a result. That is, if you use:

```
CALL sum(price,delivery,vat,total)
```

then the sum of price, delivery and vat is stored in total when the procedure ends. Thus variable parameters can be used to get information into or out of a procedure. Another way of saying that the connection between the variables is two way is to say that the parameters are *passed by reference*.

Variable parameters can be dangerous if a parameter is supposed to be used only to transfer information into a procedure. For example, in the case of the blank procedure given earlier, N is only used to transfer data into the procedure to determine the number of blank lines to be printed. But suppose the procedure, on purpose or by mistake, alters N, for example:

```
SUB blank(N)
FOR I=1 TO N
  PRINT
NEXT I
N=0
END SUB
```

In this version of the procedure any variable that was used by the calling program as the parameter would have its value altered without warning.

To get round this problem there is another sort of parameter, a *value parameter* that can only be used to pass information into a procedure. If, instead of a variable, you use a constant or an expression when you call a procedure there is no way that a connection can be made between a variable in the procedure and one in the calling program. For example, if you call blank using,

```
CALL blank(5)
```

then five blank lines will be printed but any value stored in N in the procedure will not affect anything in the calling program - how could it? In this case the value 5 is used to initialise N before the procedure is executed. This type of parameter is a value parameter and it is clearly good for getting information into a subroutine but useless for getting it out.

The same sort of thing will happen if you call a procedure using an expression. For example,

```
CALL blank(A+B)
```

will print A+B blank lines but there is no connection made between any of the variables involved, A or B and N. There is a trick that enables you to pass a single variable as a value parameter. If you enclose the variable name in brackets then it counts as an expression even though it doesn't affect the value of the variable. For example,

```
CALL blank((Count))
```

results in Count being passed as a value parameter. That is, changing the value of N within the procedure will not change the value stored in Count.

One of the most common and difficult to find errors is using a parameter within a subroutine without realising that changing its value will change the value of a variable in the calling program. The reason why this is a common error is that, within the subroutine, it is easy to forget that a variable is a parameter and not a true local variable and the reason that the error is usually difficult to find is that the subroutine will sometimes appear to work correctly with the error only making itself known later in the program.

» Local, shared and global

Exactly how variables behave in terms of where they can be used and when they exist is a subtlety that you can leave until you are completely happy with the idea of procedures. Read and return to the next two sections after you have gained some experience of using procedures.

There are two distinct and subtle ways in which variables can differ from one another. The idea of a local variable has already been described - it is a variable that is accessible only from the part of the program that defines or owns it. The area of the program that a variable is accessible from is more generally called its *scope*. In QBasic variables have *local scope* by default. However, there are times when it is useful to share a variable between a number of procedures. You can make a variable named in a subroutine identical to a variable of the same name in the main program by including a SHARED statement in the subroutine.

For example if you have a subroutine called sub1 then it can share the variable total with the main program by including the statement:

```
SHARED total
```

A variable in the main program can be shared with as many subroutines as need to use it. Any subroutine that used total that didn't start with the statement SHARED total would be using a completely separate variable from all the subroutines that did.

Taking the sharing of variables to the extreme, i.e. a variable that is accessible from all subroutines is, of course another way of describing a *global variable*. You could make a variable global by including SHARED statements within every subroutine but the same result can be achieved by including the single statement:

```
COMMON SHARED variable
```

in the main program. For example, the statement:

```
COMMON SHARED total
```

would make every occurrence of total in the entire program refer to the same variable. The COMMON command has other uses in controlling the way that variables can be shared between subroutines but these are advanced and a cause of many subtle errors and so are best avoided.

» Dynamic and static variables

As well as the scope of a variable there is also the question of when it exists. A variable defined in a subroutine is by default local and only accessible from within that subroutine. Not only is access restricted to the subroutine, it is only brought into being when the subroutine is started and vanishes again when the subroutine ends. That is it is *dynamic* and is created and destroyed as the program runs. In other words, by default variables are local and dynamic.

For example there is no point writing a subroutine that tries to count how many times it has been called using:

```
SUB many
count=count+1
PRINT count
END SUB
```

because each time the subroutine is called the local dynamic variable count is created afresh and so it never gets beyond the value one. You can, if need be, define a variable using a STATIC statement. A *static* variable exists for the life of the entire program even when its subroutine isn't being run. A static variable is still local in the sense that it doesn't have anything to do with any variable of the same name elsewhere in the program but it now also has a life of its own independent of the subroutine. You can also append the keyword STATIC to the end of a subroutine definition to make all of its local variables static.

For example, the many subroutine can be written:

```
SUB many
STATIC count
count=count+1
PRINT count
END SUB
```

and now the variable count does indeed count the number of times that the subroutine is called.

» Scope and existence

When you first meet local, shared, global, dynamic and static variables they can be a little confusing so perhaps it is worth summarising their properties:

Type	Accessible from	Existence
local	subroutine that it is declared in	while subroutine is running
shared	main program and any subroutine with SHARED name	always
global	main program and every subroutine	always
dynamic	one subroutine	while subroutine is running
static	one subroutine	always

» Functions

All the real work of a program is performed by the evaluation of *expressions*. The most common example of an expression is the arithmetic expression (that is simple arithmetic) as introduced in Chapter 2 but there are also string expressions, logical expressions and conditional expressions (all of which will be explained in later chapters). An expression is simply a recipe for working out a result by combining various data values. In this sense every expression is a mini-program for a calculation. For example, the expression 2*3+4*5 is equivalent to the instructions:

Step 1: multiply 2 by 3
Step 2: multiply 4 by 5
Step 3: add the results of step 1 and step 2 together

In the same way that a program can be divided down into smaller subroutines, an expression can be broken down into smaller units of calculation called functions.

For example, the calculation of sin(x) is quite involved but you can use it in an expression by simply writing the function SIN(X). When the computer encounters a function in an expression it essentially executes a subroutine that returns a single value - the result of the function. Thus functions are a special restricted form of subroutines that return one and only one value as a result, so that they can be used as part of an expression.

There are a wide range of standard functions defined as part of QBasic such as SIN(X), COS(X) and SQR(X) (square root of X) etc.. However, you can also define your own new functions in a similar way to procedures.

To define a function all you have to write is:

```
FUNCTION name(parameter list)
statements that compute the value of the function
name=result
END FUNCTION
```

A function is treated by the QBasic editor in much the same way as a subroutine. That is, you can only view one function at a time. To select a function you simply use View,SUBs or F2. To create a new function you can use Edit, New Function. In fact functions are really nothing more than subroutines that return a single value that can be used within an expression. Notice that the value that the function returns is determined by what you assign to a variable with the same name as the function.

For example, a function that adds together three numbers can be defined:

```
FUNCTION sum(A,B,C)
sum=a+b+c
END FUNCTION
```

The statement:

```
sum=a+b+c
```

is the line that actually determines the result that the function will return.

Once defined you can use the function within an arithmetic expression. For example:

```
answer=2+sum(X,4,3*36)/46
```

Although the example given above only consists of a single, very simple, line a function can consist of any number of QBasic statements. Even though a function should only return a single value, all function parameters are passed by reference and so can be changed by the function. This is undesirable behaviour and can lead to errors. It is all too easy to write a function that alters the value of a parameter and then use it in a situation where this causes an error. You should either protect yourself by always calling functions with parameters in brackets - as in sum((x),(y),(z)), which looks very messy - or you should keep to the rule of not writing functions which modify their parameters.

Remember:

» a safe function is one that never assigns a value to any of its parameters.

Notice that QBasic also supports the older type of Basic function using the DEF FN command. In all cases the new FUNCTION is to be preferred as it is far less prone to error. Only use DEF FN if you have to write programs that will work on older versions of Basic or if you have old programs to run using QBasic.

» Modular problems

The use of modules is now so well established as the right way to do things it is difficult to believe that there are languages and programmers who still do not accept that subroutines and function are a good thing. In particular old fashioned Basic did such a poor job of implementing subroutines that there was little point in using the facility. In traditional Basic all variables are global and subroutines do not have local variables or parameters. This means that a traditional Basic subroutine provides virtually no isolation between the different parts of a program and hence isn't really worth using! So if you have encountered subroutines in GWBasic or similar - forget the old way of doing things and use SUB-END SUB.

Another complaint that programmers often make about using subroutines is the way that the parameter list can grow to be so long that it is tedious to have to type it out every time the subroutine is used. This is a very real problem but the advantages of using subroutines are much greater than the inconvenience of having to type a few more characters! There is an argument for using global variables for quantities that have a central status within a program and so avoid having to list them as parameters - but this is a subtle argument that we will return to in Chapter 9.

The argument for using global variables in place of parameters is also closely related to the "one name" argument. In some languages programmers are encouraged to define variable names that are so precise that the idea of changing the name of a variable is unthinkable. For example, if you define a variable ThisYearsProfit then why call it anything else in a subroutine or module? If you are going to stick to a single name throughout your program then why bother using subroutines, local variables or parameters? The answer is that even though ThisYearsProfit is a name that you are unlikely to use for some other purpose, variables such as I, count, N, M, total, x, y and so on are. This sort of vague variable name is much more common and so using subroutines really is worthwhile. If there are names that couldn't possibly be used for another purpose within a program then there is an argument for making these particular variables global - but including too many global variables makes a program difficult to understand and modify.

» An example

Rather than give an example here to show how a program is created using subroutines, you are invited to examine every program in the remainder of this book! Subroutines and stepwise refinement are not to be turned on for the sake of an example - they are the very stuff of everyday programming! For this reason they have been introduced as early as possible so that they can be used from the word go. However, there are still lots of ideas that have to be described before you can create really useful programs. At the end of the Chapter 6 you will find a short example that shows how the bubble sort program listed at the end of Chapter 3 can be written using subroutines. This is the first of many modular programs listed in this book.

Relics of the past

QBasic is more powerful than standard Basic in that its procedures and functions are more sophisticated. Traditional Basic has only a very crude way of forming a module based on the use of the commands GOSUB xxx and RETURN. The GOSUB xxx command acts rather like a standard GOTO xxx command except that it remembers its location in the program so that a RETURN command can transfer control back to it. This is a very poor method of constructing modules and when you add to this the fact that that are no local variables - i.e. all variables are shared - there seems little point in using GOSUB and RETURN in preference to SUB and CALL statements. However, QBasic still supports the use of GOSUB and RETURN and extends their definition to allow line labels to specify where subroutines begin.

Traditional Basic also has functions but generally only definitions that take a single line are allowed. Once again this is more restrictive than QBasic functions and so there is little reason to conform to the old standard. However, QBasic does include the older form of function and has extended it to include multi-line functions. To define an FN function you would use:

```
DEF FNname(list of parameters)
list of instructions that work
out the result of the function
FNname=result
END
```

For example, the function to add three numbers given earlier in this chapter would be:

```
DEF FNsum(a,b,c)
FNsum=a+b+c
END
```

and would be used as:

```
answer=2+FNsum(X,4,3*36)/46
```

Notice that this FN function is not recognised by the editor and so can be included in any part of the program without clearing the editor window. It also passes parameters by value and all its variables are shared with the main program.

Key points

» A large program is easy to write only if it is split up into small modules. Each module should be small enough to be understood almost on sight.

» QBasic supports modular programming by providing subroutines and functions. The QBasic editor recognises both types of module and will only allow you to edit one module at a time. You can select which module is being edited or delete an existing module using the command View,SUBs. You can create a new subroutine or function using Edit,New SUB or Edit,New Function.

» Variables within a subroutine or function are local to that module by default. That is, they have nothing to do with any other variables of the same name defined in other parts of the program. Variables can be defined to be shared with the main program or global using common shared.

» Variables within a subroutine or function are dynamic by default. That is, they are created each time the module is executed and destroyed when the module is finished. Variables can be defined to be static and they then hold their values between uses of the module to which they belong.

» Information can be passed in and out of a subroutine or function using parameters. All parameters are passed by reference which makes it possible to use them to return values.

» Functions should return only a single result by using a statement that assigns a value to the function's name. To avoid errors do not change the values of function parameters. Alternatively pass them by value by enclosing each in brackets when the function is used.

» Older versions of Basic used GOSUB and RETURN to form modules and FN for functions. These are supported in QBasic but should not be used without good reason.

Chapter 5

The Importance of Data

Every program is made up of instructions and the data with which those instructions work. In this chapter and the next the spotlight falls on the data and here the idea of variable type is introduced.

Building up a program out of procedures, as described in Chapter 4, is a very important idea but it is only half of the story. A program is a list of instructions but there is also the question of what the instructions refer to. In the same way that every sentence has a verb (a doing word) and a noun (what the doing is done to!), so a program has an action part (the instructions) and an object part (the data that the instructions manipulate).

At the moment the only sort of data that our programs can manipulate is numbers and the only sort of actions amount more or less to arithmetic. To write programs that go beyond this we need to look in more depth at data and variables.

» Types of simple variable

The sort of data you can store in a variable depends on its *type*. Due to practical and other considerations a variable cannot store any type of data. For example, a simple or *single precision* variable can be used to store numbers to six significant digits. So far this is the only sort of variable that we have used, but QBasic supports five different types of variable in all, distinguished from one another by the particular symbol which is used to end their names.

- » Names ending with ! are single precision numeric variables and store six significant digits

- » Names ending with # are double precision numeric variables and store 16 significant digits

- » Names ending with % are integer variables and can only be used to store whole numbers in the range -32,768 to +32,767

- » Names ending with & are long integer variables and can only be used to store whole numbers in the range -2,147,483,648 to 2,147,483,647

- » Names ending with $ are string variables and can be used to store any string of characters (up to a maximum of 32,767 characters).

If a variable name doesn't end with any of the above characters then it is assumed to be a single precision variable. (In fact it is the custom to drop the ! for single precision variables.) For example:

PAY and PAY!	are single precision variables
PAY#	is a double precision variable
PAY%	is an integer variable
PAY&	is a long integer variable
PAY$	is a string variable

» Defining variable types

Most Basic programmers are used to the idea of using the special type indicating characters at the end of a variable's name but there are other methods of defining a variable's type. If you want to set up a default convention that all names beginning with a particular letter should default to a particular type then you can use the statement:

```
DEFtype letter range, letter range, etc..
```

where type is one of

```
INT   integer
SNG   single precision
DBL   double precision
LNG   long integer
STR   string
```

For example, following the statement:

```
DEFINT I-N
```

all variables beginning with I through N are automatically integer variables. A letter range applies to both upper and lower case characters and it can be overridden by the use of a type indicating character. For example, following the previous example, i and I are both integers but I! is a single precision variable and I$ is a string.

If you have used a language such as Fortran you will be familiar with this idea of default variable types based on the first letter of the variable's name but this is not the tradition in Basic. Defining types by first letter carries with it the risk of accidentally using the wrong variable type. It is much better to use explicit type indicating characters and not risk misidentification of a variable's type.

You can also set the type of an individual variable, irrespective of any naming conventions, using the command:

```
DIM variable AS type
```

don't worry for the moment about the strange use of the word 'DIM' to start the command, it does mean something but this will only become clear in the next chapter. The command defines the variable named to be the type indicated where *type* is one of INTEGER, LONG, SINGLE, DOUBLE and STRING.

For example, the command:
```
DIM name AS STRING, count AS INTEGER
```
defines the variable name to be a string variable and count to be an integer. As in the case of identifying type by initial letter this is an error prone way of defining variable type. However, there are languages, Pascal for example, where every variable must be declared in this way. Notice that this style of declaration is only safe when every variable is included and if you choose to use it then use it without exception. In most cases the Basic method of type identifiers is more than adequate.

» Using numeric variables

Of the newly introduced variable types four are just different types of numeric variable and so these should be reasonably familiar. The fifth new type - the string - needs rather more explanation and so an extended discussion is given below.

Single precision variables will do for most jobs unless you need the extra accuracy afforded by double precision. Most scientific or statistical computations benefit from the use of double precision but notice that each double precision variable takes twice as much memory as a single precision variable and double precision arithmetic is slower.

Integers have the advantage that they take slightly less memory to store but the most practical reason for using an integer is that integer arithmetic is much faster than single or double precision arithmetic. So if program speed is of importance you should use integer variables wherever possible. The speed increase gained by using integer variables in FOR-NEXT loops is also usually very significant. Perhaps an even deeper reason for using integer variables, however, is when the value to be stored cannot have a fractional part. In this case it makes good sense to use an integer variable.

Long integer variables can be put to good use for recording money values in pence accurately and doing arithmetic without losing pennies due to rounding errors.

You can use the usual arithmetic operations on integer variables but there is also a special integer division symbol \. Integer division is fast and always produces an integer as its result by ignoring any fraction or remainder after the division. For example, 7/2 is 3.5 but 7\2 is 3 exactly. If you want to know the remainder after dividing x by y then you can use the MOD operator. The result of

$$x \text{ MOD } y$$

is the remainder after x has been divided by y. For example,

$$7 \text{ MOD } 2$$

is 1, i.e. the remainder after dividing 7 by 2. The MOD operator is surprisingly useful and occurs more often than you might expect in a wide range of programming tasks.

It is possible to write expressions that involve mixed numeric types. In this case the rule is that all of the variables are converted to the most precise type used in the expression. For example, I%*A, i.e. an integer times a single precision variable, results in the integer being converted to a single precision value before the multiplication is carried out. This of course implies that the result of an expression is always at the highest precision of the variable used. When you assign a value of one type to a numeric variable of other type the value is automatically converted. For example, in D#=A the single precision value is automatically converted to double precision. Notice that the conversion from single or double precision to integer is performed by rounding up.

If you want to perform a type conversion explicitly then there are a range of functions that can be used for just this purpose. For example, function FIX(A) converts the single or double precision value in A into an integer by simply ignoring any fractional part. You can use explicit type conversion either when the default isn't quite what is required or to draw attention to the fact that conversion is being performed. A full list of type conversion functions is given later in this chapter.

» Strings

In Chapter 1 the idea of a string - a collection of letters within double quotes - was introduced as a way of printing messages and prompts. In fact, what we have been calling a string is really a *string constant*. The use of the word constant might alert you to the fact that there are such things as string variables. A *string variable* is similar to a simple variable in that it is a named area of memory that can be used to store information. In this case, the information is a collection of characters instead of a number.

You can store a string constant in a string variable by using assignment and the PRINT statement can be used to print its contents:

```
A$="This is a string"
PRINT A$
```

In fact, a string variable can be used anywhere that a simple variable can as long as it makes sense. For example, you can use INPUT A$ to store a string typed in from the keyboard while a program is running but SUM =3+A$ is obviously nonsense (you cannot add a string of characters to a number!). Notice in particular the difference between:

```
A$="1"
```
and
```
A$=1
```

The first line is fine because the 1 is enclosed in double quotes and is therefore a string but the second will give an error message because A$ is a string variable and 1 is a number. You can convert numbers to strings using the STR$ function. For example, STR$(6) is a string composed of one digit, i.e. "6". Also notice that the number of characters that are stored in a string variable can change.

The introduction of string variables is exciting because it opens up the possibility of handling text and even dialogues. So far, however, the only sort of program that you can write is :

```
INPUT "what is your name ?",N$
PRINT "hello ";N$;", I am your friendly computer"
```

which is OK for a start but it can result in unnatural dialogues like:

```
What is your name ? Fred Bloggs
Hello Fred Bloggs, I am your friendly computer
```

The trouble is that although you can INPUT, PRINT and store strings you have no way of changing them. This is rather like being able to INPUT, PRINT and store numbers but having no way of doing arithmetic - it's obvious that this would limit the programs that could be written! The answer lies in inventing operations that can be used to construct *string expressions*.

» String expressions

Before introducing the facilities for handling strings it is worth considering what sort of things you might like to do. If a program had someone's first name in F$ and their last name in L$ then it would be useful to be able to join them together to form one longer string. Such joining together of strings is known as concatenation. Another operation that would be useful is the ability to extract part of a string. For example, you could extract the last name from a string consisting of an initial and a surname i.e. extract "Bloggs" from "F. Bloggs". A string that is part of another string is often called a substring. For example, if we were trying to keep F.Bloggs a secret we might want to replace the surname by asterisks giving "F.******". Finally, it would be a great advantage to be able to test for the presence of a particular substring in a string. For example, to see if the substring "BLOGGS" occurred in the name stored in N$ you would need to search for the substring "BLOGGS" in N$.

To recap, the string operations that we would like to perform are - concatenation, substring extraction, substring replacement and substring searching.

» Concatenation

Our first requirement, string concatenation, is immediately satisfied by QBasic's concatenation sign "+". If A$ contains the string "ABCD" and B$ contains "EFGH" then after:

   C$=A$+B$

C$ contains "ABCDEFGH". Notice that we now have two uses for the symbol "+", as the sign for addition and as the sign for concatenation.

You can use the "+" sign more than once in a string expression. For example:

```
C$="MR "+F$+" "+L$
```

will join up the four strings involved and if F$ contains a first name "FRED" and L$ a last name "BLOGGS" then C$ will contain "MR FRED BLOGGS". Notice the use of the single space between the two strings to avoid the result being "MR FREDBLOGGS"!

» The MID$ function

Extracting or changing a substring can be done by using a single new function MID$. Functions were introduced earlier and it should come as no surprise that there are string functions as well as numeric functions. The result of a string function is a string. If s$ is a string of characters:

```
MID$(s$,m,n)
```

is the substring consisting of n letters starting with letter m. For example:

```
PRINT MID$("12345678",3,4)
```

will print "3456" i.e. the substring consisting of four characters starting at the third character. The MID$ operation is easy to understand and use as long as you remember that the first number indicates where the substring should start and the second number indicates how many characters should be in the substring.

MID$("HELLO",2,3)

character 2

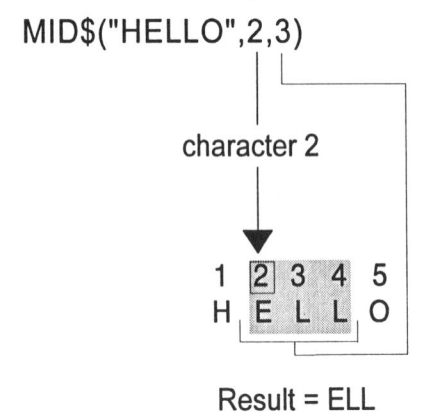

1 2 3 4 5
H E L L O

Result = ELL

Figure 5.1
MID$ extracting a substring

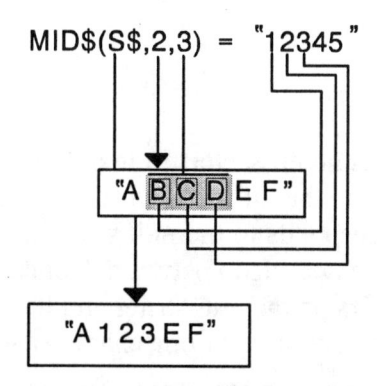

Figure 5.2
MID$ changing a substring

You can use arithmetic expressions to specify m and n, for example:

```
MID$("ABCD",FIRST,2)
```

or

```
MID$("ABCD",I,L+3)
```

You shouldn't be frightened to write complicated string expressions just as you wouldn't be frightened to write complicated arithmetic expressions, however always remember that simplicity is best.

In the same way that you can use MID$ to extract a portion of a string you can also use it to change a portion. The command:

```
MID$(s$,n,m)=string
```

will replace the portion of the string s$ specified by n and m by the first m characters in *string*. For example, following:

```
S$="ABCDEF"
MID$(S$,2,3)="12345"
```

S$ will contain the string "A123EF". That is the substring in S$ starting at letter 2 is replaced by the first 3 characters of the second string.

You can't really make a mistake using MID$. If you specify that the substring should be longer than the number of letters to the left of the starting position then you will just get as many letters as there are! For example MID$("12345",4,10) is just "45". If you leave n out then the substring will consist of all the letters to the end of the string s$. For example, MID$("12345",4) is also "45". If you specify a negative starting point or a length of 0 then the MID$ function will return a very special string - the *null string*.

» The null string

The null string has no characters in it and plays a very similar role in string expressions to that of zero in arithmetic expressions. The string constant that corresponds to the null string is written "" i.e. a pair of double quotes with nothing in between. Notice the difference between "" and " ". The first is the null string and has no characters in it, the second is a string consisting of one character - a blank or space.

From the point of view of a computer, a space is just as much a character as a letter of the alphabet, it takes up one position to print and it needs just as much computer memory to store! If you print a null string it has no effect whatsoever. The statements PRINT A;B and PRINT A;"";B produce the same result.

» Month names - an example

As an example of using MID$ consider the problem of printing the name of a month of the year given its number. i.e. printing Dec for 12 and May for 5 etc. Try the following short program:

MONTHS.BAS

```
Y$="JanFebMarAprMayJunJulAugSepOctNovDec"
DO
   INPUT "Month number ",MON
   PRINT "Month ";MON;" is ";MID$(Y$,1+3*(MON-1),3)
LOOP
```

If you enter a number in the range 1 to 12 the program will print the correct abbreviation for the month in question. The way that it works is by automatically extracting the three letter name from the long string Y$ using the numeric value in 'MON'.

The best way to understand the use of MID$ in the print line is by working it out by hand for a few values of 'MON'. If 'MON' is 4 then (1+3*(MON-1)) is 10 and the substring is given by MID$(Y$,10,3) which gives the three letters "Apr".

» LEN, LEFT$ and RIGHT$

The MID$ operation will extract any substring from a string and in this sense it is all you need. However, there are two other ways of extracting substrings that have become common and indeed popular in traditional Basic - LEFT$ and RIGHT$.

LEFT$(s$,n) will extract the substring with n characters in it starting from the first character in s$, in other words the leftmost n characters. You should be able to work out that LEFT$(s$,n) is the same as MID$(s$,1,n).

RIGHT$(s$,n) will extract the last or rightmost n characters from the string s$. You may think that this has no equivalent MID$ operation but once you know that the LEN(s$) function gives the length of a string the equivalent is obvious. For example PRINT LEN("ABCD") will print 4 on the screen. Now you should be able to work out that RIGHT$(s$,n) is the same as MID$(s$,LEN(s$)-n,n).

» String insertion

You can use the MID$ function to change any portion of a string for another but you cannot use it to insert a new string into another. That is, you cannot change the length of a string using MID$. However, using MID$ you can take the string apart and insert the new letters using concatenation. For example, to replace the 3 in S$="AB3D" with C you could use :

```
S$=MID$(S$,1,2)+"C"+MID$(S$,4,1)
```

The first MID$ extracts "AB" and the second the final "D". Putting them all together gives "ABCD" as required.

Similarly, to delete part of a string you have to use MID$ to extract the two parts of the string that you want to keep and then join then back together. For example, to remove the 3 from the string "AB3D" you would use:

```
S$=MID$(S$,1,2)+MID$(S$,4,1)
```

Which you should compare to the example above which replaces the "3" by a "C".

» Searching strings - INSTR

The only thing left from our initial list of string handling requirements is testing to see if a particular substring is present in another string. QBasic provides a direct method of achieving this - the INSTR operation.

INSTR(n,t$,s$) will search for the string s$ in the string t$ starting the search at character n. So for example INSTR(3,t$,"FRED") will search t$ starting at the third character for the string "FRED". If the string is not found INSTR produces the result zero otherwise it produces the position of s$ in t$.

» Comparing strings

The INSTR operation is very useful but it is often more than you really need. Most of the time all you need to know is if two strings are equal or different. The meaning of "=" and "<>" are easy enough to understand. Namely, two strings are equal if they are of the same length and contain the same characters in the same order, otherwise they are not equal. However, what do the relations "<",">","<=" and ">=" mean when applied to strings? QBasic defines A$<B$ to be true if the string in A$ comes before the string in B$ in an alphabetically ordered list of strings.

The trouble is that we are all so familiar with alphabetically ordered lists that we tend to forget how they work! If the two strings being compared are single letters, then A$<B$ if the letter in A$ comes earlier in the alphabet than the letter is B$. For example ,"A"<"B" is true but "D"<"B" is false. What about comparing strings that contain single characters that are not necessarily letters, i.e. what do we make of "*"<"$"? In the case of the letters, the alphabet provides us with a ready- made order so what we need is to extend this order to include all the other symbols that can be used. This is already defined for the PC. It is a list which associates a number - its ASCII code - with each character. If you don't have the manual to hand, or if you are just interested, you can print all the characters in their proper order by using the following program:

```
FOR I=32 TO 127
  PRINT "Character";I;" = ";CHR$(I)
NEXT I
```

The first line specifies 32 as the starting point as the characters before that are unprintable. The CHR$ function converts the ASCII code for a character to the character that it represents. Similarly the function ASC(s$) returns the ASCII code for the first character in the string s$. Coming back to the question of whether or not "*"<"$" is true or false, "*" is character 42 and "$" is character 36 so "$" comes before "*" in the order and "*"<"$" is false. You can decide the truth or otherwise of any relation in the same way.

If the two strings contain more than one character they are compared one character at a time until the first pair of different characters is found. The relationship between the two strings is then decided on the basis of those two characters. For example, "ABCD"<"AZCD" is true because the first pair of letters that are different is "B" and "Z" and "B"<"Z" is true. If one of the strings is the same as the other apart from the addition of a few extra characters then the comparison is based on length, i.e. "ABCD"<"ABCDEF", because there is no pair of letters that is different and "ABCD" is shorter than "ABCDEF".

Comparing strings in this way is fairly trouble free apart from one annoying detail. In the ASCII code all of the upper case characters come before the lower case characters and so if you compare two strings containing mixed upper and lower case characters you might be surprised at the result. For example, "ZBCD" comes before "aBCD". This sort of behaviour can be a problem in a program that sorts lists of words typed in upper and lower case. One solution to this is to convert all strings to upper case using the UCASE$ function or to lower case using the LCASE$ function. For example instead of IF a$>b$ THEN ... use IF UCASE$(a$)>UCASE$(b$) THEN...

» Type conversion functions

The introduction of strings completes the set of QBasic variable types and so it is now worth making a list of functions that perform type conversion:

```
ASC(char)     = ASCII code corresponding to char
CDBL(value)   = double precision
CHR$(ASCII)   = char corresponding to ASCII code
CINT(value)   = integer by rounding
CLNG(value)   = long integer by rounding
CSNG(value)   = single precision by rounding
FIX(value)    = integer by truncating fractional part
INT(value)    = integer less than or equal to value
STR$(value)   = string of digits representing the value
VAL(string)   = the value corresponding to the string of digits
```

The only tricky conversion functions are FIX and INT. For positive values FIX and INT return the same results and are equivalent to chopping off or *truncating* the fractional part of a value. For example, FIX(9.9)=INT(9.9)=9. For negative values the two functions differ. The FIX function still operates by truncating the fractional value, i.e. FIX(-9.9)=-9. This seems reasonable until you realise that -9 is bigger than -9.9 (recall that negative numbers get less as you go from -1 to -2, to -3 and so on.) The INT function maintains the action of truncating positive values in that it always returns an integer smaller than or equal to the given value, i.e. INT(-9.9)=-10.

» The type of a function

Functions were introduced in the previous chapter as a way of working out a result. The result was returned to the program by assigning the result to the name of the function. Now that we know about different types of variable it should come as no surprise that you can define functions that return different types of result. For example, max% could be defined to be an integer function and del$ a string function. String functions are particularly useful because they enable you to define new string operations very easily. For example, the function del$(a$,s,e) can be defined so as to delete the characters from s to e from the string a$:

```
FUNCTION del$(a$,s,e)
IF s<e THEN
   del$=MID$(a$,1,s)+MID$(a$,e,LEN(a$))
ELSE
   del$=""
END IF
END FUNCTION
```

You can, if you want to, define new functions for string handling operations common in other programming languages, so making program conversion easier. Indeed there is a style of programming where the first job is to write functions that perform the basic operations likely to be useful in the program that is about to be written. This is called *bottom-up* programming by contrast with the top down approach inherent in stepwise refinement.

» Procedures, functions and data types

In the previous chapter the only sort of variable used in procedures and functions was the simple single precision variable. Now that we know about different data types it is worth re-examining the way data is passed into procedures and functions. The first thing to say is that a parameter can be of any type. For example, CALL test(a%,b,c$) is perfectly correct as long as the type of each variable used in the call matches the type of the corresponding variable used in the procedure definition. If you want to you can also define parameter types without using special names, for example:

```
SUB test(a AS INTEGER,b AS SINGLE,c AS STRING)
```

This could be confusing if you forget that a is an integer, b is a single precision value and c a string. As in the case of defining simple variable types the use of an explicit type symbol is to be recommended.

» Prototypes - DECLARE

Now that you know all about the idea of passing parameters to subroutines and functions that can vary in type you might realise the scope for error that this provides. If you call a subroutine with the wrong type, or even the wrong number, of parameters then the results can vary a lot but they are never what you intended. To help guard against this QBasic allows you to include subroutine and function prototypes in the main program. A prototype is defined using the DECLARE statement:

```
DECLARE subroutine/function name (parameter list)
```

The parameter list should be exactly like that used in the subroutine or function definition. When all subroutines and functions are declared in this way QBasic can check that every use of the subroutine or function in your program is correct in terms of the number and types of parameter. For example:

```
DECLARE SUB test(i%,name AS STRING)
```

defines the subroutine test as needing an integer and a string in its parameter list when it is called. You can also make use of DECLARE statements to find out how to call a particular subroutine or function. You can also call subroutines without the need to precede the name by CALL if it is named in a DECLARE.

Adding DECLARE statements for every function and subroutine that is in your program would be something of a chore but fortunately the QBasic editor will do the job for you. When you save a program to disk the QBasic editor scans the program for all function and subroutine definitions and adds suitable DECLARE statements to the start of the program. What could be easier?

If you make a change to a subroutine or function's definition such that the parameters are different then you will see an error message when you run the program if you also forget to change the corresponding DECLARE statement. Often the quickest way to make such a change is to delete all of the DECLAREs at the start of the program and save the program to disk. This automatically regenerates all of the missing DECLAREs according to the current subroutine and function definitions.

» Constants

Although the focus of this chapter has been on variables and their type it is equally obvious that a constant has a type. For example, 1 is an integer constant and "Fred" is a string constant. In general when you assign a constant to a variable the constant will be converted to the type of the variable. For example, I%=1.6 assigns 2 to the integer variable I% because 1.6 is rounded up to give an integer value.

It is also worth knowing that you can specify integer constants using octal or hexadecimal. If you start a value with &O, &o or & then the value is treated as an octal value. In the same way starting a value with &H or &h results in it being treated as a hexadecimal number. If you want to use long octal or long hexadecimal constants then use a trailing & following the value. Don't worry if you don't know what octal or hexadecimal values are all about - they don't make any sense until you need them.

Many programs make use of constants to set their operating limits or characteristics. For example, you might set a limit of 5 bars in a bar chart that a program produces. In this case what you would discover is the use of the constant 5 throughout the program in tests to make sure that the limit isn't exceeded. This is fine, but imagine what happens when you have to alter the limit. You have to edit every line that contains the value 5 and the chances of getting it right first time are small. As an alternative you could define a variable called MaxBars, store the constant 5 in it and use it throughout the program. This has the advantage that the variable name tells you what the value 5 is controlling and changing it is just a matter of altering one assignment statement. However, variables are slower, take more storage than a constant, and what if the variable is changed accidentally? As a way of keeping the benefits of using a variable without the disadvantages, QBasic allows you to define *named* or *symbolic constants*. These are very like variables but you cannot change their value during the program. To define a named constant you have to use the command:

```
CONST name=value
```

For example:

```
CONST MaxBars=5
```

defines MaxBars to be the constant 5. The type of a constant is defined either by the use of a type symbol at the end of its name, or by the type of the value being assigned to it. Named constants are not affected by DEF*type* statements and once you have a constant with a particular name you cannot have a variable with same name, irrespective of type. Named constants are global if declared in the main program, and local otherwise. You should always use a named constant in preference to the repeated use of a value throughout a program.

» Another five easy pieces

The next five easy pieces all deal with strings, but don't miss the opportunity to use other variable types!

1. Read in a word and print it out letter-by-letter. (One letter per line).

2. Read in a word and print it out letter by letter in reverse order.

3. Instead of printing each letter out on a separate line build up a new word in reverse order. For example, if the input is HELP the output should be PLEH.

4. Convert the program written in the solution to Task 3 to test for palindromes - i.e. words/phrases that are the same forwards as backwards such as "rotor".

5. Write a program to replace all of the vowels, a,e,i,o,u in a string with asterisks.

» Suggested solution 1

This problem has a number of minor difficulties. Reading the entire word into a string variable is easy, but how do you extract a single letter. The solution is to notice that MID$(s$,i%,1) is character i% in the string. After this, all that remains is to realise that a FOR loop can generate values of i% from 1 to the length of the string:

```
INPUT s$
FOR i%=1 TO LEN(s$)
  c$=MID$(s$,i%,1)
    PRINT c$
NEXT i%
```

EASY21.BAS

Extracting single characters from a string is one of the most common uses of the MID$ function. An alternative approach, often used in dialects of Basic that don't have a MID$ function, is to use

```
c$=$ LEFT$(s$,1)
```

to extract the first character and then

```
s$=RIGHT$(s$,LEN(s$)-1)
```

to reduce the length of the string by one. Using MID$ is easier!

» Suggested solution 2

This seems like a difficult problem until you realise that printing the characters in reverse order is just a matter of running the FOR loop in reverse!

```
INPUT s$
FOR i%= LEN(s$) TO 1 STEP -1
  c$=MID$(s$,i%,1)
    PRINT c$
NEXT i%
```

EASY22.BAS

Always remember that if you can process a string in one direction you can reverse the order by making the loop run backwards!

» Suggested solution 3

There are a great many ways of writing this program, and if yours works then that is sufficient. The basic principle of all of the methods, however, is to build up the new string, character by character using concatenation. If the letters of the old string are provided in reverse order then this amounts to:

```
INPUT s$
c$=""
FOR i%= LEN(s$) TO 1 STEP -1
   c$=c$+MID$(s$,i%,1)
NEXT i%
PRINT c$
```

EASY23.BAS

Notice the use of c$=c$+MID$(s$,i%,1) to add the next letter to the string. What happens if you change this to c$=MID$(s$,i%,1)+c$? Can you use this to alter the program to make the FOR loop run from 1 to LEN(s$)?

» Suggested solution 4

This is just a matter of adding the test to the end of the previous program:

```
IF c$=s$ THEN
   PRINT "Palindrome"
ELSE
   PRINT "not a Palindrome"
END IF
```

EASY24.BAS

Notice that c$ has to be initially set to the null string - that is "" and not " ".

» Suggested solution 5

This is the most difficult of the problems, but it is still relatively easy once you realise that you can reverse the test for a vowel in s$ by searching for each letter in S$ in the string "aeiou". This means that if the current letter of the string is in c$ you can discover if it is a vowel using INSTR(1,"aeiou",c$) which is 0 if c$ isn't in "aeiou" and its position in the string if it is. Using this combined with MID$ to extract c$ from s$, and MID$ again on the other side of the equals sign to change any vowel to "*", the program is easy.

```
INPUT s$
c$=""
FOR i%=1 TO LEN(s$)
   c$=MID$(s$,i%,1)
   IF INSTR(1,"aeiou",c$)<>0 THEN
      MID$(s$,i%,1)="*"
   END IF
NEXT i%
PRINT s$
```

EASY25.BAS

Key points

» What you can store in a variable depends on its type. QBasic supports five types identified by the last symbol of the variable name: !=single precision, #=double precision, %=integer, &= long integer, and $= string.

» Variables can also be typed using DEF*type* and DIM *variable* AS *type* statements but in most cases explicit type identifiers are to be preferred.

» Type conversion between numeric variables is automatic but there are explicit type conversion functions.

» You can perform all string manipulation using concatenation, the MID$ function and the LEN function. In addition the LEFT$ and RIGHT$ functions make some operations easier.

» String comparison is supported for =, <,>, <=,=> and <>. You can also search for one string within another using INSTR.

» Functions can be typed and can return a result of that type.

» Parameters can be typed and their types are checked when they are called as long as a DECLARE statement is included in the main program. The QBasic editor will automatically add DECLARE statements to the start of the main program when the file is saved to disk.

» Numeric constants are converted to the type of the variable to which they are assigned. You can use octal and hexadecimal constants.

» Named constants behave like variables that cannot be altered and make a program easier to understand and modify.

Chapter 6

Data Structures

Arrays and records are groups of simple variables that can be used to store lists of data. This chapter examines how to define and use arrays and records.

Single variables can be used to store single values of a given type but programs often need to store and process large quantities of data. In this case you need to organise single variables into data structures that can be used as a single entity. The best known and most useful of all such data structures is the *array*.

» Arrays

Consider for a moment the apparently simple problem of reading in three numbers and printing them out in the reverse order. So far the only method that we could use is:

```
INPUT A1
INPUT A2
INPUT A3
PRINT A3
PRINT A2
PRINT A1
```

which is not too bad for three numbers but think what the program would look like if the problem was to reverse 100 numbers!

What we need to be able to do is to refer to a variable like 'A(I)' where I can take values from 1 to 3 in a FOR loop. Then we could write:

```
FOR I=1 TO 3
   INPUT A(I)
NEXT I
FOR I=3 TO 1 STEP -1
   PRINT A(I)
NEXT I
```

This is in fact exactly what QBasic allows you to do. The collection of variables A(1) to A(3) is called the array A, and a particular variable A(I) is called an *element* of the array and I is called the *index* variable. The only complication is that before you can use an array you must declare how many elements the array is going to have. This is done using the DIMension statement:

```
DIM A(3)
```

which should be added to the start of the previous program. (In fact the program will work without the DIM statement because QBasic will supply a ten element array by default if you forget it.)

If you define an array as having only five elements and then try to use A(6) then you will get an error message for trying to use something that doesn't exist! It is tempting to think that it is better to define arrays larger than you need to try to avoid such error messages but be warned - arrays can quickly use up all the memory that your machine has to

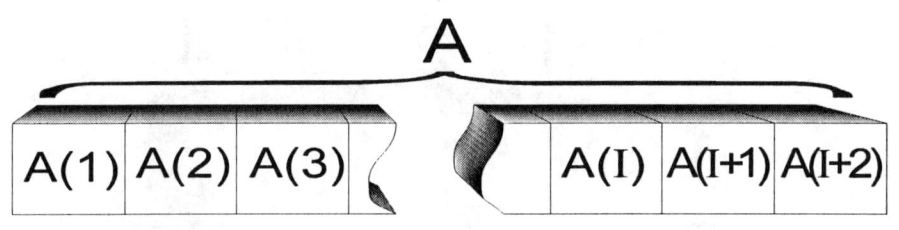

Figure 6.1
A one dimensional array

offer! You can define the size of an array using an expression or a variable. For example:

```
INPUT N
DIM A(N)
```

is perfectly correct and will set the array to whatever size you type in when the program is run. (Although see static and dynamic arrays later.)

You can think of an array as a collection of variables of a particular type all sharing the same name - A in this case. You can also think of the action of the array index as picking out a particular member of the array - see Figure 6.1.

» Two-dimensional arrays

In addition to being able to define arrays that can be thought of as rows of variables, you can define arrays that correspond to organising variables into tables made up of rows and columns. For example:

```
DIM table(10,10)
```

defines a collection of variables organised into 10 rows and 10 columns. A particular element of this array can be referred to as table(I,J) where the two indices select the row and column.

The idea of a two-dimensional array can be extended to three-, four- or more dimensions, but it is difficult to think of an arrangement of variables that corresponds to the higher dimensional arrays. For example:

```
DIM A(10,20,5)
```

is a three-dimensional array and a sample element is A(2,1,4). There is not much use for arrays with dimensions greater than two. This is fortunate because they tend to use memory very, very quickly!

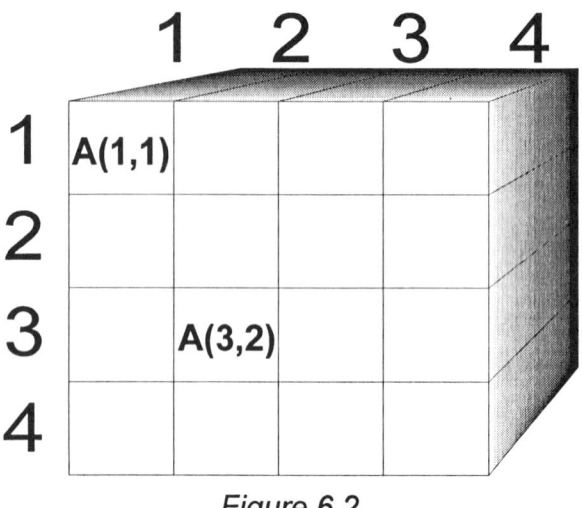

Figure 6.2
A two-dimensional array

» The type of an array

You can form arrays from integers, single precision, double precision and string variables. For example DIM count%(10) is an integer array of 10 elements. String arrays are particularly important because they can be used to store and manipulate lists and words. For example:

```
DIM S$(10)
```

is a string array composed of 10 different strings. Each element of a string array behaves exactly like a standard string and can be used to store a variable number of characters. For example, the number reversing program can be used to reverse a list of words:

```
DIM A$(5)
FOR I=1 TO 5
   INPUT A$(I)
NEXT I
FOR I=5 TO 1 STEP -1
   PRINT A$(I)
NEXT I
```

You can use MID$, LEFT$, etc. and any other string operations on any element of a string array. Indeed an element of any array behaves exactly like a simple variable of its type. For example, a%(i) can be used anywhere an integer variable can.

An alternative way of specifying the type of an array is to follow the definition with AS *type*. For example:

```
DIM A(10) AS INTEGER
```

creates an array of integer variables. This method was introduced in the previous chapter as an alternative way of defining the type of a simple variable. For example:

```
DIM A AS INTEGER
```

defines A as a simple integer variable. In most cases it is better not to use this method as it creates arrays and variables with names that do not convey their type. For example, if you didn't see the DIM statement listed above how would you know that A was an integer? In this case A% is a much clearer way of expressing the same idea. However, AS *type* comes into its own as soon as user defined types are introduced - see later.

» Upper and lower bounds

So far it has been assumed that the first element of any array corresponds to an index value of 1. In fact, the first element corresponds to an index value of 0. For example, if you define DIM A(10) there will be eleven elements from A(0) to A(10). You can alter this by using the statement OPTION BASE *n* which sets the lowest element created to A(*n*). So following OPTION BASE 1 a DIM A(10) statement would only create a ten-element array A(1) to A(10). For mathematical programs having the first element of the array indexed by 0 is usually more natural than starting from 1.

Most of the arrays that you will ever want to use will have a first element with an index of 1 or 0 but just occasionally it is useful to start with a different initial index value. It is possible to specify a different starting index for an array using

```
DIM array(s:f)
```

or

```
DIM array(s TO f)
```

where *s* is the first index value and *f* the last. For example, DIM age(18:30) or DIM age(18 TO 30) creates an array whose first element is age(18) and final element is age(30). Similarly different starting points can be set for each dimension of an array. For example, x(15:30,5:20) is an array x(i,j) and i has to be between 15 to 30 and j between 5 to 20. You might be wondering why you would want to do this? The answer is that arrays are often used as lookup tables and in this case it is simpler if the index range is natural. For example, if you wanted to keep a table of hours worked on each day of a week you would probably use an array DAYS(1:7). On the other hand if you wanted to record the number of days that the temperature was at a particular value you might use an array like DAYS(-10:30). Being able to specify the starting and finishing value of the index is sometimes a great advantage but most of the time you can ignore it.

» Index tricks

Arrays and FOR loops were made for one another. A suitably constructed FOR loop can be used to step through and process each element of an array. For example, if the array days stores the number of days that the temperature has been t% then you print the results using:

```
DIM days(-10 TO 30)
FOR t%=-10 TO 30
   PRINT days(t%)
NEXT t%
```

In languages that don't support definable upper and lower bounds for arrays, programmers have to be good at working out how to transform an index value so that it accesses the correct array element.

For example, if the days array is defined as DIM days(40) then the element corresponding to a temperature t% is given by days(t%+10). (Try working out which array elements are used for a range of temperatures.) In practice, index expressions can become very complicated and they are a source of potential error. Always try to simplify index expressions by using sensible upper and lower array bounds. Even so there are still times when you cannot avoid an index expression.

» Scope and existence of arrays

Just as with simple variables you can ask where an array is accessible from, and when it is created and destroyed. Arrays follow the same scope rules that simple variables do. That is, arrays defined in subroutines or functions are local unless you add the keyword SHARED to the DIM statement. Local arrays are, by default, *dynamic*. That is, the array declaration DIM A(10) within a subroutine or function creates a local dynamic array, i.e. it can only be used within the subroutine or function, and it doesn't keep its values between subroutine or function calls. By contrast, the array declaration DIM SHARED A(10) creates an array that is shared with the main program and so by definition this must be a *static array*.

A *global array* (i.e. one that is shared with all subroutines and functions) can be created by naming the array in a COMMON SHARED statement. If you want to create a local static array then you have to declare that the entire subroutine or function is static. For example:

```
SUB test STATIC
DIM A(10)
```

will create an array A that is local to subroutine test and static, i.e. it retains its values between calls to test. Notice that all this implies that all arrays declared in the main program are static but there is an exception to this rule.

If an array is declared using a variable or expression to give its size, e.g. DIM(N) then it cannot be created as static because its size isn't known until the DIM(N) statement is reached. In this case the array is dynamic. Finally you can change the default for arrays from static, where possible, to dynamic by including the command:

```
'$DYNAMIC
```

at the start of a program. Similarly if you want to restore the default back to static you can use the command:

```
'$STATIC
```

(Notice the use of the single quote to make the statement a remark, see Chapter 9. In this case it acts as an instruction to the compiler.)

The set of rules that govern the existence of arrays is complicated and you might be wondering why you really need to know if an array is static or dynamic? The answer is that in many cases you can ignore this subtlety but static and dynamic arrays do behave differently. The most obvious difference is that only a local static array will keep its values between subroutine calls and this is important if you are using the array as a lookup table. Static arrays are also slightly faster in use than dynamic arrays. For these two reasons, static arrays are to be preferred to dynamic arrays. However, the dynamic array does have one big advantage - you can change its size. Although you can only dimension a static array once, you can re-dimension a dynamic array any number of times that you like. The command REDIM is used like DIM but it always creates a dynamic array and it will remove any existing array of the same name. You can also remove a dynamic array and so free the storage that it used by way of the ERASE command. For example:

```
REDIM A(10)
```

creates a dynamic array with 10 elements. A subsequent:

```
REDIM A(20)
```

recreates the array with 20 elements. Notice that any data that the original array contained is lost. Finally, if you want to get rid of the array completely you would use:

```
ERASE A
```

Notice that if you try to ERASE a static array then the result is that all of the data stored in the array is erased but the array still exists and can be used later in the program.

To summarise:

» arrays declared in subroutines or functions are, by default, local and dynamic.

» Only arrays that are dimensioned with a constant, e.g. A(10), can be static. Such arrays are static, by default, if declared in the main program, a static subroutine or static function.

» This default can be changed using '$DYNAMIC or '$STATIC

» REDIM always creates dynamic arrays

» Arrays as parameters

You can pass single array elements to a function or a subroutine just as if they were simple variables. For example, CALL test(A%(5),X(7),Z$(I)) is perfectly correct as long as test expects an integer followed by a single precision then a string variable. In this case the arrays only need to be dimensioned in the calling program as the subroutine that the elements are passed to really does think that they are nothing more than simple variables.

Passing an entire array is only marginally more tricky. To pass an array into a procedure all you have to do is to indicate in the subroutine definition that it is an array by following its name by brackets. For example:

```
SUB test(A())
```

is enough to inform test that A is an array. Following this you can use the array A within test without needing to dimension it, for example:

```
SUB test(A())
FOR i=1 TO 100
   A(i)=0
NEXT i
END SUB
```

Notice that the subroutine has no idea of the size of the array and if A is not dimensioned to at least 100 elements in the calling program it will cause an error. Indeed, the subroutine doesn't even have any idea of the number of the array's dimensions. It is usual for the size of an array to be passed as a separate parameter, for example:

```
SUB test(A(),n)
FOR i=1 TO n
   A(i)=0
NEXT i
END SUB
```

If you pass a two-dimensional array it is usual also to pass two additional parameters giving its size, for example:

```
SUB test(A(),n,m)
FOR i=1 TO n
   FOR j=1 TO m
      A(i,j)=0
   NEXT j
NEXT i
END SUB
```

Notice also that array parameters are always passed by reference and never by value. In simple terms this means that if you change the value of an array within a subroutine or function then the value is changed in the main or calling program.

If you want to write subroutines that work correctly with arrays of any size without having to pass the size of the array as parameters, then it is worth knowing about:

```
LBOUND(array,dimension)
```

and

```
UBOUND(array,dimension)
```

These functions return the lower and upper legal range for an array's index in the specified dimension. Using these, the previous subroutine could be written:

```
SUB test(A())
FOR i=LBOUND(A,1) TO UBOUND(A,1)
   FOR j=LBOUND(A,2) TO UBOUND(A,2)
     A(i,j)=0
   NEXT j
NEXT i
END SUB
```

To enable type checking of array parameters you have to include the array in the DECLARE statement at the start of the program. For example:

```
DECLARE SUB test(A())
```

You can also indicate the number of dimensions that the array has by including a value between the otherwise empty brackets. For example:

```
DECLARE SUB test(A(1))
```

declares the array A to be one-dimensional.

» Fixed sized strings

For most purposes the string variable as described in the previous chapter is the most useful of all variables. It is more powerful than the string variables that you can find in other languages because it will use as much storage as needed to store the current string. That is, if you define A$ and assign a single letter to it, A$="X", then the amount of storage used is just enough for that one letter. If you later store 10 letters in it then more storage is allocated to it. This dynamic allocation of storage makes strings easy to use but this ease of use comes at a price. Dynamic strings are difficult to implement and they are slow in use. There are also situations where the amount of storage needed for a variable cannot be allowed to change. To cope with these problems QBasic also supports fixed length strings.

A fixed length string is declared using a statement like:

```
DIM Surname AS STRING*length
```

For example:

```
DIM Surname AS STRING*25
```

defines Surname to be a fixed length string capable of holding 25 characters. Fixed length strings behave just like ordinary strings with, of course, the one obvious difference that they always hold the specified number of characters. If you assign a string longer than 25 characters to Surname then only first 25 characters are stored. If you assign fewer than 25 characters then the deficit is made up by padding the string with blanks. To see the difference you can try the following program:

```
DIM test1 AS STRING*10
DIM test2 AS STRING
test1="X"
test2="Y"
PRINT test1;"Z"
PRINT test2;"Z"
```

When test1 is printed it produces X followed by nine spaces which explains the position of the final Z. When test2 is printed only the X is printed followed immediately by the final Z.

Fixed length strings are faster but their real use is as part of record data types.

» Records

An array is very useful when you need to store a set of values of the same type. In practice it doesn't take long to discover an example where the data is very definitely a single entry but it is made up of different variable types. For example, if you want to record an employee's name and salary you need a string variable and an integer. Groups of variables of different types are generally referred to as *records* because of their similarity to traditional card records. QBasic allows you to define a record type using the statements:

```
TYPE name
    element name AS type
    etc..
END TYPE
```

Each element of the record can be defined to be one of INTEGER, LONG, SINGLE or DOUBLE. You can also define an element to be a string but only a fixed length string as described in the previous section.

For example, suppose you need a record that can be used to store name and salary then you might declare a new record type using:

```
TYPE PayRec
    Surname AS STRING*25
    Pay AS INTEGER
END TYPE
```

This record has two elements, or *fields* as they are also known, Surname, a fixed length string, and Pay, an integer.

At this point you may think that you have defined a variable that you can use - you haven't. All you have done is to define a new data type which can be used as a template to create as many variables as you like. That is, in the same way that INTEGER is a type and you can create as many integer variables that you need, so PayRec is a type and you can create as many pay records as you need. To define a PayRec variable you have to use the standard method of declaring a simple variable to be a particular type. For example:

```
DIM Rec AS PayRec
```

declares Rec to be a variable of type PayRec. You can think of this statement as being very similar to using a DIM statement to define an array of a particular size. In this case you are defining a record of a particular type.

The next question is, how do you gain access to the elements of a record? The answer is that you use a qualified name. For example:

```
Rec.Surname
```

is the element of Rec that is the fixed length string. In the same way Rec.Pay is the integer.

By using qualified names you can access any element or field of a record. As is the case with an array element, a field behaves just like a simple variable of the same type, i.e. you can use them in expressions, assignment statements and pass them as parameters. Notice that the qualified name method of accessing a field doesn't lend itself to automatic processing using a FOR loop in the same way that an array does. This usually isn't a problem because the sort of processing to which records are usually subject is different for each field.

» Arrays of records

You can define arrays of record types in a perfectly natural way. For example:

```
DIM Company(1 TO NumEmployed) AS PayRec
```

creates an array with 1 to NumEmployed elements. Each element of this array is a variable of type PayRec. That is Company(i%) is a record of type PayRec and Company(i%).Surname is the name field and Company(i%).Pay is the integer pay field.

» Records within records

Being able to define arrays of records is a powerful feature of QBasic but it isn't symmetric, i.e. you cannot use an array as an element of a record. Surprisingly, you can use another record type as a field of a record. For example:

```
TYPE details
   Pay AS INTEGER
   Years AS INTEGER
   NatIns AS STRING*25
END TYPE

TYPE employee
   Surname AS STRING*30
   Job AS STRING*25
   JobInfo AS details
END TYPE
```

defines two record types. The first is a perfectly normal record but the second uses the first as the type of its last field. That is, JobInfo is a field that is itself a record. If you define a new record variable as:

```
DIM rec1 AS employee
```

then rec1.JobInfo.Pay is the pay element from the details record.

Record types have to be defined in the main program and type definitions are global to the entire program and can be used by any subroutine or function. However, variables of the type that are declared in subroutines or functions are local and dynamic (i.e. they do not retain their values between calls). If you want to make a local record static you have to declare the entire subroutine or function static by including the keyword STATIC at the end of the SUB or FUNCTION statement. In addition, you can define record variables to be shared or global just in the case of arrays or simple variables.

You can pass entire records to subroutines or functions as parameters. To do this all that is necessary is to declare the parameter to be of the required type. For example:

```
SUB test(rec2 AS PayRec)
```

Notice that this is no different from passing an array except that you have to use AS to define the type. (There is no alternative way of making a variable a user defined type other than by using AS type.) The declaration of the subroutine also has to have the type of the record parameter shown using AS type.

Record types are not a difficult idea and they have many simple applications. In many cases you can choose to use either an array or a record and it is up to the programmer to decide which is more appropriate i.e. which leads to the simpler program. However, record types make dealing with information stored in a disk file so much easier that they are more or less the only sensible choice.

» Bubble sort revisited

The example given at the end of Chapter 3 of a bubble sort was written before procedures, data types or arrays were introduced. As a result, it was not really representative of a well written QBasic program. Using stepwise refinement to write this program is fairly easy and you should have no trouble in producing a main program something like:

BUBBLE2.BAS

```
INPUT "how many numbers "; n
DIM a(n)
CALL RandData(a())
PRINT "This is the unsorted array "
CALL PrintArray(a())
CALL SortArray(a())
PRINT "This is the sorted array"
CALL PrintArray(a())
END
```

Basically all this main program does is to use three subroutines - RandData to generate some test data, PrintArray to print the array and SortArray to sort it. Easy? Yes, but the next step is to write the subroutines!

RandData depends on the use of the RND function which returns a random number in the range 0 to less than 1. Once you know about RND then the subroutine is easy enough:

```
SUB RandData (a())
n% = UBOUND(a, 1)
FOR i% = 1 TO n%
   a(i%) = RND * n%
NEXT i%
END SUB
```

Notice the use of UBOUND to find the upper limit of the array passed. Also notice that this subroutine can store random values in any array - all you have to do is call it.

PrintArray is trivial:

```
SUB PrintArray (a())
PRINT
FOR i% = 1 TO UBOUND(a, 1)
   PRINT a(i%)
NEXT i%
END SUB
```

The only interesting point in this routine is, again, the use of UBOUND to find the upper limit of the array.

Finally we come to the major subroutine SortArray. To understand this, you have to remember how a bubble sort works, so if you have forgotten turn back to Chapter 3.

```
SUB SortArray (a())
DO
   noswap% = 0
   CALL scan(a(), noswap%)
LOOP UNTIL noswap% = 0
END SUB
```

In this case, the actual scan and swapping of array elements is performed by subroutine scan. SortArray uses noswap% as a flag to discover when a scan has resulted in no swaps. When this is the case the DO-LOOP finishes and the array is sorted.

To complete SortArray we need subroutine scan. Once again this is easy enough:

```
SUB scan (a(), noswap%)
FOR i% = 1 TO UBOUND(a, 1) - 1
   IF a(i%) > a(i% + 1) THEN
      SWAP a(i%), a(i% + 1)
      noswap% = 1
   END IF
NEXT i%
END SUB
```

This subroutine scans the array, comparing adjacent elements and swapping them over if they are in the wrong order. Notice the use of the block IF statement to swap and set the flag. Also notice the use of the command SWAP to swap the variables. The existence of this command was only mentioned in Chapter 3 because every programmer should know how to swap two variables without its help, but once you do know about it there is little point in using any other method. SWAP will swap the values of any two variables of any type - integer, long, single, double, string or record - and will do it faster than the equivalent assignments. The only other point worth noticing is the way noswap% is passed to the subroutine to carry the result of the scan back to the calling program.

The DECLARE statements generated when the file is saved are:

```
DECLARE SUB scan (a!(), noswap%)
DECLARE SUB SortArray (a!())
DECLARE SUB RandData (a!())
DECLARE SUB PrintArray (a!())
```

Of course, you don't have to add these statements yourself, they are just listed for completeness.

Subroutine SortArray is fairly general purpose in that it will sort any one-dimensional array you care to pass it. Very often it can be difficult to see what assumptions you have made when writing a program. In this case the array has to be single precision and its first element has to be 1. The first assumption is obvious but the second is often overlooked. Writing subroutines that can work in all situations is very difficult.

If you want to know more about sorting then see the section on sorting in Chapter 10 where faster and more sophisticated methods are described.

Key points

» An array is a collection of variables of the same type. It is declared using:
    DIM *name*(*lower* TO *upper*) AS *type*
If the type is given by the use of type symbols then AS *type* can be omitted. If *lower* TO *upper* is also omitted the array starts at 0 or 1 depending on the last setting of OPTION BASE.

» Arrays declared in a subroutine or function are local and dynamic. Local arrays can be made static by declaring the entire subroutine or function as STATIC. Arrays can be shared with the main program using the SHARED statement.

» Arrays declared in the main program using constants are static. REDIM always creates a dynamic array. The size of a dynamic array can be changed using subsequent REDIMs. The default use of static arrays can be changed using '$DYNAMIC and restored using '$STATIC.

» Elements of an array are specified using an index expression and can be used exactly like variables of the same type.

» Entire arrays can be passed to subroutines or functions.

» Fixed length strings are declared using:
    DIM *name* AS STRING*size
They work like standard strings apart from always storing the specified number of characters.

» Records are collections of variables of mixed type. To declare a record you first have to define a new variable type using:
    TYPE *name*
        element name AS *type*
    END TYPE
and then declare a variable or any number of variables of that type using:
    DIM *variable name* AS *name*

» Elements of a record are specified using qualified names. They behave like simple variables of the same type. You can pass entire records to a subroutine or function.

Chapter 7

Graphics and Sound

Graphics is an important aspect of any program. This chapter describes how QBasic's graphics commands work.

QBasic provides a large number of commands for the production of both low and high resolution graphics. Of course, the sort of results that you can achieve depend on exactly what type of hardware you have. There are a bewildering number of graphics modes and this is one of the first problems that faces any prospective graphics programmer.

» Graphics modes

The type of graphics that you can produce depends very much on the sort of display adapter that your machine has. The original PC could only produce monochrome text, and the only graphics that it supported were produced using a range of graphics characters. Following on from the monochrome display adapter (MDA) IBM introduced the Colour Graphics Adapter (CGA). This could produce text and low- to medium-resolution colour graphics. Following CGA, which is the lowest standard of colour graphics, IBM introduced EGA (Extended Graphics Adapter) and VGA (Versatile Graphics Array). The current standard is SVGA (Super VGA). All of the graphics cards, CGA, EGA VGA and SVGA are backward compatible in the sense that all of the graphics modes offered by CGA are supported by EGA, VGA and SVGA and so on.

The only real problem that is likely to arise is the use of any graphics adapter that is not supported by IBM. Perhaps the best known of all these is the Hercules graphics adapter (HGA) which is a high resolution monochrome graphics card. QBasic does support the Hercules graphics card, but only with the addition of a driver included in MS-DOS. It also works reasonably well with the non-standard graphics cards included in the Olivetti range of machines.

The current state of PC graphics hardware is summarised below:

Adapter	Highest resolution	Max colours in highest resolution	Supported by QBasic
MDA	Text only	Monochrome	Yes
CGA	640x200	2	Yes
EGA	640x350	16	Yes
VGA	640x480	16	Yes
HGA	720x348	Monochrome	Via driver
SVGA	up to 1024x768	256	Only in VGA

» Resolution

Before you can begin writing any sort of graphics program you have to select the graphics mode in which you are going to be working. The command:

SCREEN *type,colour*

must be used to select which mode is used. *Type* is a number that selects the mode as shown in the table below. The second parameter, *colour* is either 0 for no colour if you have a CGA card and a monochrome monitor, or 1 if you are using a colour display. There are a number of other additional features of the SCREEN command that make it possible to go a little further and these are described later.

Screen #	Resolution	Colours/Palette	Adapters
0	Text only	16/16 (64 EGA)	All
1	320x200	4/(16 EGA VGA)	CGA/EGA/VGA
2	640x200	2/(16 EGA VGA)	CGA/EGA/VGA
3	720x348	2/2	HGA
4	640x400	2/16	Olivetti M24/28
7	320x200	16/16	EGA/VGA
8	640x200	16/16	EGA/VGA
9	640x350	16/64	EGA/VGA
10	640x350	4/9 (monochrome)	EGA/VGA
11	640x480	2/262144	VGA
12	640x480	16/262144	VGA
13	320x200	256/262144	VGA

Notice that you need to load the MSHERC program before starting QBasic to make use of mode 3.

» Using the text screen

Although in some senses the text screen is the least exciting of the graphics modes, it is also often proves the most useful. When you first start a QBasic program running you are in text mode by default. You can alter the number of lines and columns displayed on the screen in mode 0 using the command:

```
WIDTH columns, lines
```

Columns can be either 40 or 80. The number of lines that you can display depends on the type of display adapter that you are using but you can try 25 (standard), 43, and 50. It is also worth knowing that

```
CLS
```

clears the screen.

Any text produced by a print statement always starts from the current cursor position and this can be altered using the LOCATE command:

```
LOCATE y, x
```

moves the cursor to row number *y* (1-25) and column number *x* (1-40 or 1-80). The LOCATE command can also be used to change the shape of the cursor and determine whether it is visible or not. The full LOCATE command is:

```
LOCATE y,x,c,a,b
```

which positions the cursor at *x,y* makes it invisible if *c* is 0 and alters its size so that starts on scan line *a* and ends on scan line *b*. You can discover the current position of the cursor using the POS, row position, and CSRLIN, column position, functions. For example:

```
y=POS
x=CSRLIN
```

gives you the current x,y position of the cursor.

You can gain a great deal of control of the text screen using nothing more than the PRINT statement. You can print more than one item on a line by separating each one by a semi-colon. If you separate print items using a comma, then each item is printed at the start of a standard print zone (each print zone is 14 characters wide).

To see the difference compare the two statements:
```
PRINT A;B;C
PRINT A,B,C
```
The first prints the values one after another and the second spaces them out across the screen. To make horizontal positioning more accurate you can use the TAB(*n*) function which will move the printing position to column *n*, as long as the printing position hasn't already passed column *n*, when it has no effect. For example:
```
PRINT A;TAB(10);B;TAB(25);C
```
will print A in the first column, B starting at column 10 and C in column 25. Clearly the TAB function can be used to construct tables of results. If you want to leave a given number of spaces between items then you can use the SPC(*n*) command. For example:
```
PRINT A;SPC(10);B
```
which will always leave 10 spaces between the value printed by A and the start of B. Notice that you cannot use TAB or SPC outside a print statement.

Normally each print statement moves the screen cursor to a new line after it has printed its list of print items. In most cases this is what you want, but you can suppress the move to a new line after each print statement. All you have to do is finish it with a trailing semi-colon or comma. For example:
```
PRINT A;
PRINT B
```
is equivalent to PRINT A;B

» Print Using

Perhaps the ultimate in print output control comes from the command:
```
PRINT USING "format"; print list
```
The format string defines how each item in the print list should be printed. The format string consists of special characters which form a 'picture' of how you want each print item to look. For example, the special symbol # stands for a digit or a space and the picture ###.##

specifies three digits, a decimal point followed by two digits. If the number doesn't have enough digits then spaces are printed before the decimal point and zeros after the decimal point. For example, the value 10.2 would be printed as:

```
space space 10.20
```

The special characters that can be used to create pictures of numeric values are shown in the table below.

For example,

```
PRINT USING "###.##",A
```

will print the value in A with up to three digits before the decimal point and two following it.

Symbol	Meaning
#	a single digit - always printed either as a digit, blank or zero as appropriate
.	a decimal point - if a digit (#) precedes the decimal point then a digit rather than a space is always printed, numbers are always rounded
+	forces the sign of the number to be printed either before or after the number
-	prints a negative value with a trailing minus sign if included at the end of a picture
**	causes asterisks to be printed in place of leading spaces also specifies two digits as in ##
$$	includes a leading $ sign and specifies a single digit
**$	combines ** and $$, i.e. a leading $ is printed after leading spaces have been printed as * also specifies two digits
^^^^	exponential format
,	places commas after every third digit

There is a smaller number of formatting characters used for strings and text in general

Symbol	Meaning
&	prints entire string
!	prints only the first letter of the string
\ \	prints as many characters of the string as there are spaces between the slashes plus two for the slashes
-	prints the next character exactly as it appears

You can mix the formatting characters to print both numbers and text. You can also include other characters in the formatting string to appear as prompts. For example:

```
PRINT USING "The answer is   ###.##",A
```

will print the value in A complete with the prompt "The answer is". One of the advantages of using a formatting string is that it can be stored in a variable and used as a standard format for more than one PRINT USING statement. For example:

```
F$="The result is ###.###"
PRINT USING F$,A
```

This allows you to create a set of standard formats, at the start of a program say, to be used throughout the rest of the program.

» Text as graphics

Although text mode is not very good for graphics, you can gain access to a range of special purpose and graphics characters using the CHR$ function. You can find a list of characters and ASCII codes at the back of most PC manuals and there is also a full list in the QBasic help file when you select Contents, Quick Reference, ASCII Character Codes. Once you have identified your desired graphics characters as having ASCII code c you can print it on the screen at row y column x using:

```
LOCATE y,x
PRINT CHR$(c);
```

For example, the program in Listing 7.1 bounces a face character around the screen. Some of the techniques used in this program are explained in detail later. The basic principle of the program is to print the character at its new location and then print a blank to remove it. The IF statements detect the edge of the screen and reverse the ball's velocity appropriately.

You can alter the colour or display attribute of a text character using:

COLOR *foreground, background, border*

where *foreground*, *background* and *border* are colour/attribute codes as shown in the following table.

Colour code	CGA/EGA/VGA	MDA
0	black	black
1	blue	underline
2	green	white
3	cyan	white
4	red	white
5	magenta	white
6	brown	white
7	white	white
8	grey	black
9	light blue	bright underlined
10	light green	bright
11	light cyan	bright
12	light red	bright
13	light magenta	bright
14	yellow	bright
15	bright white	black

Listing 7.1

```
REM bounce
CLS
COLOR 2
v% = 1
w% = 1
x% = 1
y% = 1
DO WHILE INKEY$ = ""
    LOCATE y%, x%
    PRINT " ";
    x% = x% + v%
    y% = y% + w%
    IF x% = 80 THEN v% = -v%
    IF x% = 1 THEN v% = -v%
    IF y% = 24 THEN w% = -w%
    IF y% = 1 THEN w% = -w%
    LOCATE y%, x%
    PRINT CHR$(2);
    t = TIMER
    DO WHILE TIMER - t < .05
    LOOP
LOOP
END
```

BOUNCE.BAS

In CGA mode the colour can be made to blink by adding 16 to the colour code. In MGA mode the code only apply to the foreground attribute. The background codes produce black for 0-6 and 7 produces white.

» Graphics modes

If you select one of the true graphics modes described earlier then you immediately have access to a very wide range of graphics commands and the text commands described above still work! The basic principle of all graphics is specifying a point or *pixel* (from picture element) on the screen using x,y co-ordinates. You can think of this as being similar to specifying the current position of the text cursor in terms of columns

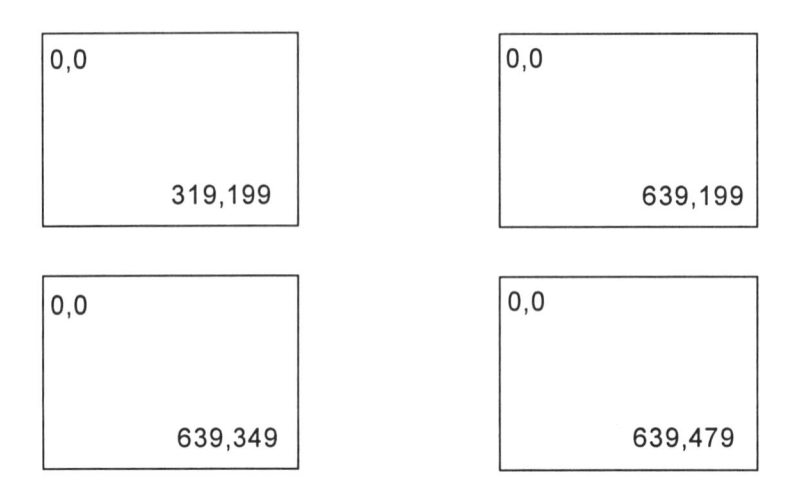

Figure 7.1
Graphics co-ordinates

and rows. The only real difference is that the first column of pixels is column 0 and the first row of pixels is row 0. The maximum x or y co-ordinate that you can use depends on the resolution of the graphics mode selected. The four possible screen co-ordinate layouts can be seen in Figure 7.1. The similarity between text and graphics co-ordinates extends to the idea of a cursor marking the current position. In the case of the graphics screen, the graphics cursor is always invisible but it is moved around by the graphics commands so that it is always at the last point referenced.

» Controlling colour - COLOR and CLS

The principle of colour control in high resolution graphics is that no matter how many colours are available for use, only two are active. One of the colours available must be designated as a background colour and another must be designated as a foreground colour. Most of the high resolution commands automatically produce points in the currently selected foreground colour. You can think of all high resolution commands as drawing in the foreground colour against the background colour.

In the graphics modes the statement:

>   COLOR *foreground,background*

sets the colours to be used for the foreground and background colours in all subsequent hi-res commands. It is important to realise that COLOR changes nothing that is already on the screen, it only sets the colours to be used in future operations. In screen modes 4,12 and 13 you can only set the foreground colour. In mode 1 the COLOR statement doesn't select a foreground-background pair of colours but sets which group of four colours is actually available for use. As this is equivalent to the use of the PALETTE statement which is described later, COLOR in mode 1 is dealt with there. All of the graphics commands to be described allow you to specify the colour in which something should be drawn, but if you leave out an explicit colour specification then the foreground colour is used as a default. The statement:

>   CLS

will clear the screen to the currently selected background colour.

» Drawing points

The simplest of all the high resolution graphics commands is:

>   PSET(*x,y*),*c*

This changes the point at *x,y* to the colour given by the colour code *c*. If you leave *c* out the current foreground colour is used. Just as PSET changes a pixel's colour to the foreground by default so the command:

>   PRESET(*x,y*)

changes the colour of the point at *x,y* to the currently selected background colour. Notice that PRESET(*x,y*) produces exactly the same result as PSET(*x,y*),*c* if *c* is the colour code of the current background colour. Although PRESET can always be replaced by an appropriate PSET it is slightly easier to use when setting a lot of points to the background colour or where your program doesn't keep track of the current background colour.

» Drawing lines

Perhaps the most useful high resolution command is:

```
LINE (x1,y1)-(x2,y2),c
```

This produces a straight line between the point at *x1,y1* and the point *x2,y2*. The colour of the points on the line are determined by *c*. For example:

```
LINE (0,0)-(100,100)
```

will draw a line from the point 0,0 to the point 100,100 in the current foreground colour and:

```
LINE (0,0)-(100,100),2
```

will set all the points on the line to colour 2.

If you leave out the first pair of co-ordinates then the line is drawn from the current position of the graphics cursor. For example:

```
LINE -(x,y)
```

will draw a line from the current position of the graphics cursor to the point *x,y*.

» Drawing boxes

Although it may seem out of keeping with its name, the LINE command can also be used to draw boxes. If you add the letter "B" to the end of a LINE command, then instead of drawing a line between the two points it will turn them into the opposite corners of a box. Thus the command:

```
LINE (x1,y1)-(x2,y2),,B
```

draws a box in the current foreground colour with the points *x1,y1* and *x2,y2* as opposite corners. You can also draw filled in boxes using LINE. If you add a BF to the end of the command you not only get the outline of a box it is also filled in with the current foreground or the colour you specify.

Dotted lines

As well as solid lines you can also draw dotted lines but unfortunately the method of specifying the pattern of dots is slightly complicated. Technically, what you have to do is specify a 16-bit mask that controls when a pixel will and will not be plotted. In practice this amounts to writing a pattern of 1s and 0s to show the dashes and spaces. For example:

```
1100110011001100
```

specifies a dotted line with two pixels plotted followed by a two-pixel space followed by two pixels plotted and so on. This idea of using the pattern of 1s and 0s to control the pattern of dots and spaces is easy enough, what is more complicated is how you write this specification within the LINE command. To draw a dotted line you use the command:

```
LINE (x1,y1)-(x2,y2),c,,style
```

where *style* is the 16-bit mask. (Notice the two commas marking the optional B or BF attributes.) The problem is that QBasic cannot accept binary numbers in commands and so you have to convert the bit pattern into a decimal, hex or octal value. If you know how to do this then all well and good, if you don't then you can use the following function to convert the binary string in b$ into a hexadecimal number:

BINCONV.BAS

```
FUNCTION BinToHex$ (b$)
b& = 0: p& = 1
FOR i% = LEN(b$) TO 1 STEP -1
        b& = b& + VAL(MID$(b$, i%, 1)) * p&
        p& = p& * 2
NEXT i%
BinToHex$ = HEX$(b&)
END FUNCTION
```

Once you have the hexadecimal number you can use it in the LINE command by prefixing it with &H, which means 'this is a hexadecimal number'. For example, 1100110011001100 converts to CCCC (hexadecimal numbers can include the characters A, B, C, D, E and F) and so the required LINE command is:

```
LINE (x1,y1)-(x2,y2),c,,&HCCCC
```

» Drawing circles and ellipses

The command:

```
CIRCLE (x,y),r
```

will result in a circle centred on the point *x,y* and with a radius *r* being drawn on the screen. For example:

```
CIRCLE (100,50),40
```

draws a circle in the current foreground colour centred at 100,50 and radius 40.

The circle command as given above is simple, easy to use and remember. However, it is not the complete form of the circle command, there are other parameters that can be included to gain more control over exactly what is produced. If you just want a simple circle then try just the simple form of the command but if you want something more complicated try:

```
CIRCLE (x,y),r,c,start,end,hw
```

As we have already seen, the first three parameters, *x,y* and *r*, control the position of the centre of the circle and its radius. All the other parameters are optional - you can leave one out by just writing a comma to mark the place it should have been. The fourth parameter *c* is the colour code of the colour in which the circle will be drawn. This can be useful if you just want a single circle in some colour other than the foreground colour.

The start and end parameters in the CIRCLE command can be used to draw parts of circles. The parameter *start* defines where the circle will start and *end* where it will finish! *Start* and *end* are in radians. Negative angles will cause CIRCLE to draw a complete segment, see Figure 7.2.

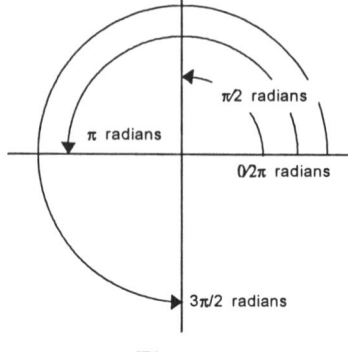

Figure 7.2
Segments

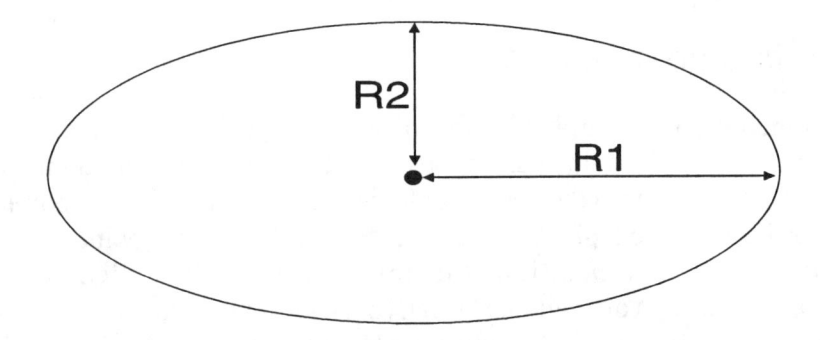

Figure 7.3
An ellipse as a squashed circle!

Notice that the angles have to be specified in radians. To convert from degrees to radians simply multiply by 180/3.14159.

The final parameter, *hw*, can be used to produce 'squashed' circles or ellipses. The way that the *hw* (height/width ratio) parameter works is easy to understand once you have noticed that you can specify two radii for a shape like a circle, see Figure 7.3. If you imagine a flattened circle, then how flattened it is could be described by giving its horizontal radius and its vertical radius. In the CIRCLE command the *r* parameter specifies the horizontal radius or width of the circle drawn and the *hw* parameter gives the ratio of the vertical radius or height to the width - hence its name *hw* or *aspect ratio*. If you set a value of *r* equal to 50 and *hw* equal to 2 then the horizontal radius will be 50 and the vertical radius will be *r*hw* or 100. This would produce a long thin vertical ellipse. However, if you use *r* equal to 50 and *hw* equal to .5 the horizontal radius will again be 50 but the vertical radius will be 50*.5 or 25. This will produce a thin horizontal ellipse.

To summarise:

» The horizontal radius is specified by *r* and the vertical radius is given by *hw*r*.

» Values of *hw* greater than 1 produce vertical ellipses and values of *hw* less than 1 produce horizontal ellipses.

» A value of *hw* equal to 1 produces a circle and this the value that is assumed if you leave *hw* out of the CIRCLE command.

» Relative co-ordinates

Sometimes it is useful to be able to specify a position in terms of how far it is away from the current position. For example, you might want to draw a line from the current graphics cursor position to the point 10 pixels down and 5 pixels to the right. Such references to points relative to the current position are not unreasonably called *relative co-ordinates*. You can use relative co-ordinates in any graphics command in place of standard *absolute co-ordinates* by writing STEP(*x,y*) in place of (*x,y*). For example:

```
LINE -STEP(x,y)
```

will draw a line from the current graphics cursor position to the point *x* pixels below and *y* pixels to the right. You can use negative relative co-ordinates to signify points above and to the left.

The real value of relative co-ordinates comes from the fact that if you use them to draw a shape then that shape is drawn relative to the starting point and that makes it very easy to shift it to any other point on the screen. For example, if you want to write a procedure to draw an equilateral triangle with a corner at *x,y* and side *s* using absolute co-ordinates is quite difficult to work out how - try it! But using relative co-ordinates it is fairly easy:

```
SUB triangle(x,y,s)
   PSET (x,y)
   LINE -STEP(s/2,s)
   LINE -STEP(-s,0)
   LINE -STEP(s/2,-s)
END SUB
```

Notice the use of the initial PSET to position the graphics cursor at *x,y* before the subsequent relative commands are used to draw the triangle. Notice that this subroutine will draw a triangle anywhere on the screen. Always use relative co-ordinates if you want to write a set of graphics commands that will draw a shape at any location.

» The DRAW command

The DRAW command is a mini-graphics language in its own right. It works as if you were controlling the position of a pen, in this case the graphics cursor, that is drawing on the screen and moving according to the instructions that you give it. The instructions are all of the form 'move x units across' or 'move y units down' but written in an abbreviated form. For example you can draw a square by:

```
DRAW "U20R20D20L20"
```

where U20 means up 20, R20 means right 20, D20 means down 20 and L20 means left 20. The square would be drawn from wherever the imaginary pen found itself at the start of the command. The full list of DRAW directions can be seen in Figure 7.4. Obviously it is important to be able to start a drawing from any given point and to this end you can use the command:

```
BMx,y;
```

command which will move the pen to the point x,y without leaving any 'marks'. The letters BM stand for Blank Move and in fact you can place a letter B in front of any pen movement command to make the pen move without drawing anything. The general form of the DRAW command is:

```
DRAW "command string"
```

and the command string that follows the word DRAW contains any of the permitted draw commands shown in the table overleaf.

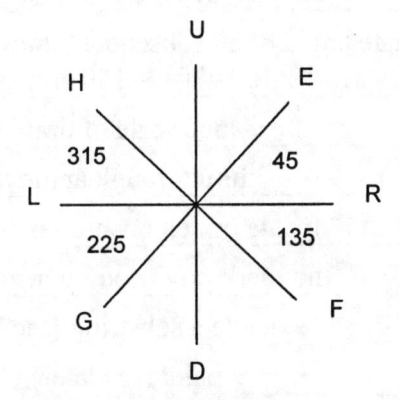

Figure 7.4
DRAW directions

Notice that there are two versions of the M command. If you specify M50,50 then the pen will move to the point 50,50, however, if you specify M+50,-50 then the pen will move to a point 50 points to the right and 50 points up from its current position. In other words, if the pen is at *x,y* then M+50,-50 will move it to *x*+50,*y*-50.

Command	Effect
\multicolumn{2}{c}{Pen Movements}
M*x,y*	move pen to *x,y* e.g. M10,20
M*sx,sy*	move pen relative to current position *s* must be either + or - e.g. M+10,-20
U*d*	move pen up *d* units
D*d*	move pen down *d* units
L*d*	move pen left *d* units
R*d*	move pen right *d* units
E*d*	move pen 45 degrees *d* units
F*d*	move pen 135 degrees *d* units
G*d*	move pen 225 degrees *d* units
H*d*	move pen 315 degrees *d* units
\multicolumn{2}{c}{Drawing attributes}
C*n*	change colour of pen to *n*
A*k*	rotate angle of all subsequent drawing commands 0=0, 1=90, 2=180 and 3=270
S*k*	change scale of drawing
TA*n*	turn through angle *n*
N	no update of pen position by next move
B	no mark produced by next move
X	execute a substring (see later)
P	paint (see later)

The drawing condition commands are fairly easy to understand. The C*n*, or colour command can be used to change the colour of the line that the pen produces. Following a C*n* command the pen will draw in the colour with the code given by *n*. So following C0 the pen will draw black lines, assuming that black is a colour that can be used in the current mode. The A command can be used to alter the angles of the drawing and the S command can be used to alter its scale. The best way to understand and use the A command is to work out the commands that produce the shape that you want and then rotate it by the desired angle. Notice that the drawing rotates around the point from which the pen starts drawing.

The S command can be used to produce larger or smaller versions of a drawing. Following an S*n* command all of the steps used by the DRAW command are effectively multiplied by *n*.

The final draw command is X, execute a substring. This command allows you to include a string variable within a draw string. For example you could write:

```
C$="S16C0"
DRAW "X"+VARPTR$(C$)+"L20E20D20"
```

which would draw the triangle four times larger and in black. The contents of the string variable following the X are treated as if they had been written directly into the draw string.

As an example of the Draw command in action the following program draws a small house:

```
SCREEN 2
x%=320
y%=100
CLS
x$="bm"+str$(x%)+","+str$(y%)
DRAW "X"+varptr$(x$)
DRAW "U40 R80 D40 L80"
y%=60
x$="bm"+str$(x%)+","+str$(y%)
DRAW "X"+varptr$(x$)
DRAW "TA-45 U15 TA0 R30 TA45 D15"
```

HOUSE.BAS

» Painting

The DRAW command is excellent for producing outlines on the screen, but apart from very small objects, filling in shapes with colour is outside of its capabilities. If you have an outline drawn in colour *b* you can fill it with colour *c* by using the command:

```
PAINT (x,y),c,b
```

where *x,y* must be a point inside the outline (it can be any point but it must be inside the shape!) What happens is that it starts to fill the screen with the colour *c* from the point *x,y* and only stops when it reaches a boundary of colour *b*. The PAINT statement will fill an arbitrary shape no matter how convoluted. The colour really does seem to flow like paint into every crevice - but be careful that you don't leave any holes in the boundary because if you do the paint will flow out and fill the entire screen!

For example, adding the two commands:

```
PAINT (330,90)
PAINT (360,55)
```

HOUSEP.BAS

to the end of the house drawing program listed earlier will paint both parts of the house.

» GET and PUT

The DRAW command can be used to produce outline shapes and small solid objects anywhere on the screen. However, there are two extra commands that can be used to 'read' the contents of an area of the screen into an array and then 'redraw' the contents at some other place. In other words, you can produce a small drawing using a combination of LINE, CIRCLE, DRAW or PAINT, read it into an array and then produce it any time you need it using one command.

The command that reads an area of the screen into an array is:

```
GET(x1,y1)-(x2,y2),array-name
```

The co-ordinates *x1,y1* and *x2,y2* define a rectangle in the same way that the pairs of co-ordinates define a rectangle in the LINE command. The array must be large enough to hold all of the graphics points in the rectangle. There is a complicated way of working out the smallest array needed to store the graphics points in the rectangle but it doesn't matter if you use an array that is too big, apart from the waste of storage that is. It is easy to define an array that is always large enough using:

```
DIM (x2-x1,y2-y1)
```

In other words, by using a two-dimensional array with as many elements as there are points in the rectangle.

To redraw the shape after GETting it into an array you have to use the PUT command:

```
PUT (x1,y1)-(x2,y2),array-name,action
```

The co-ordinates once again define a rectangle, but this time the information in the array is transferred to the rectangle. You can use one of the following action parameters:

Action	Effect
PSET	Set points to the same colour that they were in in the original drawing.
PRESET	Resets each point that is set in the original i.e. background colours become foreground and vice versa.
AND	Sets a point if the point is already set and was set in the original.
OR	Sets a point if either the point is already set or was set in the original.
XOR	Sets a point if either the point is already on or was set in the original but not if it is set in both.

In most cases you have to PUT a graphic in the same screen mode that you GET it. In other words, in most cases you shouldn't change screen modes in between a GET and a PUT. Some screen modes are compatible and you can PUT a graphic in one that was drawn in another but there is always a change of scale involved.

As a simple example of the use of the GET and PUT, add the following commands to the end of the house program listed earlier:

```
DIM h%(420-320,100-10)
GET (320,100)-(420,10),h%
PUT (10,100),h%
```

HOUSEG.BAS

The GET instruction reads the house graphic into the array h% and the PUT instruction re-draws it at 10,100. You can repeat the PUT command to draw the house as many times as you like.

Advanced use of GET and PUT

The GET command acts like a screen dump program in that it simply transfers the data stored in the screen area of memory into an array. As it doesn't perform any sort of processing of the graphics data, the format of the data in the array is exactly as it would be in the video memory. Graphics modes differ in how many bits per pixel they use and the order in which these bits are stored in the graphics memory. They can either be stored so that bits that control the colour of a given pixel are next to each other in memory, or they can be organised into planes so that adjacent bits in each plane control adjacent pixels. Each plane controls a particular colour of the image. You can think of it as a complete screen full of image data but only in a single colour - e.g. a red plane, a green plane and a blue plane.

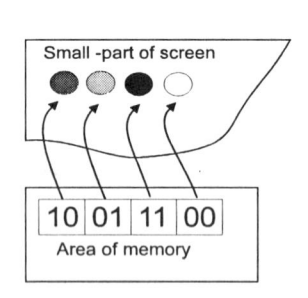

Each pixel is controlled by adjacent bits in a single area of memory

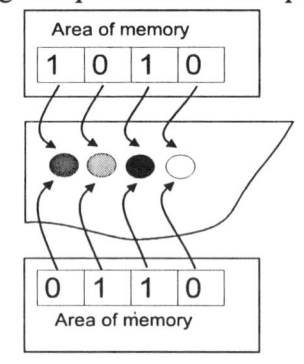

Each pixel is controlled by pixels taken from different areas of memory

This means that each pixel can be controlled by a number of adjacent bits in a single plane or a number of bits in different planes. Thus the important storage characteristics of a graphics mode can be described in terms of the number of bits per pixel in each plane and the number of planes.

Mode	Bits per pixel per plane	Planes
1	2	1
2, 3, 4, 11	1	1
7, 8, 9, 12	1	4
10	1	2
13	8	1

The format of the array used to store the graphics data is fairly simple as long as you assume that it is a standard integer array. The first two elements of the array hold the number of horizontal and vertical pixels in the GET or PUT area. The remaining elements are then used to store the image data a row at a time. The data is stored so as to make it easy to return the data to the graphics memory and so the organisation of the data depends on the screen mode in use. If you understand the way that the different types of video hardware work then the way that data is stored in the array will seem obvious. You can quite easily work out the number of array elements needed to store an area of the screen using the formula:

$$(4 + INT((w\% * bitspixel\% + 7) / 8) * planes\% * h\%) / 2$$

where the area of the screen is w% wide by h% high (in pixels), bitspixel% is the number of bits per pixel per plane and planes% is the number of bit planes. Notice that this formula gives the number of elements of an integer array needed to store the graphics data. If you understand how image bits are stored in the video memory and in the array then this formula should make reasonable sense. The 4 at the start is for the four bytes needed to hold the size of the rectangle. The w%*bitspixel% gives the total number of bits per row (per plane) and dividing by 8 gives the number of bytes needed (adding seven just makes sure that the number of bytes is rounded up - i.e. 3.2 Bytes becomes 4.) At this point in the calculation you know the number of bytes needed per row so multiplying by h% gives the total number of bytes per plane and multiplying by planes% finally gives the grand total. As there are two bytes in every element of an integer array dividing by 2 gives the size of the array.

If you know what values are stored in the array to produce a given shape then you can use this to create the shape without having to draw it and use GET to load the array. In principle this gives you the ability to create user-defined characters in QBasic but in practice it is hard work to determine the values that have to be stored in the array. A much easier solution is to write a program that allows you to paint the shape on the screen and then display the values that have to be stored in the array. This is too large an application to be included in this book but you will find such a program on the companion diskette, complete with documentation.

» The PALETTE command

So far it has been assumed that the colours that appear on the screen are fixed but if you have an EGA or VGA video card then this is not the case. In practice if you have a full function EGA or VGA card you can select the group of colours that can be displayed on the screen from a larger range of colours - the *palette*. For example, in mode 1 while you can show only four colours on the screen at one time these can be selected from a palette of sixteen possible colours. The colours that your program works with are always specified by the numbers 0,1,2,3 - these are the four logical colours that the graphics commands specify but which actual or physical colours these number specify can be altered.

You can assign a physical colour to the logical colour or attribute code using the PALETTE command. For example:

```
PALETTE 3,2
```

assigns attribute code 3 (or logical colour 3) to physical colour 2, i.e. green. Following this statement whenever you use attribute code 3 in a graphics command the colour green will appear on the screen. If you change the physical colour associated with an attribute code then not only will all future pixels that you set to that code display in the assigned colour, but so will all existing pixels set to that attribute code. This means that you can instantly change the colour of large areas of the screen by using a single PALETTE command. If you use PALETTE without specifying any attribute or physical colour codes then all attributes are reset to their original default assignments.

You can set all of the attribute to physical colour assignments with a single PALETTE USING command. To do this you have to store the physical colours that each attribute corresponds to in an integer array. The physical colour of attribute i has to be stored in array%(i), although you can also specify the array element that the physical colour of the first attribute is stored in. For example:

```
PALETTE USING x%
```

would set attribute i% to physical colour x%(i%) and:

```
PALETTE USING x%(5)
```

would set attribute i% to physical colour x%(5+i%-1). If you don't want to alter an attribute/colour assignment then simply store -1 in the corresponding array element. For the PALETTE USING statement to work you have to make sure that the array is large enough to hold the definition for all the attributes in the current mode.

CGA mode 1 is a little different in that it has two different fixed palettes of four colours:

Attribute Number	Palette 0	Palette 1
1	green	cyan (blue/green)
2	red	magenta
3	brown	white

In mode 1 you can select either palette using:

COLOUR *background*, *p*

where *p* is the palette number i.e. 0 or 1.

The example given in Listing 7.2 uses the palette command to give the impression of a ball rotating on the screen. Note the use of negative start and end points to draw the segments. The position for starting painting each segment is calculated using trigonometry to work out the co-ordinates of the centre of each segment. It has to be said that this amount of mathematics to simply find the starting point for the PAINT command seems excessive!

Listing 7.2

```
CONST pi = 3.14159
SCREEN 8
COLOR 7, 0
CLS
x% = 320: Y% = 100
S = -2 * pi
inc = 2 * pi / 8
c% = 3
FOR i% = 0 TO 8
    CIRCLE (x%, Y%), 100, , S, 2 * pi + S - inc
    cx% = 50 * COS(-S + inc / 2)
    cy% = 25 * SIN(-S + inc / 2)
    PAINT (x% + cx%, Y% - cy%), c%, 7
```

ROTATE.BAS

```
            S = S + inc
            IF c% = 3 THEN c% = 4 ELSE c% = 3
      NEXT i%
      DO WHILE INKEY$ = ""
            FOR i = 1 TO 2000: NEXT i
            PALETTE 3, 4
            PALETTE 4, 3
            FOR i = 1 TO 2000: NEXT i
            PALETTE 3, 3
            PALETTE 4, 4
      LOOP
```

» Making patterns

As well as filling in areas in a single colour the PAINT command can be used to produce patterns. The way in which this is done is quite complicated, but the results are very worthwhile. To specify a pattern the colour specification of the PAINT statement has to be a string variable or expression:

   PAINT (x,y) colour$,boundary,background$

The string variable takes the form of a number of special characters that define the pattern of pixel colours that make up the pattern, each character defining a short row of pixels up to a maximum of 64 rows. The way in which the characters define the pattern depends on the number of colours available in the mode that you are using. In modes 1 and 2 each colour is assigned a code according to the following schemes:

Mode 2		Mode 1	
Two colours		Four colours	
Colour	code	Colour	code
0	0	0	00
1	1	1	01
		2	10
		3	11

Each character in the string is defined by a string of eight zeros and ones taken from these tables. For example, in mode 2 a pattern of alternating foreground and background pixels corresponding to a single character is 01010101. In mode 1 a pattern of alternating background and colour 3 pixels corresponding to a single character is 00110011. Notice that in mode 2 a single character defines eight pixels but in mode 1 it only defines four pixels. These strings of zeros and ones are called *bit strings* or *binary numbers* and to convert bit string *b* to a character you first have to convert it to decimal (or some other number base that QBasic understands such as hex or octal). You can use the function BinToHex$ listed earlier in the chapter in the box *Dotted Lines*.

Once you have the hexadecimal value then the character is given by:

    CHR$(&H*hh*)

where *hh* is the hexadecimal value supplied by the function. For example the character that represents the bit string 01010101 is given by:

    CHR$(VAL(BinToHex$("01010101")))

Similarly, the character that represents the bits string 00110011 or 33 in hex is given by:

    CHR$(&H33)

You can build up a small pattern line by line in this way. For example the *colour$* string needed to define the two-line coloured chequerboard pattern is:

    *colour$*=CHR$(&H33)+CHR$(&HCC)

Notice that this pattern is a small rectangle four pixels by two - see Figure 7.5. You can of course make more complex patterns by adding more characters up to the limit of 64 - each character defining a row of dots.

The *background$* string can be used in the same way to define a background pattern that the painting is performed over. If you don't specify *background$* then it is assumed to be just uniform background points, i.e. unpatterned.

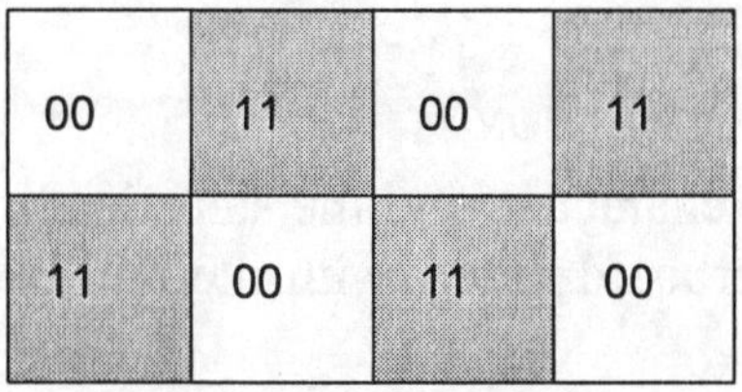

00	11	00	11
11	00	11	00

Figure 7.5
Chequerboard pattern

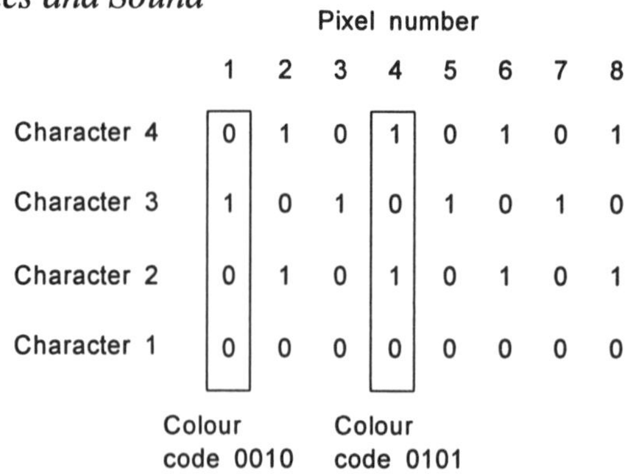

146 *Graphics and Sound* *Chapter 7*

```
                        Pixel number
                1   2   3   4   5   6   7   8
Character 4    [0]  1   0  [1]  0   1   0   1
Character 3    [1]  0   1  [0]  1   0   1   0
Character 2    [0]  1   0  [1]  0   1   0   1
Character 1    [0]  0   0  [0]  0   0   0   0
               Colour       Colour
               code 0010    code 0101
```

Figure 7.6
Defining a chequerboard

In modes that make use of more than one graphics plane, i.e. 7 to 10 and 12, the operation of the *colour$* string is a little different. In these modes each character defines the partial colour of eight pixels as in the case of mode 1. Modes 7, 8, 9 and 12 need four characters to completely define the colours of eight pixels and mode 10 needs two. The way that this works is that the colour of the first pixel is given by the first bit of each character read together to give a colour code. The colour of the second pixel is given by the the second bit in each of the characters read together to give a colour code and so on, see Figure 7.6. Using the following function you can find out the pattern of bits to which each colour code corresponds:

```
FUNCTION dec$ (d)
dt = d
d$ = ""
DO UNTIL dt = 0
  IF (d \ 2) * 2 = dt THEN
    d$ = "0" + d$
  ELSE
    d$ = "1" + d$
  END IF
  dt = dt \ 2
LOOP
dec$ = d$
END FUNCTION
```

For example, the characters and the steps leading up to them needed to define a chequerboard pattern with alternate pixels at colour 2 (0010)

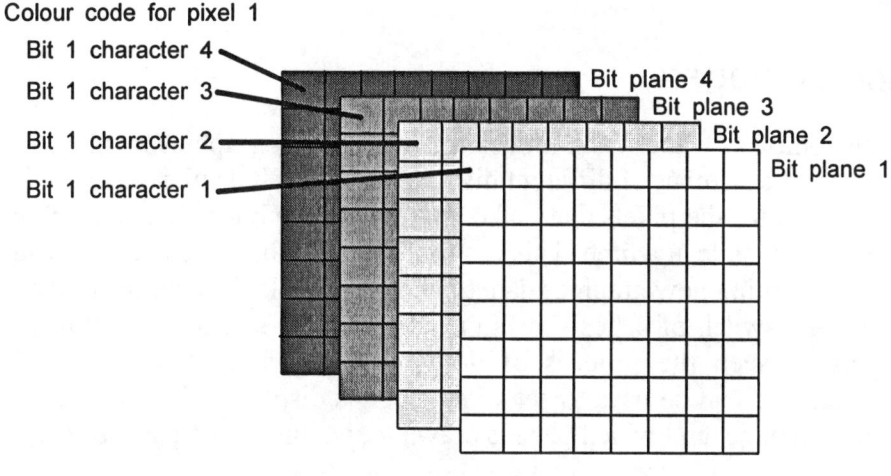

Figure 7.7
Bit planes

and colour 5 (0101) can be seen in Figure 7.7. The bin function listed below will convert a binary number as a string into a decimal value.

```
FUNCTION bin (b$)
  b = 0
  p = 1
  FOR i% = LEN(b$) TO 1 STEP -1
    b = b + VAL(MID$(b$, i%, 1)) * p
    p = p * 2
  NEXT i%
  bin = b
END FUNCTION
```

Bin is useful when you want to specify patters in binary directly to functions that expect a decimal value. For example, the following program fills in a circle with the pattern specified above:

```
screen 2
cls
colour$=chr$(bin("00010011"))+chr$(bin("11001100"))
circle (320,100),50
paint (320,100),colour$
```

CHEQUER.BAS

» Screen pages

In some EGA and VGA modes there is enough graphics memory to support a number of different display pages. Each display page holds the data for the pixels that make up a full screen but only one display page is visible at a time. This is a useful facility because it allows you to be writing new graphics data to one page while displaying another. Then a switch of pages shows the user the new screen without them having seen the process of drawing the update. The SCREEN command can be used to set which page is displayed, i.e. the visible page, *vpage*, and which page is drawn to, i.e. the active page, *apage*:

    SCREEN mode,colour,apage,vpage

where *apage* and *vpage* are integers in the range 0 to 7. For example, following the command:

    SCREEN 8,,1,0

page 1 is the active page and page 0 is the visible page. Mode 7 can have between 2 and 8 pages depending on the amount of graphics memory installed, mode 8 can have 1,2 or 4 pages and modes 9 and 10 have either 1 or 2 pages. Although all of these figures depend on the amount of memory fitted to the graphics card. Text mode 0 also has up to 8 pages which can be used to switch text displays very rapidly.

» Changing the co-ordinate system

Using pixel co-ordinates is fine for many applications but it is a nuisance to have to keep on changing your co-ordinate system to cater for different resolutions. For one thing it makes it very difficult to write a graphics program in one mode and then change to another without extensive rewriting. You can in fact avoid this problem by setting up your own co-ordinate system which is independent of graphics modes. Following the command:

    WINDOW (x1,y1)-(x2,y2)

where all the variables are single precision, the top left-hand corner of the screen is (x1,y1) and the bottom right is (x2,y2) so establishing a new co-ordinate system - see the left-hand diagram in Figure 7.8. The

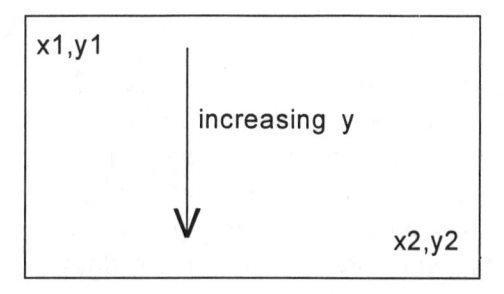

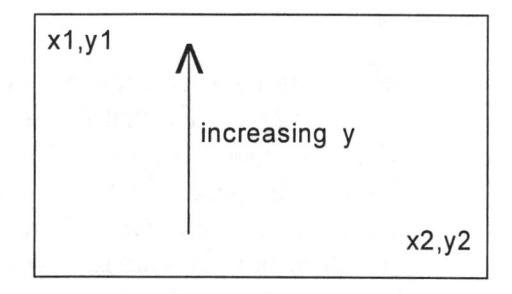

Figure 7.8
A new co-ordinate system

y co-ordinate still runs from low values at the top of the screen to high values at the bottom. This is, of course, the exact opposite of the way co-ordinates run in a graph or in many other situations.

If you want to use the more normal convention of y increasing as you move up the screen then use:

```
WINDOW SCREEN (x1,y1)-(x2,y2)
```

which results in a co-ordinate system as shown on the right of Figure 7.8. A WINDOW command with no parameters restores the default pixel co-ordinate system.

There are a wide variety of uses for the WINDOW command. As already mentioned, you can define a new co-ordinate system to make the conversion of programs written for other machines easier. For example some graphics systems use co-ordinates in the range 0 to 1 or -1 to +1. You can also use a change in co-ordinate system to zoom in or out on an existing graphic.

» Viewports

The WINDOW command redefines the co-ordinate system over the entire screen but sometimes it is an advantage to be able to confine the graphic area to a small *viewport* (more commonly referred to as a *window*). You can do this using the VIEW command:

```
VIEW (x1,y1)-(x2,y2),colour,border
```

which defines a rectangular viewport with opposite corners at (*x1,y1*) and (*x2,y2*). Notice that the co-ordinates are with respect to the full screen. If *colour* is specified it is used as the viewport's background. If *border* is specified a line is drawn around the viewport to delimit it. Once defined the viewport is treated as if it was the full graphics screen and all co-ordinates are relative to its boundaries. That is, it really does behave like a small version of the entire screen. This is ideal when you want to draw a graphic in a part of the screen while using other parts of the screen for other purposes.

As well as creating miniature screens it is also sometimes useful to be able to define a *clipping window* that marks a region of the screen where graphics are visible. That is it is a window or viewport onto the whole screen. To define a clipping viewport you have to use the command:

```
VIEW SCREEN (x1,y1)-(x2,y2),colour,border
```

following which all co-ordinates are still relative to the whole graphics screen so you only see graphics objects that fall within the window. The difference between the two forms of viewport is not difficult to understand if you consider a shape drawn using the full screen. Following a VIEW command you will still see the full shape but reduced in size to fit inside the viewport. Following a VIEW SCREEN command you will only see the part of the original shape that now fits into the viewport.

To restore the viewport to the full screen simply use the command VIEW without any parameters. If you precede the VIEW command with a WINDOW command, then the viewport will be created using the new co-ordinate system.

Many users are initially confused by the WINDOW and VIEW commands. This is mainly due to the way the names of the commands seem to have been assigned in an arbitrary way so that they are almost a random coupling of the words WINDOW, VIEW and SCREEN! As long as you remember that the WINDOW command establishes a new co-ordinate system, VIEW creates a complete graphics window and VIEW SCREEN creates a clipping viewport onto the graphics screen you should be able to make some sense of it all.

The example program in Listing 7.3 calls the house procedure defined earlier in this chapter to draw a house using high resolution graphics commands in four different screen situations. First on a normal high resolution graphics screen, then with a clipping viewport onto the full screen. The final two houses are drawn using the VIEW SCREEN command so that co-ordinates are relative to the start of the window, first with a very large co-ordinate system specified by a window command, then with a window which only just contains the picture.

Listing 7.3

WINDOWS.BAS

```
SCREEN 2
CALL house
INPUT a$
CLS
VIEW SCREEN (100, 50)-(200, 150), 0, 1
CALL house
INPUT a$
CLS
WINDOW SCREEN (0, 0)-(1000, 600)
VIEW (100, 50)-(400, 190), 0, 1
CLS
CALL house
INPUT a$
WINDOW SCREEN (0, 0)-(200, 120)
VIEW (100, 50)-(400, 190), 0, 1
CLS
CALL house
INPUT a$
END

SUB house
LINE (0, 120)-(200, 50), , B
LINE (0, 50)-(75, 30)
LINE -(200, 50)
LINE (88, 120)-(112, 90), , B
LINE (40, 110)-(62, 95), , B
LINE (138, 110)-(160, 95), , B
LINE (40, 80)-(62, 65), , B
LINE (138, 80)-(160, 65), , B
END SUB
```

» Physical and world co-ordinate systems

The new co-ordinate system that you set up using WINDOW is often referred to as the world co-ordinate system. Before anything can be plotted QBasic has to convert world co-ordinates to pixel co-ordinates to find out which pixel to change. The PMAP function can be used explicitly to discover the pixel co-ordinates that correspond to a given pair of world co-ordinates and vice versa:

```
PMAP(x,0) converts world x to pixel x
PMAP(y,1) converts world y to pixel y
PMAP(x,2) converts pixel x to world x
PMAP(y,3) converts pixel y to world y
```

It is obvious, but still worth pointing out, that you cannot increase the resolution of a mode by changing its co-ordinate system - it always has the same number of pixels! Indeed this is one of the problems that you are bound to encounter if you make use of other co-ordinate systems. For example, if you are working in the physical or pixel co-ordinate system for the graphics mode then you can be sure that the two commands:

```
PSET (x,y) and    PSET (x+1,y)
```

will set two different pixels to the foreground colour. However, if you have changed the co-ordinate system using WINDOW then you cannot be sure that adding one to x increases the co-ordinate sufficiently to move to a new pixel. You might not think that this is very important but it can result in features that are below the resolution of the screen vanishing and reappearing depending on the position of the graphics object. For example, suppose that in mode 2 you set up a co-ordinate system that runs from 0 to 1279. In this system each pixel is referred to by two integer co-ordinate values because there are only 640 pixels but 1280 integer co-ordinate values. That is, in the new co-ordinate system (0,0) and (1,0) both refer to the pixel at physical co-ordinate (0,0). Now imagine the effect of:

```
FOR i%=0 TO 100 STEP 2
  PSET(i%,10)
  PRESET(i%+1,10)
NEXT i%
```

This is supposed to create an alternating black and white line but its actual effect is to set all of the pixels to the background colour. The reason is that (i%,10) and (i%+1,10) are the same pixel. Now repeat the argument but this time change the loop to:

```
FOR i%=1 TO 100 STEP 2
```

In this case the result is a solid line in the foreground colour. The reason is that now the last operation to affect each pixel is the PSET command. Notice that you get completely different results from these two programs - i.e. no line or a solid line - depending on the starting position of the loop i.e. (0,0) or (1,0). You have to keep effects like this in mind whenever you are tempted to draw something that exceeds the actual resolution of the screen while using world co-ordinates.

» Text windows

As well as the ability to create graphics windows you can also create a text window, although the facility is far less sophisticated. The command:

```
VIEW PRINT top TO bottom
```

will create a text window the full width of the screen starting at the line number given by *top* and finishing at the line number given by *bottom*. The text window will automatically scroll to accommodate new text. The easiest way to understand this is to see it in action by trying the following program:

```
VIEW PRINT 20 TO 24
DO
    PRINT i
    i = i + 1
LOOP
```

TEXTWIND.BAS

This program creates a small text window at the bottom of the screen and then prints a stream of numbers to it to show the automatic scrolling.

» Finding out what's on the screen - POINT

The function POINT can be used to find out what colour is on the screen at any given high resolution position. The general form of the POINT function is:

```
POINT(x,y)
```

This will return the colour code of the point at *x,y*. If either *x* or *y* are out of range (i.e. the point *x,y* is off the screen) then POINT will return -1.

There is a second form of the POINT function that can be used to discover the current position of the graphics cursor. If you use POINT(0) it will return the current *x* position of the graphics cursor and if you use POINT(1) it returns the current *y* position of the graphics cursor. There is also a version of POINT that returns world co-ordinates:

```
POINT(0) returns pixel co-ordinate x
POINT(1) returns pixel co-ordinate y
POINT(2) returns world x
POINT(3) returns world y
```

» Sound

Although QBasic's music commands are not directly connected with graphics, sound and music do tend to go together. The simplest sound producing commands are:

```
BEEP
```

which makes the speaker go beep and:

```
SOUND frequency, duration
```

which produces a tone of the specified *frequency* and *duration*. The frequency is specified in Hertz (cycles per second) and must be in the range 32 to 32767 and duration is specified in system clock ticks. Given that there are 18.2 system clock ticks in one second you can see that a value of 18 gives a duration of roughly one second.

» Music

The main sound command is also very like a musical equivalent of the DRAW command. The command:

```
PLAY commandstring$
```

will produce sound from the machine's loudspeaker (often a very small and quiet loudspeaker) according to the commands stored in the *commandstring$*. The music commands can be seen in the following table.

Command	Action
O*n*	set octave to *n* where *n* is 0 to 6
>	increase current octave by 1
<	decrease current octave by 1
A to G	notes A to G - # in front means sharp and - means flat, a number following the note name indicates the length of the note, see L*n*, and you can also lengthen a note by *n*3/2 by following it by *n* dots
N*n*	note *n* where *n* is 0 to 84 with 0=rest
L*n*	length of note 1=whole note, 2=half note etc.
M*x*	tempo *x*=N, L or S standing for Normal, Legato or Staccato
P*n*	pause for length of note given by *n* (see L*n*)
T*n*	tempo *n*= the number of quarter notes in one minute
X*string*	execute the commands stored in *string*
M*x*	foreground *x*=F background *x*=B - see Chapter 9

The PLAY command gives you access to 84 notes that can be specified as a note number or as a note name A-G in a given octave. There are two ways to play the entire scale. You can set the octave to 0 and then play the musical scale using notes from C to B, shift the octave up by one and repeat as in:

```
c$ = "L16CDEFGAB>"
PLAY "O0"
FOR i% = 1 TO 7
   PLAY c$
NEXT i%
```

SCALES.BAS

The alternative is to simply play notes 1 to 84 as in:

```
FOR i% = 1 TO 84
   c$ = "L16N" + STR$(i%) + " >"
   PLAY c$
NEXT i%
```

See Chapter 9 for an example of playing music in the background.

Key points

- » The PC is a complicated machine on which to program graphics because of the large number of graphics modes that it can support depending on the hardware.

- » The basic text formatting commands are: PRINT, PRINT USING, LOCATE, TAB and SPC.

- » Graphics modes are selected using SCREEN.

- » The basic graphics commands are: PSET, PRESET, LINE, and CIRCLE.

- » There are three more complex graphics commands: PAINT, GET and PUT.

- » The DRAW command is a complete drawing language in its own right.

- » A knowledge of the way data is stored in the different graphics modes helps understand how PAINT, GET and PUT work.

- » Colour control can be extended to setting which physical colours are associated with the attribute codes used to specify colours in the graphics commands.

- » You can create a custom co-ordinate system using WINDOW.

- » The VIEW command creates viewports that can either restrict the graphics screen to a small area or can be used for clipping graphics displayed on the full screen.

- » The PLAY command can be used to produce music. BEEP and SOUND are sometimes useful for simpler sound effects.

Chapter 8

Data Files

This chapter looks in detail at how disk files are organised and used. The principles of simple sequential files are introduced first and then direct access files are described.

Some programmers are of the opinion that serious work only really begins when you start to make use of disk storage! While this may be a slightly biased viewpoint there is no doubt that the use of disk files opens up a wider range of applications than just processing the small amounts of data that can be held in memory.

» What makes disks different

The simplest way of storing data is to use an array. In an array each item of data is available at any time and data can be stored and retrieved in any order. In other words, if you want to work with data item i% you can simply refer to element a(i%). Arrays are so familiar that they tend to be taken for granted, but as soon as you are forced to move to disk storage it is clear how powerful and convenient they are. The main characteristic of disk storage is that it is a block storage device. That is, data can only be written or read in chunks or blocks - usually referred to as *sectors* or *clusters*. For example, a typical PC disk drive works with blocks of 512 characters at a time. Each time you see the disk light go on at least one 512 character block is transferred to or from the disk.

Of course, you may not want to read or write a whole 512 characters at once and the solution to this problem is to use a *buffer*. A buffer is an area of memory set aside specially to hold the blocks of data on their way to or from the disk drive (or any other block oriented device). For example, if you want to read a single character from disk then 512 characters are read into a buffer and you are given the first character in the buffer. If you then want another character the disk isn't read again because the second character is already in the buffer and so on. Each time you ask for a character it is retrieved from the buffer until all 512 characters are 'used up' and the buffer is 'empty'. Of course, when you want to read the 513th character the disk is read again and the buffer refilled, and so on.

Writing characters to a disk using a buffer works on exactly the same principles but each character written is added to the buffer and the buffer is written out to disk when it is full. The creation and management of the buffers is something that QBasic and MS-DOS look after, and normally you can use disk storage without worrying about them. However, knowing about buffers and blocks can help explain many of the otherwise arbitrary ways that disk storage works.

» Files - sequential, random and indexed

There are many different types of file according to what is stored in the blocks and the way that the data is organised to make access possible. For example, a binary file can be used to store any type of data, but a text or ASCII file can only store codes which correspond to valid character codes. This is just a trivial difference in what is considered legal data for a file. More important differences stem from the way that files can be processed. For example, the data stored in a *sequential* file can only be read back in the order in which it was written. However, in a *direct* or *random access* file you can read data back in any order, irrespective of the order in which it was written. Clearly, random access files are more powerful than sequential files and you might be wondering why we bother with sequential files? The answer is that sequential files are very often all that is needed to solve a data processing problem and they have the additional advantage of being efficient and very easy to use.

Direct access files in many languages, including QBasic, are just the starting point for implementing a more advanced and useful type of file. A direct access file only gives you the power to access any item of data that you want. For example, you might ask to read record 56. The only way to do this with a sequential file is to start at the beginning and read records 1 to 55 to reach 56. A direct access file doesn't have to waste time in this way because it can move directly to record 56 and read it. This sounds powerful but it leaves out the problem of discovering that it was record 56 that you needed to read.

That is, the problem is not so much one of storage and access, but of locating the data that you need. For example, you could quite easily use a direct access file to store a list of names and telephone numbers, but how would you go about finding the telephone number that corresponded to a particular name. The simplest way of finding the required telephone number is to read the file from the beginning and compare each name to the name that you are searching for until you find it - this is called a *linear search* and it is very inefficient. There are ways of improving the speed of search by sorting the file into order, but this takes time and a file can only be sorted into one order at a time.

For example, a file that is sorted into order on name makes it faster to find someone's telephone number given their name, but to find their name quickly given their telephone number the file needs to be sorted into telephone number order.

An alternative to sorting a file is to use an *index*. An index is simply a way of finding the location of the information that you are interested in and it works in the same way as the index to a book. If you want to find all the references to "computers" in a book you look up "computers" in the index and this tells you the page numbers at which the information is to be found.

A disk file index works in roughly the same way. It is a separate file that contains the data items - the keys - used to form the index and the location of the information associated with each key value. For example, you could index the name and telephone number file on name by creating an index file that listed the names in order and along with each name the location of the telephone number, address and any other personal data kept in the main file. This type of file is generally referred to as an *indexed sequential* file.

In file processing you are only supplied with the basic tools to do the job. It is up to you to construct subroutines that implement the mechanisms that organise the data in the file so that it can be found easily.

» Sequential files

Before looking in detail at direct access files it is essential to have a good grasp of the way sequential files work. It is also the case that if a problem can be solved using a sequential file then this is usually the best method.

Items of data written to a sequential file can only be read back in the same order in which they were written. The best way to think about sequential files is to imagine that each file corresponds to a tape. Initially the tape is blank and each item written to it causes it to advance so that there is always fresh tape available for more data. To read the tape you first have to rewind it, and then reading each item of data back

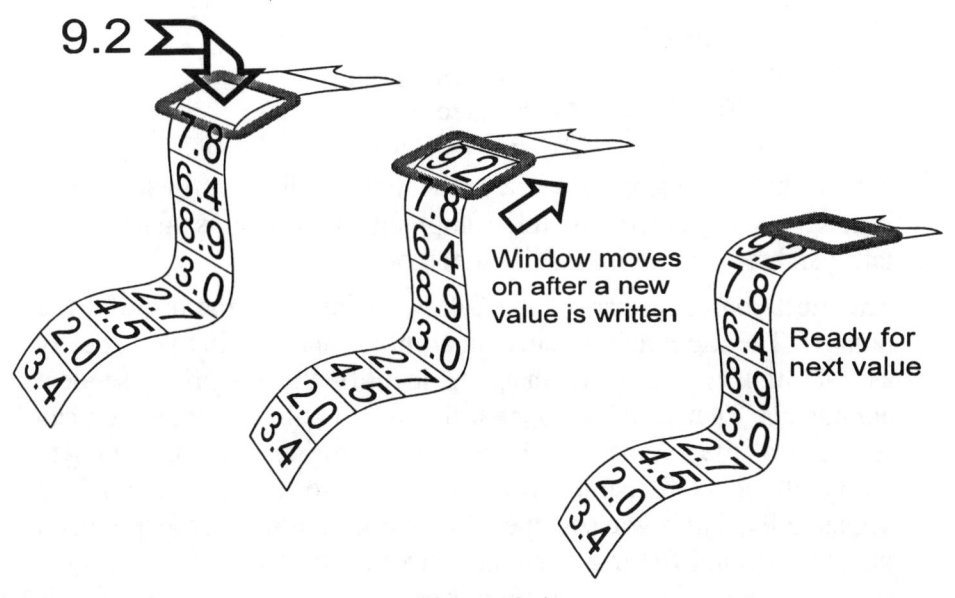

Figure 8.1
A sequential file

advances the tape so that a fresh item of data is available. With this tape model of a sequential file it becomes obvious why data is read back in the same order in which it was written to the file.

QBasic provides a number of standard commands to control sequential files. Before you can use a sequential file you have to inform QBasic of its filename and whether you intend to read or write it using the OPEN statement which is available in two different forms:

> OPEN *filename* FOR *mode* AS *filenumber*

or:

> OPEN *mode*, *filenumber*, *filename*

The only difference between the two forms is that the first version is wordier and so easier to read. The second version is the one more likely to be used in other dialects of Basic.

In each case the filename is just the usual filename that appears in a directory listing i.e. it is an MS-DOS filename. That is, it can have up to eight letters followed by a three letter extension, e.g. MYFILE.TXT. If you don't specify a three letter extension then .DAT is added by default.

Mode can be one of:
- INPUT   if the file is to be read
- OUTPUT   if the file is to be written
- APPEND   to write data at the end of the file

Notice that you cannot open a sequential file for both reading and writing, although there is nothing stopping you from closing a file (see later) and re-opening it in a different mode.

The most confusing part of the OPEN command is the use of a file number. The file number is just an arbitrary number that you specify as part of the OPEN command to identify the file in subsequent commands. That is, if you open a file as file number 1 then you can refer to it as file number 1 in the rest of the program without having to worry about its filename. You don't have to assign file numbers sequentially, that is you can open file number 1 and then file number 3 without opening file number 2 in between. The only rule is that you cannot assign a file number to more than one file at a time - this is obvious as the file number is used to identify the file to which you are referring! Although it isn't strictly necessary, most programmers use the convention of adding a # in front of a file number. The OPEN command will work with or without the # so it is entirely a matter of preference. For example, #1 would be read as "file number 1".

If you open a file for output and it already exists then it will be deleted so that you can create a brand new version. In the case of reading it is obvious that the file must already exist. If you are writing a subroutine that makes use of files then it can be difficult to know which file numbers are currently free and unused by other parts of the program. To solve this problem you can use the function:

```
FREEFILE
```

which returns the next unused file number. This would be stored in a variable, f%=FREEFILE, and then f% would be used as the file number in subsequent commands.

To write data to a file you can use a modified form of the PRINT command:

```
PRINT# filenumber, printlist
```

where *filenumber* is the number that was used to OPEN the file and *printlist* represents anything you could write in a standard PRINT statement. The PRINT# statement works in exactly the same way as the PRINT statement but it sends the data to the disk file rather than to the screen. For example PRINT#1,"HELLO" sends the word HELLO to the disk file OPENed as file number 1.

To read data back from a file you can use the INPUT# statement which once again works in the same way as the INPUT statement but instead of reading data from the keyboard it reads it from the disk file specified. For example, INPUT#2,A$ reads a string from the disk file OPENed as file number 2 and stores it in A$.

The most important thing to understand about the way that the INPUT# and PRINT# commands work is that they are identical to the INPUT and PRINT commands except for the fact that they work with a disk file. For example, you can use the TAB command within a PRINT# command and if you end the print list with a semi-colon then the automatic new line is suppressed in the usual way. There is even a disk file equivalent of the PRINT USING command:

```
PRINT# filenumber USING format
```

which sends data to the disk file formatted exactly as it would be on the screen.

After you have finished with a file you can free the buffer and other resources that it was using with the command:

```
CLOSE filenumber
```

If the file was open for reading then the CLOSE statement simply frees the file buffer for further use, but if the file was open for writing the CLOSE command ensures that any data in the buffer is first written out to disk. Thus it is very important to CLOSE a file that is open for writing if you want to avoid losing data!

» A simple example

Just to show how the above commands would actually be used consider the problem of writing out 10 random numbers to a file, closing it and then reading them back.

```
                                              Comments
OPEN "random.dat" FOR output AS 1  open for output as #1
FOR I=1 TO 10                      write 10 random numbers to file
  A=RND                            generate random number in A
  PRINT#1,A                        write A to file
NEXT I
CLOSE 1                            write any remaining data in
                                   buffer 1 to disk and release it
OPEN "random.dat" FOR input AS 1   open for input using buffer 1
FOR I=1 TO 10                      read 10 numbers from the file
  INPUT#1,A                        read A from file
  PRINTA                           display A on screen
NEXT I
CLOSE 1                            release file number 1
```

These are very simple programs but they do show most of the features of file handling. Although file number 1 is used for both reading and writing the file, any file number could be used for either activity.

DWRITE1.BAS
DWRITE2.BAS

In this example the file name is fixed as "random.dat" but in most real applications the name of the file that the program processes changes each time it is used. The key to coping with this problem is to notice that the filename used in the OPEN command can be specified by a string variable, for example, by:

```
OPEN f$ FOR input AS 1
```

where f$ contains the filename. Notice that all of the specifications within the OPEN command can be provided by variables.

» Records and fields

The fact that the PRINT# and INPUT# statements work in exactly the same way as the familiar PRINT and INPUT statements makes using sequential files easy, as long as you are aware of one subtle trap. If you write out a string and a number to a file, i.e.:

```
PRINT#1,A$,N
```

and then try to read it back using a similar INPUT# statement:

```
INPUT#2,A$,N
```

you will find that it doesn't work! The reason is clear if you think about what would appear on the screen as a result of an identical PRINT statement. If a$ contained "QBasic" and N contained 123.4 then PRINT A$,N would print "QBasic   123.4" on the screen with the space being generated by the comma. This is exactly what is written to disk. The INPUT# statement then tries to read this back and it does this just as if the contents of the disk file were being typed on the keyboard. First it tries to read data into the string A$ and so it reads "QBasic" a number of spaces and then 123.4 because all of these are perfectly valid input for a string, and there is nothing to delimit the end of the string except the end of the line - i.e. input to the string A$ stops after the 4. This means that there is nothing left to read into the numeric variable N and so an error is reported.

The problem is that there is no indication of where the string ends. One solution to the problem is to use a separate PRINT# statement for each item of data. This automatically places each item of data on a new line and implies that it has to be read back in using a separate INPUT# statement for each item. For example:

```
PRINT#1,A$
PRINT#1,N
```

can be read back correctly using:

```
INPUT#1,A$
INPUT#1,N
```

Many programmers use this simple solution and nothing else, but there is another way of solving the problem which is more like the way you have to work when it comes to direct access files. Instead of using the end of line marker to separate each data item you can use a comma. For example, instead of PRINT#1,A$,N you could use:

```
PRINT#1,A$;",";N
```

which writes QBasic,123.4 to the file. (Notice the quoted comma between the A$ and the N.) When this is read back the comma automatically stops the reading in of the string A$ so leaving the 123.4 to be read into the variable N. If you want to see this in action try the equivalent INPUT statement and type the data with and without the comma. The comma is the default delimiter for the INPUT statement.

Indeed, if you want to read a line of data without taking account of the comma as a delimiter you have to use the command:

```
LINE INPUT string variable
```

or:

```
LINE INPUT#filenumber, string variable
```

which reads in a whole line of data into the string variable irrespective of commas or other delimiters. Obviously once you have the line in the string variable you can then process it to separate out items of interest.

The only trouble with the delimiter solutions is the need to include quoted commas which makes the PRINT# statement untidy and prone to error. There is an additional output statement, WRITE#, which will write data to a disk file automatically inserting commas and deleting unnecessary spaces. It also goes a little further in formatting the data and will enclose string data in double quotes so that commas can be included within a string. For example, if A$ contains QBasic, N contains 123.4 and F$ contains "Hello" then:

```
WRITE#1,A$,N,F$
```

will write "QBasic",123.4,"Hello" to the file - notice the added quotes and commas. This can be read back correctly using a matching INPUT# statement i.e. INPUT#1,A$,N,F$. Clearly, if you are going to write multiple data items on a line then use the WRITE# command.

There is a single unifying idea that links the way data items are grouped together in any type of file. Files are generally organised as a number of records. A *record* is simply a group of data items and each data item is called a *field*. That is, a file is a collection of records and a record is a collection of fields.

For example, you might create a file of name and address records with each record having three fields :

    field 1   Name   a string
    field 2   Address a string
    field 3   Id Number an integer

This way of thinking of files is based on the familiar idea of a traditional card file. That is, a box of cards - the file - with each card - the record - containing a fixed number of items of data - the fields. You should also recognise this as being exactly the data structure discussed in

Chapter 6 - the *user-defined* type. In other words, you can define a record as a user-defined type. For example, the name and address record could be defined as:

```
TYPE address
    fullname   AS STRING*20
    address    AS STRING*20
    idnum      AS INTEGER
END TYPE
```

You should also be able to see that inserting commas as delimiters is a way of imposing a record structure on the data. Each data item was made into a field by adding a comma and each record was on a new line. This is a very simple and, as will be explained, versatile way of constructing a file.

Thinking about data files as being made up of records, which are themselves made up of fields, provides a good organising principle for the programs that process the file. The record and field structure usually corresponds to the way that the file is processed. It is common to read a record, process it and then perhaps write it back out. When it comes to direct access files you have no choice but to use records and fields but you are free to organise (or disorganise!) sequential files as you like. However, you can make your sequential file programs easier to write and debug if you organise them around the concept of a record. For example, you should write a subroutine that reads a whole record and another that writes a whole record and never access the file by any other method. In this way you will never accidentally read or write part of a record and so damage the structure of the file or the natural order of processing of your program.

» Fixed and variable length records

So far two distinct ways of constructing records have been described: user-defined types and using commas as field separators. You might be wondering what the difference is between the two? The answer is that user-defined types implement a fixed length record and field delimiters are used to implement a variable length record. A file containing fixed length records, as you might imagine, is composed of a set of records each one taking exactly the same amount of storage. If you don't have enough information to fill a field in a given record then the data is simply padded to fit. This may sound like a terrible waste of space but it has huge advantages if you are trying to implement direct access methods. Fixed length records and user-defined types are described in more detail later in connection with direct access files.

The alternative scheme, variable length records, are really only easy to implement for sequential files. By marking the end of each field and each record by using a special character there is no need specify the length of either. The program simply reads data until it meets a field delimiter when it knows that it has read a complete field. In the same way when it bumps into the end of record marker it knows that it has read an entire record. In other words using delimiters allows you to write variable length records. For example:

```
WRITE#1,FullName$,Address$,IdNum%
```

writes a single variable length record consisting of four fields. Why is the length of the record variable? The answer is that the amount of data stored in the strings FullName$ and Address$ can be anything from 0 characters to 32,767 characters each! The records in the file will look something like:

```
"Fred Bloggs","1 Acacia Avenue",1234
```

Notice once again the way that the commas act as field separators (as long as they are outside the quotes) and the end of line acts as a record separator. The records can be read back in using an INPUT statement something like:

```
INPUT#1,FullName$,Address$,IdNum%
```

» File export

Notice that the organisation of this file is entirely unsuitable for viewing on the screen or working with in a text editor. It is sometimes useful to abandon the whole idea of a record structure and simply create a file that contains formatted data as it would appear on the screen or the printer. Such formatted files are useful if you want to export data to a word processor, DTP package or just for sending to a printer at a later date. However, if you want to export data to an application such as a spreadsheet or a database then the variable length record format just described is ideal because it is a standard data exchange format usually referred to in this role as a Comma Separated Values or CSV file. By the same token you can read records from a CSV file using an INPUT# statement.

» Some file practicalities

One problem that has to be solved in nearly every sequential file handling program is knowing when you have read to the end of the file. Fortunately this is easily solved using the End Of File function, EOF(*filenumber*). This is a logical function which returns the value true when you are positioned at the end of the file and the next read would result in an error. You can use EOF in a loop such as:

```
DO UNTIL(EOF(f))
    INPUT#f,variable list
LOOP
```

One of the most common requirements for a sequential file is being able to add more records. This used to be quite difficult in early versions of Basic because files could only be opened for reading or writing but in QBasic you can open a file for APPEND. If you open an existing file for APPEND then you will start writing new records at the very end of the file without having read, or indeed being able to read, any of the preceding records.

» Direct access files

The direct access file forms the basis for nearly all the advanced data handling usually referred to as database. On the other hand the direct access file is not a solution in itself. It has to be used carefully to create workable solutions.

In a sequential file each field within a record can be of any length, given that it is possible to determine where one field starts and another begins. In a direct access file you could use the same system of field and record separators except for the need to find a given record starting from any point in the file. This is easy if each record is exactly the same length but almost impossible otherwise. For example, if each record is always exactly N characters long then to find the 5th record, say, all you have to do is to make the current position in the file 5*N characters from the start of the file. In other words, fixed length records make it possible to find where any given record is stored using nothing more complicated than multiplication - hence the connection between fixed length records and direct access files. In practice the arithmetic to find any particular record is performed by QBasic, all you have to do is specify the record number.

» The old and the new

One of the complications of using direct access files in Basic is that there are two different ways of going about it. The original method is based on the direct use of a record buffer. This is the method that most Basic programmers know and also is the method used in most existing Basic programs. So it cannot be ignored. However, the new method is much simpler and based on the use of user-defined types and so it should be the preferred method for all new programs. In this chapter the new method based on user-defined types is described but you will find details of the use of the record buffer in the box, *Using record buffers*.

» Opening a direct access file

To open a direct access file you not only have to supply the file name, and file number but also the length of each record. The reason for this is obviously so that QBasic can work out where to move to to find a given record number. The OPEN statement for a direct access file is:

OPEN *filename* FOR RANDOM AS *filenumber* LEN=*recordsize*

where *filenumber* and *filename* are as for a sequential file and the RANDOM option means that you want to use or create a direct access file. You can work out the size of the record by simply counting up the number of bytes needed to store each field but this is a slightly technical and error prone way of doing it. As all direct access file I/O is performed by reading and writing user-defined records it is much easier and safer to use the LEN function to discover the amount of storage needed for a record variable. For example, if you have defined a variable called RecordCard to hold names and addresses, then you could use the function LEN(RecordCard) to set the record size in the OPEN command:

OPEN *filename* FOR RANDOM AS *filenumber* LEN=LEN(*RecordCard*)

When you open a direct access file it is created if it doesn't already exist but, unlike a sequential file opened for writing, it is not deleted and recreated if it already exists. This is because a direct access file can be both written and read at the same time. In many ways it is better to think of opening a direct access file for updating rather than for reading or writing. If you want to open a brand new version of a file that already exists then you have to delete it before opening it. As with all files, once you have finished with a direct access file you should close it using the usual:

CLOSE *filenumber*

You should always close a direct access file that has been modified or added to so that any data in the record buffers is actually written to disk.

» Reading and writing a record

Storing and retrieving data from a direct access file is done entirely in terms of complete records as defined by a suitable user-defined type. The command:

PUT *filenumber, recordnumber, recordname*

writes the current contents of the user-defined type *recordname* as the specified *recordnumber*. For example, if you have just opened a new direct access file as file number 1 the command:

PUT 1,100,RecordCard

will write the contents of RecordCard as record 100. If records 1 to 99 are not yet written then they will be created but their contents will be undefined. Thus a direct access file is automatically extended to accommodate the highest record number that you write to it.

In the same way the command:

    GET *filenumber, recordnumber, recordname*

will read the specified *recordnumber* into the user-defined type *recordname*.

You can detect the end of a direct access file by using the EOF function in the same way as for a sequential file.

The GET and PUT commands can also be used to read in records sequentially from a file from a given point. The command:

    GET *filenumber,, recordname*

reads the next record and:

    PUT *filenumber,, recordname*

writes the next record.

» An example

In this simple example the 'name' of the item that the record stores is taken to be the same as the record number. For example, if you wanted to keep stock control records for 100 items then you might as well assign part numbers in the range 1 to 100 and store the information about part number *x* in record *x*. This is, of course, highly artificial but it is difficult to organise files in a way that makes it easy to find the record number of any item you are interested in. For a fuller example see the database application in Chapter 10.

Suppose that each stock control record has to hold the following information:

    part name   a string of less than 25 characters
    stock level   an integer
    re-order level   an integer

This immediately translates into a user-defined record as:

```
TYPE stock
  PartName     AS STRING*25
  StockLevel   AS INTEGER
  ReOrderLevel AS SINGLE
END TYPE
```

Notice that this only defines the record type, you still have to declare a variable of the type:

```
DIM StockRecord AS stock
```

The next step is to open the file:

```
OPEN "stock"  FOR Random AS 1 LEN=LEN(StockRecord)
```

The final stage is to read in records and save them to the file:

```
DO
   INPUT "item number";item%
   IF item%=-1 THEN CLOSE 1:EXIT DO
   INPUT "item name";StockRecord.PartName
   INPUT "stock level";StockRecord.StockLevel
   INPUT "reorder level";StockRecord.ReOrderLevel
   PUT 1,item%,StockRecord
LOOP
```

WRITER.BAS

The program to read records back in is very much like a sequential file program except for the need to specify the record being written. To find the information on a particular item all that is necessary is to supply its item number and read the corresponding record:

```
TYPE stock
   PartName    AS STRING*25
   StockLevel  AS INTEGER
   ReOrderLevel AS SINGLE
END TYPE
DIM StockRecord AS stock
OPEN "stock"  FOR Random AS 1 LEN=LEN(StockRecord)
DO
   INPUT "item number";item%
   IF item%=-1 THEN CLOSE 1:EXIT DO
   GET 1,item%,StockRecord
   PRINT "item name";StockRecord.PartName
   PRINT "stock level";StockRecord.StockLevel
   PRINT "reorder level";StockRecord.ReOrderLevel
LOOP
```

READER.BAS

This example is very simple, and in practice you would need a menu from which the user could select operations and, most importantly, some method of organising the file so that a record could be found on the basis of a more natural identification number or even on the basis of its name. You will find a large database example along these lines in the final chapter.

Using record buffers

The traditional way of effecting Basic direct access is to work with the record buffer directly. The record buffer exists even if you use the GET and PUT commands to transfer data to it using user-defined types. You can access the record buffer directly by giving parts of it names. This is achieved by using the FIELD statement to associate parts of the record buffer with particular character variables, i.e. fixed length strings. The FIELD statement has the general form:

FIELD *filenumber, fieldsize*1 AS *fieldname*1$, *fieldsize*2 AS *fieldname*2$, ...

You can think of the FIELD statement as slicing up the fixed length record buffer into a number of fixed length fields. For example, if you have OPENed a direct access file with a record length of 30 this creates a record buffer 30 characters long. This can be explicitly divided up into fixed length strings using something like:

FIELD 1,10 AS A$,15 AS B$,5 AS C$

to define three fields as shown:

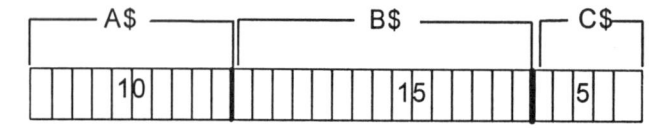

For advanced applications you can even use more than one FIELD statement to divide up a single record buffer in different ways. This provides QBasic with something like Pascal's variant record facility. It is even possible to implement sophisticated schemes that allow variable length fields within a fixed length record structure.

To transfer character data from a field variable to an ordinary variable all you have to do is use an ordinary string. So, for example:

    N$=A$

transfers the 10 characters of A$ to a standard string variable N$.

However, you cannot transfer character data to a field variable by simply assigning a string to it. If you do then the field variable is converted into a standard string variable and loses its association with the record buffer. Instead you have to use one of the three special functions:
```
LSET field variable =string expression
RSET field variable =string expression
MID$(field variable,s,n)=string expression
```
The LSET and RSET functions store the string in the field variable, left or right justified respectively, truncating or padding with blanks as required. The MID$ function stores *n* characters of the string expression starting at position *s* in the field.

Numeric information can be stored in a field variable, but only after it has been converted to a string of characters. The most obvious way of converting a number to a string is to use the STR$ function, but this has the disadvantage that the length of the string that it produces varies according to the number of digits in the number. To overcome this difficulty there are four functions which will convert numbers to fixed length strings. There are also four inverse functions which will convert the character representation back to numeric form.

MKI$(n%) converts an integer to a two-character string
CVI(s$)   converts a two-character string to an integer

MKL$(a&) converts a long integer into a four-character string
CVL(a$)   converts a four-character string into a long integer

MKS$(a)   converts a single precision number to a four character string
CVS(s$)   converts a four-character string to a single precision number

MKD$(a#) converts a double precision number to an eight character string
CVD(s$)   converts an eight-character string to a double precision number

Using these functions you can store a character representation of a number in a field variable, but it is important to remember to still use one of LSET, RSET or MID$. For example:
```
    LSET A$=MKI$(I%)
```
The MK*x*$ and CV*x* functions are also useful in performing bit manipulation.

Once you have stored the data in the record buffer you can use:
    GET#*filenumber, recordnumber*
and:
    PUT#*filenumber, recordnumber*
which in the absence of a named record variable simply read and write the record buffer.

There is one small problem caused by a recent change in the way numeric values are stored by most MS-DOS programs. Older versions of Basic used the Microsoft format and current versions, including QBasic, use the IEEE format. This change only affects single and double precision values. This isn't a problem unless you try to read files written using an older version of Basic. The solution is to use conversion functions suitable for Microsoft format numbers as follows:

MKSMBF$(*a*)   converts a single precision value to a four-character Microsoft format string.

CVSMBF(*s$*)   converts a four-character Microsoft format string to a single precision (IEEE format) value.

MKDMBF$(*a#*) converts a double precision value to a eight character Microsoft format string.

CVDMBF(*s$*)   converts an eight-character Microsoft format string to a double precision (IEEE) number.

Direct manipulation of the record buffer coupled with its requirement to convert numeric values to fixed length strings makes this approach to direct access files much more complex and time consuming than using user-defined types. However, it does have advantages for the advanced user in that it allows more flexible record handling schemes to be implemented.

For example, you can define two different divisions of the record buffer and use one or the other depending on, say, the first value stored in the record. This makes it possible to have a file with two different types of record. You can even implement record structures that overcome the fixed length limitation to some extent. However, all of these schemes are tricky to implement and you should use the user-defined data type approach wherever possible.

» Useful commands and functions

Although you already have enough information to work with direct access files there are a few commands and functions that make the task easier. The LOF(*filenumber*) function, for example, can be used to discover the length of a file in characters (i.e. bytes). The LOC(*filenumber*) function returns the current position in the file reporting the number of 128 character blocks read/written for a sequential file, the record number for a direct access file, and the number of bytes for a binary file. More useful positioning information can be obtained from SEEK(*filenumber*) which returns the number of the next byte to be read or written in all cases except for direct access when it returns the next record number.

Just in case you are writing a subroutine that needs to determine the mode in which the file it is passed is opened you can use the FILEATTR(*filenumber*) command which returns 1 for INPUT, 2 for OUTPUT, 4 for RANDOM, 8 for APPEND and 32 for BINARY.

There are also a number of useful functions when it comes to manipulating fields. The LSET command, for example, can be used to move one string of characters into another so that they are left justified, truncating or padding with blanks if necessary. The RSET command does the same job but it right justifies the characters. These commands have to be used if you are working with the record buffer directly -see the box "Using record buffers" - but they can also be useful when working with strings or record variables. For example:

```
LSET a$=b$
```

left justifies the contents of b$ into a$ so that the length of a$ remains unchanged.

The LTRIM$ and RTRIM$ functions will trim off leading and trailing spaces from a string respectively. To remove both you can use:

```
LTRIM$(RTRIM$(string))
```

» Binary files

A QBasic sequential file can only read or write valid printable ASCII characters. This means that you cannot read any system or internally formatted files such as those produced by most word processors, spreadsheets etc.. To get round this problem QBasic provides an additional type of file - the binary file. You can read or write any sort of file as a binary file but you do have to do some of the work that you would normally take for granted when using a standard sequential file. Binary files are treated as a sequence of bytes without any formatting. To open a binary file use:

```
OPEN filename FOR BINARY AS filenumber
```

A binary file is opened for both reading and writing. The bytes in a binary file are numbered from 1 up to the maximum number of bytes in the file. Before reading any given byte or group of bytes starting at byte *n* you must first position the file pointer to that byte using:

```
SEEK #filenumber,n
```

Following this you can read the *m* bytes into the string variable S$ using:

```
GET$ #filenumber,m,S$
```

The characters in S$ may be control codes and hence not be printable. It is up to the program to convert or use the information in S$ in a sensible way. The process of writing bytes to a binary file follows the same pattern of - first position the file pointer using SEEK and then use:

```
PUT$ #filenumber,m,S$
```

You have to close a binary file in exactly the same way you would close any other file. The string variables used in GET$ and PUT$ should either be fixed length strings or should have the number of characters to be read or written stored in them before being used with GET$ or PUT$.

The use of binary files depends very much on the type of file that you are trying to process. For a simple example consider the problem of writing a simple file copying program. You might think that this was just a matter of opening a sequential file for reading and one for writing and then transferring the data from one to the other. However, this doesn't work for all files because of the possibility that they might contain control codes which a sequential file will filter out. The problem is very simple to solve using binary files, as can be seen in Listing 8.1 You don't really need any SEEK commands after the first pair because the reading and writing position moves on, as in the case of a sequential file.

Listing 8.1

```
INPUT "Input file name", F1$
INPUT "Output file name", F2$
OPEN F1$ FOR BINARY AS 1
OPEN F2$ FOR BINARY AS 2
byte% = 1
T$ = " "
DO UNTIL EOF(1)
   SEEK #1,byte%
   GET #1,,T$
   SEEK #2,byte%
   PUT #2,,T$
   PRINT T$, byte%
   byte% = byte% + 1
LOOP
CLOSE 1
CLOSE 2
PRINT byte% - 1; " Bytes transferred"
```

COPY.BAS

» DOS file commands

Part of the problem in using any version of Basic is that it stops you from using the standard MS-DOS file handling commands such as ERASE, RENAME, CHDIR etc.. QBasic however does provide a range of commands that are in most cases very similar to the equivalent MS-DOS commands. These can be seen along with their MS-DOS equivalents in the following table:

MS-DOS	QBasic
ERASE *filename*	KILL *filename*
RENAME *file1,file2*	NAME *file1* AS *file2*
DIR *filename*	FILES *filename*
CHDIR *path*	CHDIR *path*
MKDIR *path*	MKDIR *path*
RMDIR *path*	RMDIR *path*

All the file and path specifications in these commands are general string expressions. For example, FILE F$+".TXT" will give you a directory of all the files with the extension .TXT if F$ contains the string "*". Also, anywhere that you can use a filename you can include a path specification. If any of these commands proves insufficient then you can use any MS-DOS command by using:

```
SHELL "command"
```

where *command* is any MS-DOS command, program or batch file name. When the command, program or batch file is complete the control is returned to the program.

» Networks

If you are working with a network, or any multi-user or multi-tasking situation, then there are some special considerations concerning the sharing of files. It is important to avoid the situation where two users attempt to update the same sequential file or record in a direct access file. The reason is simply that which set of changes take effect depend on which user saves the file last! To stop simultaneous access you can use the command:

```
LOCK filenumber, record
```

which locks the specified record number in the given file. If a record is locked another program cannot access it. If an attempt to work with the record is made then one of the errors "Bad record number" or "Permission denied" are produced. You can also lock a range of records using:

```
LOCK filenumber, start TO end
```

which locks all records from record number *start* to record number *end*. In the case of a binary file the record numbers are interpreted as characters enabling a lock to be placed on any portion of the file. A sequential file can only be locked in its entirety and any record or byte numbers specified are ignored.

Once you have finished using the record, range of characters, or file, then you should unlock it using a matching UNLOCK command:

```
UNLOCK filenumber, record
```

or:

```
UNLOCK filenumber, start TO end
```

UNLOCK statements must match the LOCK statement exactly - that is you cannot unlock part of a range that you have locked.

You should unlock files and records as soon as possible to enable maximum sharing of data on the network. Notice that LOCK and UNLOCK only work if you have loaded SHARE.EXE before starting QBasic on the workstation.

In many cases treating a lock as a complete prohibition on further file access is more than is necessary. For example, suppose a file is locked by another program, there is still no harm in opening the file as long as you only want to read it and are aware of the fact that you might be looking at a file that might be about to be up-dated. Also if you have a file opened for reading you might only want to apply a lock that stops other users from updating, i.e. writing to the file, even though it might be fine for other users to also read the file. In other words, in a more sophisticated system, access to a file should depend how the file was opened by the first user and by subsequent users. You can specify both what you are going to do with a file and what sort of lock you want to place on it using extra conditions in the OPEN statement:

OPEN *filename* FOR *mode* ACCESS *access lock* AS *filenum*

The *access* type can be any of READ, WRITE or READ WRITE and *lock* can be SHARED, LOCK READ, LOCK WRITE or LOCK READ WRITE. Also if you leave out a specification for *lock* then a default lock mode is used. Access to the file is allowed or denied depending on what type of access you are requesting and what type of lock is already in place. This is best summarised in the following table:

Type of lock already in place	Access mode requested		
	Read	Write	Read/Write
Default	Denied	Denied	Denied
Shared	Allowed	Allowed	Allowed
Lock Read	Denied	Allowed	Denied
Lock Write	Allowed	Denied	Denied
Lock Read/ Write	Denied	Denied	Denied

Key points

» The record and the field are the data structures most appropriate for working with disk files.

» File handling must follow the set sequence of opening the file, using it and then closing it.

» Sequential files are easy to work with and they allow variable length records, but they have to be read in the order in which they were written.

» The WRITE command will automatically insert field separators between data items. The resulting file format is known as CSV.

» Direct access files work with fixed length records but you can read and write records in any order simply by specifying the record number.

» The simplest way of working with a direct access file is to create a user-defined type in the format of the record and then use GET and PUT to read and write it. Alternatively, you can store values, suitably converted into character strings, directly into the record buffer.

» Binary files allow you to read any data, irrespective of whether or not it corresponds to printable characters.

» There are a range of file manipulation commands similar to those available under MS-DOS.

» Sharing data files on a network or multi-user system requires special attention to locking and unlocking files or records.

Chapter 9

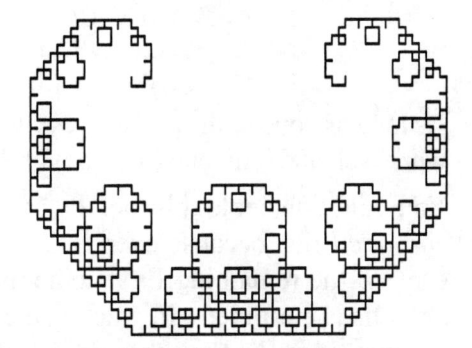

Advanced Control

This chapter describes some less common but very useful commands and techniques. It also covers the activity of testing programs.

Although you can get by using very little more than the commands and statements that have been described in earlier chapters, there are a few additional commands that make life easier - and so are worth knowing about. There are also a number of programming methods, recursion and event driven programming in particular, that every programmer should know something about. Both are described in detail later in this chapter as are general issues concerning debugging and testing.

» Multiple selections

A single IF statement can be used to select between two alternatives. To select between three or more alternatives you have to use more than one IF statement. For example, if you want to select between three alternatives depending on whether C is 1, 2 or 3 you could use:

```
IF C=1 THEN CALL sub1
IF C=2 THEN CALL sub2
IF C=3 THEN CALL sub3
```

As long as none of the procedures changed the value of C then this would work well and only one (or none) of the subroutines would be called.

You might object to this method of using IF statements, usually called *cascaded* IFs, because even if C is equal to 1, the conditions within each of the remaining IF statements are tested to see if they are true and this is inefficient. In practice the inefficiency is usually very small and cascaded IFs have the additional advantage of being a fairly clear way of expressing the choice process - subject to the warning that the value of C is not changed during the selection process.

There is, however, an extension to the IF statement that makes multiple selections of the sort described above more efficient - the ELSEIF statement. For example, you can rewrite the previous cascaded IF selection on C as:

```
IF C=1 THEN
   CALL sub1
ELSEIF C=2 THEN
   CALL sub2
ELSEIF C=3 THEN
   CALL sub3
END IF
```

This works in exactly the same way as the simple cascaded IF but the remaining ELSEIFs are skipped as soon as one of the conditions turns out to be true. For example if C is 2 then the IF C=1 is tried followed by the ELSEIF C=2 which proves to be true so the CALL sub2 is performed. On return from sub2 the ELSEIF C=3 is skipped and control passes to the instruction following the END IF.

You can have as many ELSEIF statements within a block IF as you need and you can also specify an ELSE block which will only be carried out if all of the conditions in the previous IF and ELSEIFs are false. For example:

```
IF C=1 THEN
   CALL sub1
ELSEIF C=2 THEN
   CALL sub2
ELSEIF C=3 THEN
   CALL sub3
ELSE
   CALL subremainder
END IF
```

will result in sub1 being called when C=1, sub2 when C=2, sub3 when C=3 and subremainder when C is a value other than 1, 2 or 3.

» Select Case

Although the ELSEIF statement is very useful it can be difficult to read a long list of ELSEIFs, THENs and ELSEs. A much simpler way of achieving the same effect is to use the SELECT command. There is another method of making choices between a number of alternatives but it only works if the conditions to be tested are all on the same variable or expression. For example, the multiple selection based on the value of C described in the previous section can be written:

```
SELECT CASE C
  CASE IS =1
    CALL sub1
  CASE IS =2
    CALL sub2
  CASE IS =3
    CALL sub3
  CASE ELSE
    CALL subremainder
END SELECT
```

Notice that the conditions are entered in two parts - the expression, C in this case, that gives the value of the first part of the condition and the comparison that has to be made following each CASE statement.

The type of comparisons that you can make are also extended slightly. You can use:

CASE IS <5	or any relational operator >=, <>etc.
CASE 4	short for IS =4
CASE 4,13,10	true if the expression is equal to 4, 13 or 10
CASE a TO b	true if the expression is between a and b

You can also mix these conditions as in:

    CASE 10,15 TO 20

which is true if the expression is equal to 10 or in the range 15 to 20. If none of the conditions following the CASE statements are true then the instructions following the CASE ELSE statement, if there is one, are executed. If you can use the SELECT statement then it is clearer and easier to read than the equivalent multiple IFs or ELSEIFs and safer than the equivalent cascaded IFs.

» Logical expressions

It is possible to write rather more complicated conditions within selection statements than just A>B etc.. You can use the logical operators - AND, OR, XOR, NOT, EQV and IMP - to form conditions known as *logical expressions*. For example:

    A>1 AND A<10

is a logical expression that is true only if A is both greater than one and less than ten. (That is A must be between 1 and 10.) The meaning of the logical operators can be seen in the following table:

Logical operator	Meaning
A AND B	True if both A and B are true
A OR B	True if either or both of A or B are true
NOT A	True if A is false
A XOR B	True if either A or B but not both are true
A IMP B	False if A is true and B is false
A EQU B	True if A and B are both true or both false

Of all of the logical operators only AND, OR and NOT are the most used and really the only ones you have to be sure you know how to use.

Logical expressions are expressions which evaluate to true or false. Instead of using a different form of data to represent true and false, most versions of Basic, QBasic included, use -1 to represent true and 0 to represent false. This means that you can save the result of a logical expression in a standard variable for later use. For example:

```
ANS=((Z=Y) OR (A=B))
IF ANS THEN
```

is perfectly legal. The most common use of logical results stored in variables is to allow a procedure to pass back status information to the calling program. For example you could use a variable called OK which is set to -1 if the procedure worked without error and 0 if an error occurred. You could write a test that the procedure had worked as simply as

```
IF(OK) THEN ...
```

It is also useful to define the constants TRUE=-1 and FALSE=0 at the start of every program. In practice QBasic will treat any non-zero value as being equivalent to true and this can sometimes be put to good use. For example,

```
IF(X) THEN ...
```

will carry out the THEN portion of the IF for any non-zero value of X. It is tempting to get carried away with this new way of using logical values - always remember that clarity and simplicity are your aim.

» Advanced loops

Once you have mastered them loops are simple enough and as long as you don't start trying to invent something more complicated they are trouble free! The best advice is always to keep things simple and obvious.

As already discussed in Chapter 3, there are two different types of loop *conditional* and *enumeration*. A conditional loop repeats until a condition is met and then stops. An enumeration loop repeats a given number of times. In QBasic the conditional loop is the DO-LOOP and the enumeration loop is the FOR-NEXT loop. You should always try to use the correct loop for the job. This would be easy apart from the existence of the EXIT FOR command. You can use this to leave a FOR loop before the specified number of repeats has been completed. This produces something that looks like a FOR loop but behaves like a conditional loop. This can be confusing to another programmer (or to yourself at a later date) so think very carefully about whether or not the EXIT FOR is worth using. If you don't think that you are likely to use it then consider the following very natural example:

```
FOR I=1 TO N
   IF A(I)=0 THEN EXIT FOR
NEXT I
```

This loop scans through an array until it finds the first zero element. Notice that the FOR loop is used to perform the scan from 1 TO N but if the required element is found before the loop reaches N then it is terminated early. You can tell if a zero element was found when the loop has finished by testing the value of I. If I is less than or equal to N then a zero element was found. If it is equal to N+1 then a zero element was not found. Many programmers consider this use of the FOR loop bad style. It is misleading and it relies on the value of I being N+1 when the loop ends - and this is a minor detail of implementation that might not be true in other versions of Basic and might not even remain so for future versions of QBasic. Personally I think that this use of the FOR loop is simpler and clearer than the more correct conditional version:

```
I=1
DO UNTIL A(I)=0 OR I>N
   I=I+1
LOOP
```

The problem with terminating a FOR loop early also generalises to terminating any sort of loop. There are only two things that can go wrong with a loop - the code being repeated can be defective or it can be repeated the wrong number of times. Working out what a loop should do is a very general question but how many times it is carried out is directly related to how the loop was formed. It is important that when you look at a loop you know exactly what conditions make it terminate. The best way of making this easy is to have only a single way out of a loop - an exit point - which clearly states the condition for the loop to stop. Many programmers are also of the opinion that loops are simpler if they have exit points only at the very start or at the very end. The reason is that then you are sure that all of the instructions in the loop have been obeyed the same number of times. Compare this to a loop with an exit point in the middle and ask yourself how many times the instructions before the exit point have been carried out when the loop ends compared to the number of times the instructions after the exit point.

The FOR loop is remarkably useful but there is one respect in which Basic probably goes too far in trying to make it cover all situations. The STEP instruction can also be used to specify a fractional step size but in general this is not to be recommended. Try the following loop:

```
FOR I=0 TO 1 STEP .01
     PRINT I
NEXT I
```

What would you expect the final value to be? It should logically be 1 but the correct answer depends on the way the slight rounding errors accumulate. In QBasic the actual answer is .9999993. In many programming languages loops that have fractional step sizes are thought to be in 'bad taste' and likely to lead to errors. In practice it can be easier to use a fractional step size for some applications. The crucial thing is that you should avoid the use of fractional step sizes when the final value or the exact number of times around the loop, is critical.

For example if you want to print out a table of imperial to metric conversions for every .01 of an inch between 0 and 1 inch then it is important that the table ends exactly on 1 inch. In this case the loop based on FOR X=0 TO 1 STEP .01 might give you trouble. The correct way to do this is to write the loop in terms thousands of an inch:

```
FOR X=0 TO 1000
     inch=X/1000
     metres=inch*ConversionFactor
     PRINT "Inches=";inch;"metres=";metres
NEXT X
```

» Recursion

If you want to repeat a section of program the simplest and most straightforward way is to use a loop. Programs that achieve repetition using loops are generally referred to as *iterative*. However there is another way of repeating things that doesn't involve iteration, called *recursion*. Recursion achieves the repetition of a group of instructions by using self reference. If a group of instructions can include the instruction "do this list of instructions" then this self reference will cause the list of instructions to be obeyed forever. This is a primitive form of recursion equivalent to an infinite loop. Self reference has long been a source of logical puzzles and paradoxes and hence any use of it has to be treated with great care. For example:

"This sentence is false."

is a paradox due to self reference that can keep you awake at nights!

Thus there are two ways of writing any program - using iteration and using recursion - and there are programmers who believe that only one of the ways is correct in all cases. In practice there are applications that iteration and recursion suit equally well, but there are problems to which recursion is especially suited and so it is worth trying to find out what exactly recursion provides that simple iteration does not.

Notice that there is no suggestion that there is anything that can be done by recursion that cannot be done by iteration - it's just that sometimes the recursive solution is much, much, simpler. Indeed recursion can often be so simple that its success looks like magic!

» Infinite recursion

Recursion is achieved in QBasic by allowing a procedure to call itself. It is this element of self reference that makes recursion difficult to understand at first meeting. Perhaps the best way to understand recursion is by comparing its action to the by now familiar loop. As already described, the fundamental form of the loop is the infinite loop. Consider the problem of printing the word HELLO on the screen repeatedly. Most programmers would solve this problem using a DO-LOOP:

```
DO
   PRINT "HELLO"
LOOP
```

The same problem can be solved using recursion by defining a subroutine that prints HELLO and then calls itself to print another HELLO and so on:

```
SUB DoIt
PRINT "HELLO"
CALL DoIt
END SUB
```

This second, infinite recursion, version of the program has a lot of similarities with the infinite loop but many programmers tend to panic at the sight of CALL DoIt occurring at the end of what they think of as the definition of DoIt. It is not so difficult if you think in terms of the CALL transferring control back to the start of the procedure. Notice however that it is a little more complicated than a simple loop because each call brings a new copy of the DoIt subroutine into existence - it is this that makes recursion so powerful.

» Conditional recursion

Infinite recursion is no more useful than the infinite loop, and so it is not surprising that the next idea that we have to examine is finding some way of limiting it. If we wanted to print the word HELLO on the screen n times then most programmers would find the following iterative solution very easy to understand:

```
SUB hello(n)
DO
   PRINT "HELLO"
   n=n-1
   IF n=0 THEN EXIT LOOP
LOOP
END SUB
```

Here the variable n is being used as a loop counter which is decremented each time through the loop until it is zero. That is, the loop ends when n is zero. The equivalent recursive solution is:

```
SUB Hello(n)
  PRINT "HELLO"
  n=n-1
  IF n<>0 THEN CALL Hello((n))
END SUB
```

This recursive method of repeating something has a lot in common with the previous looping program. It has a counter, in the form of variable n, which is decremented just before each repetition. It also has an IF statement which controls when the repetition should come to an end. The difference is that the looping program achieves its repetition by transferring control back to the start of the program but the recursive program says "do it all again" by transferring control to a completely new copy of the procedure Hello.

This difference can be seen more clearly if you try to follow the path through each program with your finger. In the case of the iterative solution you will find that you really do go round in circles, but in the case of the recursive solution you have to write down a completely new copy of the procedure for each repeat. The path for the recursive Hello for n equal to 2 is shown in Figure 9.1.

```
             Copy 1
               ↓
               ↓  (n=2)
           SUB hello(n)
               ↓                    SUB hello(n)
         PRINT "HELLO"                   ↓
               ↓                   PRINT "HELLO"
              n=n-1                      ↓
               ↓  (n=1)                 n=n-1
    IF n<>0 THEN CALL hello((n))  →       ↓  (n=0)
                                  IF n<>0 THEN CALL hello((n))
                                         ↓
           END SUB      ←            END SUB
               ↓
```

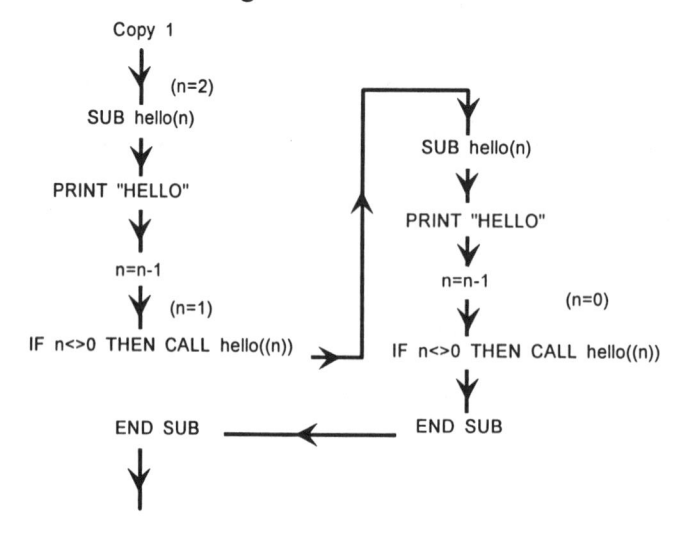

Figure 9.1
The flow of control through Hello

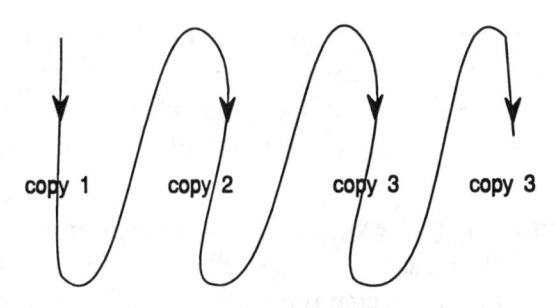

Figure 9.2
The shape of recursion

Notice that at the point when the repetition ends, that is when n=0, the latest copy of the procedure Hello comes to an end and passes control back to the copy before it and so on all the way back to the very first copy. You can think of this as 'unwinding' the recursion. Thus, if going 'round in circles' is the natural 'shape' of iteration, then a spiral is the natural shape of recursion as the flow of control passes through each new copy of the procedure - see Figure 9.2.

» Forward and backward recursion

The type of recursion described above is particularly simple because nothing extra happens during the unwinding of the recursion. That is, it is of the form:

```
Do something
if condition then Do something
end
```

and when the condition is false all the copies of the procedure just come to an end one after the other without doing anything other than go out of existence! You can use this unwinding phase of a recursion to produce some interesting results, however. Consider, for example:

```
SUB Back(n)
   n=n-1
IF n<>0 THEN CALL Back((n))
   PRINT n
   PRINT "HELLO"
END SUB
```

BACK1.BAS

Calling Back(10) will cause the machine to pause for a moment and then print out 0 HELLO, 1 HELLO, 2 HELLO etc. up to 9 HELLO. You should find this a little puzzling as the value of n decreases by one each time a new copy of the procedure is called, yet the values printed out increase!

The reason for this is that the printing out is done during the unwinding phase of the recursion and this takes you back through existing copies of the procedure in the reverse order to the one in which they were created, hence the increasing value of n. If you would like to see this more clearly try the following version of the subroutine.

```
SUB Back (n)
   n = n - 1
   PRINT n
   IF n <> 0 THEN CALL Back((n))
   PRINT n
END SUB
```

BACK2.BAS

In this case calling Back(10) prints 10,9,8 down to 0 and then 0,1,2 back up to 10. The decreasing values are printed going down the recursion and the increasing values going back up again.

In general, recursions that involve doing something during the unwinding are more complicated and difficult to understand, and of course recursions that do something in the forward and reverse directions are even more complicated! The most general form of recursion is:

```
SUB xxx(parameter list)
    list of instructions 1
 CALL xxx(parameter list)
    list of instructions 2
END SUB
```

The first list of instructions will be obeyed on the way up the recursive spiral and so will process the parameters in the order in which the copies of the routine are activated. If we assume that parameters are passed by reference then the second list of instructions processes the parameters as passed back from later activations as the spiral unwinds.

» Local variables and passing by value

One of the conditions that has to be satisfied for recursion to work is that each time you call a subroutine a completely new copy is brought into existence. So far this 'new copy' principle has been implicitly assumed to work, and indeed it does as long as all of the variables used are local variables and all parameters are passed by value. The reason for having to use local variables is simply that these are created afresh each time a procedure is started and destroyed when it ends. Most parameters have to be passed by value for the same reason. This can be achieved by placing brackets around the parameter or by passing an expression. However if you want the recursive call to a subroutine to return a result then the parameter used should be passed by reference.

Knowing when to pass by value or reference is the hardest part about using recursion. So if you are writing a recursive program and it doesn't seem to work as you would expect then the chances are that you are passing something by reference that should be passed by value or vice versa.

Another problem that sometimes crops up with recursive procedures or functions is running out of stack space. The stack is an area of memory where QBasic keeps track of where to return after each subroutine. It also allocates local variables on the stack each time a new subroutine starts. Normally running out of stack space isn't a problem but each recursive call brings into existence another copy of all of the variables etc. that are used by the procedure or function and the necessary storage is taken from the stack. To increase the amount of memory allocated to the stack you can use the command:

```
CLEAR,, size in bytes
```

The two commas are needed to keep QBasic compatible with earlier dialects of Basic. Note that as the CLEAR command deletes all variables and closes all files it should be placed at the start of the program unless you want to re-initialise everything.

» When is recursion useful?

Now that we are able to see recursion as nothing more than an alternative way of repeating something, the question that remains is, what good is it? Some enthusiastic programmers see applications for recursion everywhere. Indeed some computer languages such as Logo have been designed with recursion as the only way of achieving repetition. The truth of the matter is that most types of repetition are better dealt with using iteration. However, there are times when recursion is ideally suited to a problem. In particular there are some data structures for which a recursive definition seems natural and this makes them good candidates for recursive processing.

For example, there are a group of particularly intricate curves that are best described, and therefore generated, recursively. The C-curve is obtained by recursively replacing a straight line between two points by a pair of lines at right angles, see Figure 9.3. Obviously this process of replacement would continue forever to finer and finer lines but to make the recursion practical it is stopped when the lines reach a given size. The program in Listing 9.1 uses the recursive procedure drawcurve to produce a C-curve like the one in Figure 9.4. If you would like to experiment then try changing the values of lngth% and angle.

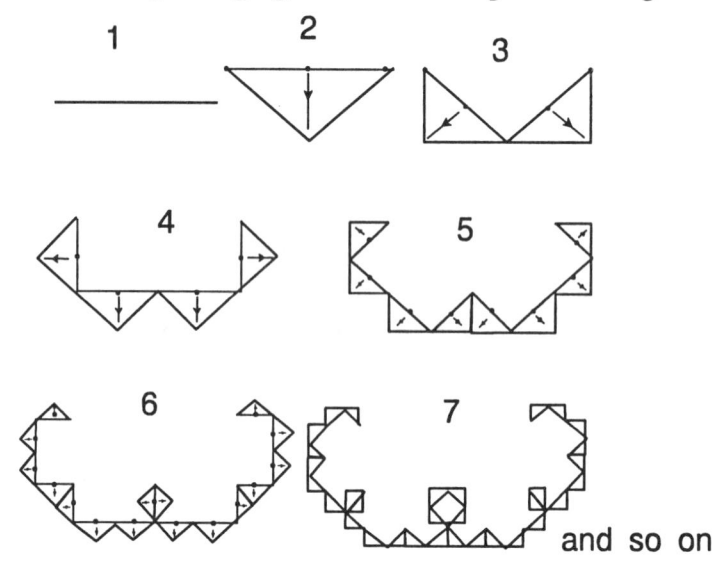

Figure 9.3
Building up a C curve

Listing 9.1

```
CALL init(lngth%, angle)
CALL drawcurve((lngth%), (angle))
END

SUB init (lngth%, angle)
SCREEN 2
CLS
angle = 0
lngth% = 150
PSET (100, 40)
END SUB

SUB drawcurve (lngth%, angle)
IF lngth%<5 THEN
   x = lngth% * COS(angle) * 1.8
   y = lngth% * SIN(angle)
   LINE -STEP(x, y)
ELSE
   lngth% = INT(lngth% / 1.4142)
   CALL drawcurve((lngth%), angle + 3.14159 / 4)
   CALL drawcurve((lngth%), angle - 3.14159 / 4)
END IF
END SUB
```

CCURVE.BAS

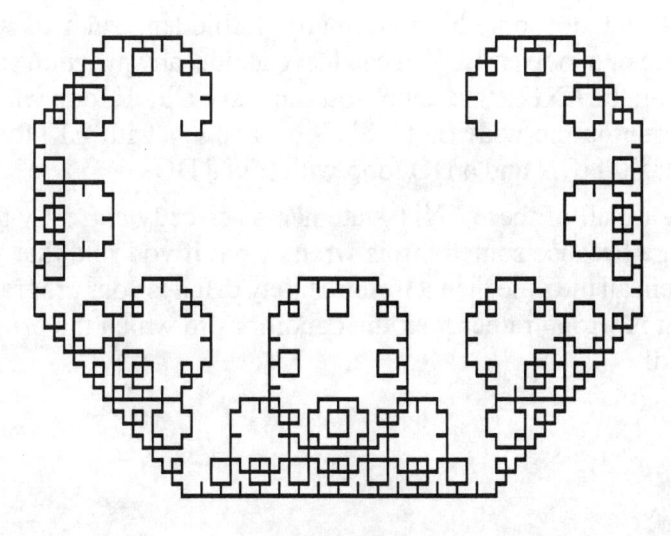

Figure 9.4
A sample C-curve

» Exceptions

After you have been writing large programs for a little while you will discover that occasionally a condition occurs within a program that makes you think that it would be nice if there was some way of ignoring the program's normal structure and doing something exceptional. For example, if you have written a well structured modular program and are several subroutines down only to discover that it is possible for an error to occur, such as a file not existing or some calculation being capable of overflowing, what should you do? Your entire program has been constructed on the basis that everything will work and suddenly something out of the ordinary can occur which really needs to go outside of the ordinary structure of the program. It can be argued that this should never happen in a well designed program, but it is often difficult to think of every eventuality when designing a program.

Such out of the ordinary occurrences are usually called *exceptions* and currently no programming language has come up with a really good way of dealing with them. The best that you can do is to try to 'unwind' the procedure structure that you have produced by returning early from each subroutine with a flag set to indicate that an error has occurred.

The most important feature of exceptions is that they are nearly always easier to deal with if you can temporarily ignore the structure of the program and do something normally forbidden, such as leave a subroutine or a loop early. You can leave almost any program structure early using the EXIT statement. You can leave a FOR loop with EXIT FOR, a subroutine with EXIT SUB, a function with EXIT DEF or EXIT FUNCTION and a DO loop with EXIT DO.

You can use all of these EXIT statements perfectly correctly to leave a structure because something is wrong - but if you find that you are using them all the time then it is more likely that it is your programming style that is wrong rather than the conditions to which the program is subjected!

» Event driven programming

There is a connection between handling unexpected errors and dealing with events that are generated in the outside world. This is because both the pressing of a particular key and the occurrence of an error condition can occur at any time and neither take account of the structure of your program.

With the methods you have available at the moment, the only way that you can respond quickly to the pressing of a key is to write a *polling loop* that continually checks the state of the key. An alternative and much simpler method is to use event driven programming. This is based on the hardware idea of an *interrupt*. An interrupt is a transfer of control to a particular point in a program caused by some external event. That is, an interrupt can cause transfer of control from any point in the program without you having to write an explicit transfer statement such as GOTO, GOSUB or CALL. Usually an interrupt is a transfer of control, initiated by the hardware, from any point in the program to a specially written piece of program called the *interrupt handler*. For example, when a disk drive is ready to transfer data it signals an interrupt which causes your machine to stop doing whatever it is doing and to transfer control to a routine that will read data from the disk drive into memory.

In QBasic a similar idea is implemented in the form of event handling. There are a number of statements of the form:

```
ON xxx GOSUB label
```

which when the event *xxx* occurs cause control to be transferred to the point in the program indicated by *label*. For example, following:

```
ON KEY(1) GOSUB functionone
```

control will be transferred to the part of the program labelled 'functionone' whenever key one i.e. the F1 key, is pressed. Notice that this transfer of control will occur no matter what position has been reached in your program. Once you have completed that action that is supposed to happen when F1 is pressed, you can resume the execution of your program from where it was interrupted by using the command:

```
RETURN
```

For example:
```
ON KEY(1) GOSUB functionone
KEY(1) ON
DO
   PRINT "hello"
LOOP
END

functionone:
   PRINT "function key one"
   BEEP
   RETURN
```

EVENT1.BAS

This program will print Hello on the screen in an infinite loop unless it is interrupted by someone pressing the F1 key, when control is transferred to the subroutine it prints the "function key one" message and beeps. The RETURN statement then returns control back to the point at which the program was interrupted.

Events are very useful and have the potential to make a program capable of dealing with complex occurrences in a flexible way and with minimum effort. There are a number of problems to be aware of. Firstly QBasic's event handling restricts you to the use of traditional Basic subroutines with all their problems of global variables. Secondly event handling follows none of the basic guidelines of structured programming and it is very easy to produce a program that is simple on the surface but in practice very complicated in the way that it works.

The general form of the event handling statement is:

    ON x GOSUB *label*

where *x* is one of the possible events listed in the following table:

Event	Description
COM(n)	character is received on serial port n
KEY(n)	key n (n = 1 to 31) is pressed
PEN	light pen button pressed
PLAY(n)	less than n notes are left in the music buffer
STRIG(n)	joystick button n is pressed
TIMER(n)	an event every n seconds

All these events have a corresponding statement to switch handling on and off:

COM(*n*)	ON/OFF/STOP
KEY(*n*)	ON/OFF/STOP
PEN	ON/OFF/STOP
PLAY	ON/OFF/STOP
STRIG	ON/OFF/STOP
TIMER	ON/OFF/STOP

Following an *event* OFF statement the event is still checked for but it is ignored if it occurs. An ON *event* GOSUB statement only has effect following an *event* ON statement. An *event* STOP statement has a similar effect to *event* OFF but any event that occurs will be remembered and cause a transfer of control as soon as the next *event* ON statement is encountered. Whenever control is transferred by an ON *event* GOSUB statement that event is switched off until the next RETURN. This avoids multiple events from interrupting the event handling subroutine until it is finished.

For the key assignments in ON KEY(*n*) see Chapter 10 where a number of other keyboard control commands and functions are discussed and an example of keyboard control using events is described.

» A musical event

It is worth noticing that the ON PLAY(*n*) command only makes sense if you are using the PLAY in the background, i.e. if MB is included in the command string. In this case the note buffer is loaded with the commands specified and the program continues. The note data is sent to the speaker while your program is working and the ON PLAY(*n*) command can be used to transfer to a subroutine that re-loads the music buffer to keep it going.

As an example of event handling other than keyboard events, you might like to try the following simple program. It plays a random tune continuously while drawing random boxes in random colours on the screen.

202 *Advanced Control*   *Chapter 9*

```
SCREEN 1
GOSUB fillbuf
ON PLAY(5) GOSUB fillbuf
PLAY ON                                    MUSEVENT.BAS
DO
   FOR j% = 1 TO 500: NEXT j%
   LINE (rndx, rndy)-(rndx, rndy), rndc, BF
LOOP

fillbuf:
s$ = "MBL16"
FOR i% = 1 TO 10
   s$ = s$ + "N" + STR$(INT(RND * 84))
NEXT i%
PLAY s$
RETURN

FUNCTION rndc
   rndc = INT(RND * 4)
END FUNCTION
FUNCTION rndx
   rndx = INT(RND * 320)
END FUNCTION
FUNCTION rndy
   rndy = INT(RND * 200)
END FUNCTION
```

The fillbuf subroutine is called whenever the notes in the music buffer fall below 5 when it adds a further 10 notes to it. If you increase the number of notes placed in the buffer then the fillbuf subroutine is called less often but when it is there is more of a pause in the line drawing. Try altering the number of notes added and the level at which fillbuf is called. Also notice the MB command at the start of the play string. This makes the music play in the background. Try changing MB to MF to see the difference.

» Error handling

The ON ERROR GOTO *label* statement is a special sort of event handling command because it allows a program to respond to a wide range of runtime errors without crashing. When a runtime error occurs control is passed to the point in the program indicated by the label. Although this is not formally a subroutine it is generally referred to as the error handling routine.

The way in which an error is dealt with obviously depends on the type of error and where it occurred in the program. The ERL function will return the line number, but not line label, of the line that caused the error. Of course, if you have been using QBasic without line numbers ERL will be of little use as it will always return zero. The ERR function will return the code of the error that has just occurred. This is generally more useful in deciding what the error handling subroutine should do. In the case of errors relating to external devices such as disk drives, communications ports etc. then the pair of functions ERDEV and ERDEV$ are useful. ERDEV returns the error code (low byte is the MS-DOS error code and the high byte contains device attribute information) and ERDEV$ gives the name of the device.

You can give up trying to handle an error, or cause a runtime error to be reported, from any point in your program by using the ERROR *n* statement. This causes QBasic to behave as if error number *n* has just occurred. You can also define your own custom errors by using values of *n* that aren't already used to report errors.

If your error handling subroutine can deal with the error then it has the option of restarting the program at the place where the error occurred using the RESUME statement, at the statement following the line that caused the error by using RESUME NEXT, or at any given line by using RESUME *label*. Unlike the other ON *event* statements, ON ERROR handling is disabled by ON ERROR GOTO 0. This implies that you shouldn't use 0 as a line label.

Writing error handling routines always seems simple in theory but in practice it turns out to be virtually impossible to write a routine that deals with even the majority of common errors sensibly. In most cases programs are written to deal with a few of the most frequent errors and then the remainder are dealt with by some sort of general restart of the entire program. This may not be entirely satisfactory but it is generally preferable to a program crash.

The short program below uses an on error routine which prints a suitable message if the program attempts a division by zero, which is one of the most common causes of errors:

```
ON ERROR GOTO zero
INPUT x
INPUT y
z=x/y
PRINT z
END
```

ERRORDEM.BAS

```
zero:
  IF err=11 THEN PRINT "you cannot divide by zero"
  RESUME NEXT
```

The big problem with event handling is that it forces you to make use of old style Basic subroutines with all of their problems. Error handling isn't quite as bad as event handling in this respect in that you can write a single error handling routine that is tagged on to the end of the main program and carry on using subroutines in the usual way. Notice that if you are in a subroutine when an error occurs then you are still in the subroutine after the GOTO *error handler* and so you should be careful about using RESUME *line label*.

» Interacting with MS-DOS

There are a range of commands that you can use to call on the services that MS-DOS provides. The file handling commands, FILES, NAME, MKDIR and RMDIR have already been discussed in Chapter 8. The SHELL command was also briefly discussed but it is worth stressing that it can be used to run another MS-DOS program or command from within a QBasic program. For example:

```
        SHELL "DIR"
```

will give you a standard MS-DOS style directory. Control is passed back to your program when the MS-DOS program or command finishes. Notice that SHELL only works in MS-DOS Version 3 and later implementations.

The MS-DOS environment is a specially reserved area of memory where programs and batch files can set up and examine parameter strings of the form "PATH=\" "COMSPEC=A:" etc.. These parameter strings are often used to establish operating conditions or the current state of the operating system, but in practice they can be used for any purpose that you like. You can discover the setting of any parameter in the environment area using, for example:

    S$=ENVIRON$("PATH=")

This would return the current setting of the parameter PATH. If you would just like to know the setting of the *n*th parameter use:

    S$=ENVIRON$(*n*)

To change the setting of any parameter use:

    ENVIRON "PATH=\SW"

and to remove a parameter use:

    ENVIRON "PATH=;"

Although the examples given above use PATH, you can set and read any parameter string, even if it has no predefined meaning to MS-DOS. For example:

    ENVIRON "TEST=ON"

will store the parameter string in the environment area even though it presumably only makes sense to the QBasic program that stored it there or a batch file that you have written to make use of it. There is one problem that it is important to be aware of - you cannot increase the number of characters stored in the environment area. If you need to add a parameter string then you must delete one to make room for it.

» Low level and BIOS interface

The full QBasic package provides a wide range of facilities to support a low level interface to machine code programs, hardware and the PC's BIOS (Basic I/O System) software. Some of these commands are not available in the QBasic interpreter and if you are particularly interested in these features then it is worth buying the full compiler.

To make use of some of these features you need to know about assembly language and this is beyond the scope of this book. However, some of the statements can be used even if you don't know much about machine code and hardware. It should be stressed that many of these commands give you direct access to your machine's memory and as such are capable of crashing not only QBasic but MS-DOS.

The command:

```
POKE offset,value
```

will store the single byte specified by *value* in the memory location at the address given by *segment+offset*. The value of *segment* is specified by the most recent DEF SEG=*segment* statement. Older versions of Basic running on machines limited to 64K of memory didn't need a segment address specifying because the full 64K of memory could be addressed using just the offset. Machines such as the PC treat their larger amounts of memory in 64K segments and to specify any given memory location you have to give the starting address of the segment and the offset. The POKE command doesn't do any sort of checks to make sure that it is permissible to store a value at the given location in memory, and so it is easy to crash the system by mistake. The function PEEK(*offset*) returns the value stored in the memory location specified by *segment+offset*.

One fairly safe application of PEEK and POKE is to store single-byte values in an array. If you dimension an integer array of size *n* then QBasic reserves a block of 2*n memory locations. The address of this block can be found using VARSEG and VARPTR. VARSEG(*variable*) returns the segment address of the variable and VARPTR(*variable*) returns the offset from the start of the segment. So to examine byte i% of the array you would use :

```
DIM a%(100)
DEF SEG=VARSEG(a%(0))
addr%=VARPTR(a%(0))
PRINT PEEK(addr%+i%-1)
```
and similarly to store *value* in byte i% you would add:

```
POKE addr%+i%-1,value
```
to the end of the program.

You can also use the command:

```
BSAVE filename, offset, length
```
to store any block of memory, starting at *offset* and *length* bytes long in a file. To load the block back into memory you can use:

```
BLOAD filename, offset
```
One of the main uses for BSAVE is to store graphics screens on disk so that they can be loaded at a later date.

As well as PEEK and POKE, the INP function and the OUT command can be used to transfer data from and to the I/O ports. These instructions are only really useful if you have special purpose hardware connected to your PC.

You can call a machine code routine using the command:

```
CALL ABSOLUTE parameters, offset
```
to transfer control to a machine code program located at *segment+offset*. You can follow the call by a number of parameters which are passed to the machine code routine as *near pointers* (i.e. offsets) on the stack.

Always remember that when you are using POKE or CALL you can crash your program and perhaps the entire system to such an extent that rebooting is the only way of regaining control - be very cautious when using these low level instructions and always save your program before testing.

» Other I/O devices

The methods used for sending and receiving data from disk described in Chapter 8 can be used to work with other devices. For example, you can OPEN a device as if it was a file using:

```
OPEN "device name" FOR mode AS filenumber
```

The device names that QBasic recognises are:

- KYBD: the keyboard - input only
- SCRN: the screen - output only
- LPT*n*:   line printer *n* (*n*=1,2 or 3) - output only
- COM*n*:   communications port *n* (*n*=1 or 2)
- CONS: the keyboard and screen

Once you have opened a device you can use the standard file I/O commands PRINT#, INPUT# etc. to send and receive data. For example:

```
OPEN "LPT1:" FOR OUTPUT AS #1
PRINT#1,"HELLO"
```

prints HELLO on the printer. Opening a device can be used as a way of altering where data is sent to or taken from. For example, if you open the screen for output using:

```
OPEN "SCRN:" FOR OUTPUT AS #1
```

and then use PRINT#1 instead of the standard PRINT then you can change the output device to be the printer simply by closing filenumber 1 and opening it again - that is:

```
CLOSE#1
OPEN "LPT2:" FOR OUTPUT AS #1
```

Communicating using the serial port can be a complicated business involving setting the transmission and reception parameters correctly. To allow you to do this from within QBasic there is the special version of the OPEN command when used with COM*n*:

```
OPEN "COMn:parameters" FOR mode AS filenumber
```

If you understand serial communications then you will have no trouble also understanding the list of parameters that you can use. In practice it can be quite tricky to get everything right so that the communications link works.

If you need to communicate directly with an MS-DOS device driver then you can use:

   IOCTL#*filenumber*,*string*

to send *string* to the device driver opened as *filenumber* and:

   A$=IOCTL$(#*filenumber*)

to read strings from it. The IOCTL function and statement allow you to send and receive status and command information as well as raw data, but to be able to use them you have to know something of how MS-DOS device drivers work.

» Debugging

If you have been using the program construction methods described in earlier chapters then you will have a head start when it comes to producing programs that work. However, it is worth saying a few words to explain the basic principles of *debugging* a program. ("Bug" is a term used by programmers to mean "error".)

There are essentially three different types of errors:

- » Syntax errors - these are simple spelling mistakes (produced by mistyping or a misinterpretation of the programming language manual).

- » Runtime errors - these are errors that only become apparent when the program is active. Runtime errors can occur because of some unforeseen, and hence not catered for, condition or because of the type of inputs a program is presented with.

- » Specification errors - these are failures of a program to meet its specification. In other words, the program may, in the usual sense, work but it doesn't do what it was intended to do. It is possible to have a complete specification error where the program solves the wrong problem but the shortcomings of a program are usually only partial.

Of the three types of errors, runtime errors are the most varied and difficult to characterise. They are also potentially the most devastating, occurring at any time during the life of the program and with consequences that range from having to re-key a few commands to a complete failure or crash. Syntax errors are easy to find and correct because the QBasic interpreter will report them to you as you type a program in. Runtime errors can remain hidden unless you find them. For these reasons it is important to examine ways of detecting and dealing with runtime errors.

» Testing methods

It is important to distinguish between knowing that there is an error in a program and knowing where it is. That is, bug detection is distinct from bug location. Bug detection is generally called *testing* and it is a phase of program development that is usually undervalued. Another problem is that testing is about proving that your program doesn't work, but most programmers test programs to prove that they do work! Even if you are prepared to attack your program in the spirit of making it fail there is always the psychological barrier against showing that the product of your own intellect is, in fact, flawed. This is the main reason why some people are better at testing than others, and why it is better to use someone other than the person who wrote the program to test it.

To test a program fully it is necessary to supply data that will take it through every possible route and this is difficult. The number of routes through even a fairly small program is enormous. Not only do you have to ensure that every route has been tested, you also have to test the program's response to extreme data values. Of course the trap in this simple idea is in the word 'extreme' because what is extreme data depends on the situation. Often included in the extreme data category are large numbers, negative numbers, zero, character data, control characters etc. But what constitutes appropriate test data relies on the judgement of the programmer to choose data that is likely to cause the program to malfunction - remember the purpose of testing is to show that the program doesn't work!

It is usual for testing to proceed as the program is developed - stepwise testing is a natural partner to stepwise refinement - but there is still a need for a final testing phase. Stepwise testing picks up problems as the program is being created, final testing makes sure that the program is fit to be used. Although it sounds as though we know how to test a program this is only a theoretical certainty, in practice testing is still a matter of judgement about how best to use the limited time available.

» After testing

Once you have determined that there is a bug in a program the next step is to locate it. The most common method of bug location in use is the 'just looking method'. All that happens is that a printout is obtained and the programmer sits and 'just looks at it' for a few minutes. This is a very effective method for a great many simple bugs. Indeed, often the bug becomes obvious in the time it takes to for the printer to produce the listing! The trouble with just looking is that it is often the only debugging method that a programmer knows and it is a property of the method that if it is going to work it works in at most a few minutes. There is no point in staring at a listing into the small hours of the night, cup of coffee in hand. Such tales of all night debugging sessions are often an indication that the programmer telling them knows little of logical fault finding!

Debugging is an activity just as logical as programming and it is based on gathering observations about how the program is working and comparing this with information about how the program should work. This predict and compare method has been in use as long as there have been programmers to create bugs. There are only two things that determine the behaviour of a program - the path taken through the statements and the values stored in the variables. If you can predict the path through the program and the values of the variables at each point then by comparing them with the actual route that is taken through the program and the actual values of the variables the bug can be located at the first place that there is a discrepancy between prediction and reality. This procedure is simple in principle but in practice there is the problem of gathering data on how the program works.

QBasic provides a TRACE on/off option in its Debug menu that is designed to allow you to follow the order of execution of a program. If you run a program with TRACE on you will be shown the statement currently executing highlighted in the text editing window. This allows you to follow the follow of control through your program. The only trouble is that between each step you will be shown the output screen for a moment and unless you are concentrating it can be difficult to follow what is going on.

Perhaps a better way to follow the flow of a program is to use the single step option. In this case an instruction is only carried out when you press F8 (or select Single Step from the Debug menu). Using Step you can work your way though your program line by line at your own speed. You can start the program going from the current point by pressing F5 (or selecting Continue from the Run menu). In between steps you can modify the program and then continue, but some modifications make it impossible to continue the program and in this case QBasic will tell you so. You can even move the point at which the program will restart by placing the cursor on the desired line and then using the command Set Next Statement. This shifts the highlight to the current line and when you select Continue from the Run menu execution starts from this line.

The main problem with single stepping is that it can take a long time to reach any particular point in the program. You can treat each procedure call as if it was a single instruction by pressing F10 (or by selecting Procedure Step from the Debug menu). You can mix pressing F8 and F10 to work your way though a program in small or big steps.

Another aid to getting to a given point in a program is the *breakpoint*. A breakpoint is simply a line in your program that stops the program running. You can set a breakpoint by placing the text cursor on the line and then pressing F9 (or by selecting Toggle Breakpoint from the Debug menu). You can remove the breakpoint by repeating the operation. You can set more than one breakpoint and they are shown in your program highlighted in red on colour monitors. (Although you can change the colour using the Options Display command.) When you run the program it will stop whenever it reaches a breakpoint. You can then single step the program or simply restart it. To clear all breakpoints simply select the option Clear all breakpoints from the Debug menu.

While a program is halted you can use the Immediate window to examine or change the contents of any variable. All you have to do is switch to the Immediate window, using F6, and then type in any command that you want. When you press Enter the command that the cursor is on will be obeyed at once. So for example, if A is a variable in the program being debugged you can discover the current contents of A by typing PRINT A in the immediate window and pressing Enter.

» Documentation

If you are writing a program for your own use then perhaps documenting is an unnecessary chore but if you plan to use the program over a number of years then you will certainly have forgotten how it works at a time when you need to change it. If you write well structured modular programs then these are virtually self-documenting. All that is generally needed is the addition of a few comments. You can enter comments by starting a line with a single quote, ' , or using the REM command. Any comments are ignored when the program is executed and are purely for you to read to discover how the program works. An exception to this is that there are a small number of instructions to the interpreter about how to run your program that take the form of comments such as '$STATIC. You don't need to add comments to every line of your program - this would make it harder to understand not easier. Add comments only where the meaning of your program isn't clear from the existing text and make sure that they add to the meaning rather than duplicate what is already obvious!

» Standalone programs

If you have a finished program you can run it without the user having to worry about loading QBasic using the command:

```
QBASIC /RUN program
```

If you leave out the /RUN then the program is loaded but not run. You can even put this command into a suitably named batch file so that you can give the impression that your QBasic program is a standard .EXE program. For example, suppose you have just finished a database program called DATA.BAS. You can write a batch file called DATA.BAT that contains the single line:

```
QBASIC /RUN DATA
```

when the user types the command DATA the batch file starts running and loads QBasic plus your program. Of course, there is nothing stopping you from including more batch file commands to customise the running of the program.

Notice that the command:

```
SYSTEM
```

used within a program will return control to the operating system i.e. to MS-DOS when the program has finished whereas:

```
END
```

will return to the QBasic editor. However while you are testing your program i.e. running it using the command Run,Start both SYSTEM and END take you back to the QBasic editor. This to avoid you constantly having to reload QBasic while you are testing a program you plan to run standalone when it is actually working.

Starting QBasic with the line:

```
QBASIC /RUN
```

i.e. with no program specified, also has the effect of removing the usual sign-on display.

» Large programs

There will come a time when the requirements of your QBasic program will exceed the available memory capacity. QBasic cannot make use of the many Megabytes of extended RAM that most modern machines have. Being a simple MS-DOS program it cannot use more than the 640KBytes of conventional memory available to MS-DOS. Even then there are restrictions on the size of arrays and strings that limit the amount of memory that a QBasic program can use. One solution to this problem is *chaining*. This works by breaking the program down into a number of modules that can be loaded into memory as they are required while the program is running. For example, suppose you have written a very large database package which can be divided into a module that allows the user to add records and a module that allows the user to look up records. You could write a main program that gives the user the choice of which action, and hence which module, is needed - see Figure 9.5. The main program clearly has to load whichever module is needed according to the selection the user makes. A module can be loaded using:

```
CHAIN "module name"
```

This loads a module into the memory space occupied by the original program. Thus chaining replaces one program in memory by another.

Obviously, for a program made up of a number of chain modules to work there has to be some way for one module to pass information to another. This problem is solved by using the COMMON statement. When a chain module is loaded into memory all the existing variables are lost and replaced by the chain module's own variable. The only exception to this are any variables listed in COMMON statements that are present in both programs - the variables so listed are treated as common to both programs. The variables may have different names in

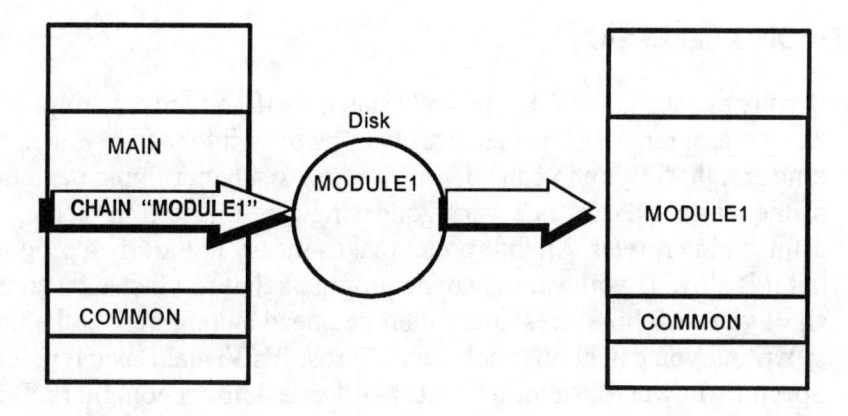

Figure 9.5
Chaining

each program and the connection between variables is made by the order in which they are listed in each COMMON statement. This is very like the way variables are matched up in parameter lists between the subroutine definition and its use. You can include arrays in COMMON statements, but you must indicate that the variable is an array by including brackets as in COMMON A(). If you include the keyword SHARED in a COMMON statement then all variables named will be accessible from subroutines and functions, i.e. they are global.

For example, suppose the main program in the database example described above uses F$ to record the name of the database file, N for the number of records, and a list of data in A(10). Also suppose that the lookup module uses FILE$, M and DATA(10) for the same purpose. To make sure that the information in F$, N and A() is inherited by FILE$, M and DATA() when the main program chains to the lookup module you have to include :

```
COMMON F$,N,A()
```

in the main program and:

```
COMMON FILE$,M,DATA()
```

in the lookup module. Notice that you have to include a COMMON statement in any chain module that needs access to the common variables.

» Beyond QBasic

If you have mastered QBasic, and especially if you are contemplating writing programs that need to use chaining to fit into memory, then the time is right for you to consider moving on to a better implementation of the Basic. QBasic is a very good language but it is implemented using an interpreter. An interpreter makes it easy to modify a program but it is slow. If you want to create programs that run fast and can use all of your machine's resources then you need a compiler. At the time of writing you can choose between Microsoft's Visual Basic for DOS, Spectra's Power Basic or a number of lesser known compilers. Both Visual Basic and Power Basic are highly compatible with QBasic and you should have no trouble writing programs using them and even converting existing programs to run using them.

Visual Basic has the unique advantage of offering an event driven programming style that includes visual elements such as buttons and text entry boxes. You can create advanced and easy to use interfaces in no time at all using it. Another advantage is that it is compatible with Visual Basic for Windows. This can be used to create Windows applications using a dialect of Basic that is essentially QBasic.

» The final stages

The only way to learn to program is to do it. In the final chapter of this book you will find a collection of applications that make use of all the ideas introduced in earlier chapters. It also takes the opportunity of introducing the more specialised ideas and techniques that would have been out of place in a more general discussion of programming. Read the descriptions, try the programs and learn by modifying them or incorporating them into your own programs.

Key points

» You can use ELSEIF and SELECT to make multiple choices.

» You can often simplify a selection using a logical expression.

» Recursion is an alternative to iteration that suits some, but by no means all, problems.

» Exceptions are the sort of conditions that arise in real programs when things go wrong.

» Event driven programming causes jumps to event handling routines to occur in response to external events.

» Error handling using ON ERROR GOTO is very similar to event handling with the error taking the place of the event.

» There are a wide range of commands that allow a program to interact with both the system i.e. MS-DOS, and the machine. In most cases you need a good knowledge of how the PC works as well as QBasic to make use of them.

» Debugging is an activity that involves predicting what you expect the program to do and comparing it with what the program actually does.

» There is a range of debugging aids included with QBasic including trace, single step and break pointing.

» Although it is possible to produce well finished, large standalone programs using the QBasic interpreter there are many advantages to moving to a true Basic compiler such as Visual Basic for DOS or Power Basic. These produce true .EXE programs that can be run from the command prompt like any other program.

Chapter 10
POW!
Applications

In this chapter all you will find a collection of larger examples that make use of all the techniques described earlier. This makes it possible to use realistic programming methods without avoiding topics that have yet to be introduced. There are even occasions when an application is the best place to introduce a new command or technique that has been ignored in the earlier chapters.

The applications that you will find in this chapter and the methods that they use and illustrate are:

Dates and times - an example of building a subroutine library that can be used to solve other problems.

Sorting - a basic operation in many programs. As an illustration of how important it can be to use the correct method, execution times are shown to range from 11 seconds to 3 hours for the same task!

Keyboard control and **Turtle graphics** - basic methods of interacting with the user and an example of simple high resolution graphics.

Qtress - a simple game showing how keyboard control and graphics can be combined to provide a good user interface.

Database - an example of file handling, sorting, searching and user interaction.

Dates and times

DATES.BAS

Working with dates in QBasic is more difficult than you might think. If you only want to record the date on which something happened then you can use a simple string variable to store it such as "01/11/95". However, problems lurk even here. For example, how can you verify that the date is valid? To do this you not only have to know the correct format but check that it doesn't go beyond the number of days in the month, taking into account leap years. Another problem is in working out how many days there are between any two dates. For example, how many days are there between 6/5/1991 and 20/2/1992. Dates are untidy because they work by counting in a mixed and irregular base. That is, years are in lots of 365 or 366 days, months are 30, 31 or 28 days or even occasionally 29 days!

The solution to most of our problems with dates is to convert the irregular date notation into the simplest possible representation - the number of days from a given fixed date usually referred to as the *date base*. The only question is, how do you convert from a date to the number of days? The following subroutines and functions will do the job for you in a way that is compatible with SuperCalc and Lotus spreadsheets. This makes it possible to read in date values correctly into a QBasic program. If you don't want to know how they work then you can just make use of them within your own programs.

The first step is to write a function, Jdate&(dd%,mm%,yy%) which will take the three integers giving the day, month and year respectively. Taking the base date as 1900 seems reasonable and fits in with most spreadsheets. Given this, converting the number of years into number of days is easy. The formula:

```
INT((yy%-1900)*365.25)
```

solves this part of the problem in one go and works for leap years. As the earth takes 365 and a quarter days to go right round the sun we have to add a leap day every four years to stop the day count going out of sync with the seasons. This takes into account leap years without having to make any tests.

Multiplying by 365.25 deals with the irregular number of days in the year very neatly and the next step is to see if there is any way of using a similar method to convert months into days.

The trouble is that the pattern is so irregular :

1	2	3	4	5	6	7	8	9	10	11	12
Jan	Feb	Mar	Apr	May	Jun	Jul	Aug	Sep	Oct	Nov	Dec
31	28/29	31	30	31	30	31	31	30	31	30	31

It is almost a 31/30 alternation, but February is a complete misfit, and sometimes has 29 days. It would be simpler if February could be moved out of the way. If you are trying to work out the number of days since the start of the year, then you only need to know the number of days in the complete months. For example, how many days have elapsed from the start of the year to 15/3/1995? The answer only involves the number of days in month 1 and month 2 because we are only 15 days into month 3. What this means is that the number of days in the month at the end of the year, i.e. December, is irrelevant. This suggests renumbering the months so that the year starts with March and ends with February:

11	12	1	2	3	4	5	6	7	8	9	10	11	12
Jan	Feb	Mar	Apr	May	Jun	Jul	Aug	Sep	Oct	Nov	Dec	Jan	Feb
31	28/29	31	30	31	30	31	31	30	31	30	31	31	28/29

which makes 1st March the new New year. As February is now the last month of the year you no longer have to worry about how many days are in it. The price of this simplification is to have to change the month and year numbers to correspond to our new numbering.

If you take the average number of days in the eleven months that matter you get 30.64 days in a month. It seems worth giving this fractional value a try in the same way as the 365.25 days in the year. However, if you try truncating the result of (month-1)*30.64 you discover that you go wrong immediately because you get 30 days for March which has 31. If you round, however, things work a lot better, as a table of cumulative days since the start of the year shows:

Month No.	1	2	3	4	5	6	7	8	9	10	11	12
Month	Mar	Apr	May	Jun	Jul	Aug	Sep	Oct	Nov	Dec	Jan	Feb
Actual	0	31	61	92	122	153	184	214	245	275	306	337
Calculated	0	31	61	92	123	153	184	214	245	276	306	337

but they are still not perfect. The calculated cumulative number of days for Jul and Dec are one day too large. This suggests trying a slightly smaller value than 30.64 and by trial and error you can discover that multiplying by 30.6 gives a perfect agreement between actual and calculated.

Putting all of this together, it is now possible to write a function that will convert a date into the number of days since 1st March 1900. To convert to our new month numbering scheme we have to subtract 3 from the month number. Negative months correspond to months 11 and 12 of the previous year in our new calendar. So finally the complete function is:

```
FUNCTION Jdate& (dd%, mm%, yy%)
yc% = yy% - 1900
mc% = mm% - 3
IF mc%< 0 THEN
   mc% = 12 + mc%
   yc% = yc% - 1
END IF
Jdate& = INT(yc% * 365.25) + mc% * 30.6 + dd%
END FUNCTION
```

Notice that this function only works sensibly for dates after 1/3/1900. This is the date base used by SuperCalc. Lotus uses 1/1/1900 as its base date. The Jdate& function as listed gives the correct number of days before 1/3/1900 as negative values so it is easy to convert from the SuperCalc to the Lotus date base - just add 60. Also notice that this date function fails for dates before 1900 and after 2100 because of these years are not leap years to allow for an even smaller correction to the calendar.

Using the function Jdate& you can now convert dates in the standard notation into the number of days since the date base. This makes it very easy to find the number of days between any two dates, that is:

```
Jdate&(dd1%,mm1%,yy1%)-Jdate&(dd2%,mm2%,yy2%)
```

To convert back from the number of days since the base date to a normal calendar date you can use the function Datevalue$ which returns a string in the format "dd/mm/yy":

```
FUNCTION Datevalue$ (dd&)
yy% = INT(dd& / 365.25)
dm% = dd& - INT(yy% * 365.25)
mm% = INT(dm% / 30.6)
d% = dm% - INT(mm% * 30.6)
E% = mm% * 30.6 + d% - dm%
mm% = FIX((dm% - E%) / 30.6)
d% = dm% - mm% * 30.6
mm% = mm% + 3
IF d% = 0 THEN
    mm% = mm% - 1
    d% = 29
END IF
IF mm% > 12 THEN
    mm% = mm% - 12
    yy% = yy% + 1
END IF
yy% = yy% + 1900
d$ = STR$(d%) + "/" + STR$(mm%) + "/" + STR$(yy%)
Datevalue$ = d$
END FUNCTION
```

If you want to use the Lotus date base then all you have to do is subtract 60 before reconverting to a calendar date.

If you need an exact inverse of Jdate&, i.e. something that returns a day, month and year number, then you can convert the Datevalue$ function into a procedure by replacing the first line by:

```
SUB dateval (dd&, d%, mm%, yy%)
```

removing the last three lines and replacing them with END SUB. In a date library you need both Datevalue$ and Dateval.

Now that we have the two basic functions for date manipulation completing a subroutine library for dates is fairly easy. For example, if you want to know what day of the week any particular date falls on then you can use the function:

```
FUNCTION wday% (d&)
wday% = (d& + 3) MOD 7 + 1
END FUNCTION
```

which returns 1 for Sunday, 2 for Monday and so on. This function relies on the fact that the 1/3/1900 was a Thursday and there are always 7 days in a week. A program that is now easy to write is one to find the day of the week on which someone was born:

BIRTHDAY.BAS

```
day$ = "SunMonTueWedThuFriSat"
INPUT "What is your birthday (dd,mm,19yy)?", dd%, mm%, yy%
d% = wday%(Jdate&(dd%, mm%, yy%))
PRINT "You were born on a "; MID$(day$, (d% - 1) * 3 + 1, 3)
```

To validate a date, for example, to make sure that someone isn't trying to use the 29th of February when it isn't a leap year you can use the function:

```
FUNCTION ValidDate% (dd%, mm%, yy%)
d1& = Jdate&(dd%, mm%, yy%)
CALL dateval(d1&, d%, m%, y%)
IF d% = dd% AND m% = mm% AND y% = yy% THEN
   ValidDate% = -1
ELSE
   ValidDate% = 0
END IF
END FUNCTION
```

which returns -1 (i.e. True) for a valid date and 0 (i.e. False) for an invalid date. It works by using Jdate& to convert to the number of days and then using dateval to convert back. As long as the day and the month doesn't change then the date must be valid.

You can use the ValidDate% function to write a short program that prints a calendar for any month:

```
INPUT "Calendar for which month and year? mm,19yy ",mm%,yy%
'What day of the week is the 1st
fd% = wday%(Jdate&(1, mm%, yy%))
'Print the title
PRINT "Sun Mon Tue Wed Thu Fri Sat"
'Print the first row
FOR i% = 1 TO 7
   IF i% < fd% THEN
      PRINT " .  ";
   ELSE
      PRINT i% - fd% + 1; " ";
   END IF
NEXT i%
PRINT
'Print the next five rows
FOR w% = 1 TO 5
   FOR i%=1 TO 7
      d1% = i% + 8 - fd% + (w% - 1) * 7
      IF ValidDate(d1%, mm%, yy%) THEN
          PRINT RIGHT$("  " + STR$(d1%), 2); "  ";
      ELSE
          PRINT " .  ";
      END IF
   NEXT i%
   PRINT
NEXT w%
```

CALENDAR.BAS

About the only missing subroutine from our collection is something that will return the current date on the system clock in a form that can be converted using Jdate&. QBasic has a built in DATE$ function that will return the current date as a string and a command:

```
DATE$="new date"
```

which can be used to set the system clock to the specified date.

The only problem with DATE$ is that it returns a string in the format specified by COUNTRY= in the config.sys file. For the UK this format is dd-mm-yyyy and it isn't difficult to write a subroutine that will parse this string to produce integer day, month and year numbers.

```
SUB today (dd%, mm%, yy%)
d$ = DATE$
s$ = "-"
i% = INSTR(d$, s$)
dd% = VAL(MID$(d$, 1, i% - 1))
j% = INSTR(i% + 1, d$, s$)
mm% = VAL(MID$(d$, i% + 1, j% - i% - 1))
i% = INSTR(j% + 1, d$, s$)
yy% = VAL(MID$(d$, j% + 1))
END SUB
```

If you want to write a more general date parsing subroutine then this isn't difficult. Notice that the string s$ is set to the date separator character "-". If you want to use a date format separated by "/" then just change s$. If you want to change the order of day, month and year in the date then shuffle dd%, mm% and yy% before leaving the subroutine!

» Times

Time is a much easier quantity to deal with than dates because although it is measured using different number bases - 60 seconds in a minute, 60 minutes in an hour and 24 hours in a day - it is very regular, assuming the leap seconds can be ignored! In most cases time calculations can be simplified by converting the usual hours, minutes and seconds into either seconds since midnight or to a fraction of a day.

For example:

```
FUNCTION Stime& (h%, m%, s%)
Stime& = CLNG(h% * 60 + m%) * 60 + s%
END FUNCTION
```

TIMES.BAS

will return the number of seconds since midnight using a 24 hour clock. The CLNG function converts the standard integers into double length integers. Without this function the arithmetic would become too big to be stored in the variables. The function:

```
FUNCTION Ftime (h%, m%, s%)
Ftime = (h% + (m% + s% / 60) / 60) / 24
END FUNCTION
```

will convert a time to a fraction of a day. To convert back from seconds use:

```
SUB SecToTime (ss&, h%, m%, s%)
m% = INT(ss& / 60)
s% = ss& MOD 60
h% = INT(m% / 60)
m% = m% MOD 60
END SUB
```

The only interesting part of this subroutine is the use of the operator:

```
x MOD y
```

which returns the remainder after dividing x by y. The subroutine:

```
SUB FracToTime (t, h%, m%, s%)
h% = INT(t * 24)
m% = INT((t * 24 - h%) * 60)
s% = INT(((t * 24 - h%) * 60 - m%) * 60)
END SUB
```

will convert the fraction of a day back to time. Notice that using fractional days isn't accurate to the nearest second - that is, you can convert a time to a fraction of a day and be as much as a second different when you convert back again. The advantage of using seconds since midnight is that it is absolutely accurate. However, using fractions of a day has the advantage that they can be added to the number you get from Jdate& to give a combined date and time number.

QBasic has a TIME$ function which returns a string in the format "hh:mm:ss" containing the current time from the system clock. You can also change the time shown on the system clock using the command:

```
TIME$="hh:mm:ss"
```

You can use the TIME$ function to write a Now function that will return the current hours, minutes and seconds in suitable integer variables:

```
SUB now (h%, m%, s%)
t$ = TIME$
s$ = ":"
i% = INSTR(t$, s$)
h% = VAL(MID$(t$, 1, i% - 1))
j% = INSTR(i% + 1, t$, s$)
m% = VAL(MID$(t$, i% + 1, j% - i% - 1))
i% = INSTR(j% + 1, t$, s$)
s% = VAL(MID$(t$, j% + 1))
END SUB
```

You can also use the TIMER function which returns a single precision value that gives the number of seconds since midnight according to the system clock. The value is accurate to 1/100th of a second. One of the most important uses of the TIMER function is to control the rate at which a program runs. If you find that a program is running too fast then you should include calls to a delay subroutine. The simplest sort of delay subroutine contains a FOR loop that does nothing. This is often called a *time-wasting loop* but it has a big fault in that the amount of time that it wastes depends on how fast the computer works.

A much better delay subroutine is based on the use of TIMER:

```
SUB DELAY (t)
s = TIMER + t
DO UNTIL TIMER > s
LOOP
END SUB
```

In most cases the time delay will be for exactly t seconds. Even this routine fails, however, if the processor is so slow, or the time interval so short, that it cannot complete even one loop before the time delay is up.

There is a built in delay command but it only works for whole seconds. The command:

```
SLEEP n
```

will pause the program for n seconds. If you don't specify how long the pause should be then the program will wait until a key is pressed or an event occurs (see later in this chapter). This is an easy way of implementing a "Press any key to continue" subroutine.

Also notice that there are the commands ON TIME, TIMER ON, TIMER OFF and TIMER STOP but these are to do with event handling and are described in Chapter 9.

Sorting

The topic of sorting lists of data into order is something that fascinates many programmers. The reason is that on the surface it looks like an easy task but when you try it the difficulties become immediately obvious. To see that this is true try to work out how you would sort a stack of 100 exam papers into alphabetical order. It is usually easier to see how to sort things systematically if you start with a smaller number of items. For example, if you were asked to put a hand of playing cards into order you might invent a method something like:

» take the first card
» take the second card and place it in front or behind the first card according to its value
» take the third card and place it in the correct place relative to the two you are already holding

and so on till you have sorted all of the cards. This method is called an *insertion* sort because each new card is inserted into its correct position in the existing order. When converted into a program the inefficiencies of the method quickly become apparent. Inserting a new data value into A(I) of an existing array of values generally means moving all of the values from A(I) and below down one place and for a realistic amount of data involves a lot of work to sort one item. Still, you might like to try to write a simple subroutine that will perform an insertion sort - it isn't that difficult. (An insertion sort is used in the Database application.)

Insertion sort and its many relatives are typical of simple sorting methods. They seem fine at first but it you quickly discover that the amount of movement of the data is much more than you anticipated. To invent a really good sorting method you have to work out a very sophisticated method of moving data to the correct position in as few moves as possible. When you compare different sorting methods what matters is not how fast they are on small quantities of data but how the time they take increases as the the data increases. For small quantities of data almost any sorting method will do - but for large quantities of data only one or two are efficient enough to cope.

The *bubble sort* was introduced in Chapter 3 and it is another of the basic sorting methods. All that happens in a bubble sort is that you start at the top of the array and compare each pair of items. If they are in the wrong order you swap them, if not you leave them alone. After one pass through the array it won't be sorted but it will be a little closer to being sorted. If you repeat the process often enough then the array will eventually be sorted. You can detect that the array is sorted into order by looking out for a pass that doesn't swap any elements. The bubble sort is attractive because it is simple but it is very inefficient. The reason is that each swap doesn't move an item very far. For example, if the data item that should be at the top of the array starts out at the bottom then it will only move up the array by one place per pass. On the other hand, if the item at the top of the array eventually needs to be at the bottom it will only take one pass to get there. This unequal treatment of moving up and down the array suggests the best known improvement to simple bubble sort - each pass should start at opposite ends of the array. That is the first pass should start from the top and compare pairs of elements moving down the array and the next pass should start at the bottom and compare pairs of elements moving up the array. This version of bubble sort is generally called a *shaker sort* and although it sounds good in practice it is almost as bad as a simple bubble sort.

There is an improvement that you can make to bubble sort but it is a bit more difficult than shaker sort. Instead of comparing and swapping elements in the array that are 1 unit apart, compare and swap elements that are k units apart. In other words use:

```
IF a(i)>a(i+k) THEN swap(a(i),a(i+k))
```

as the basis of the pass down the array. If you keep on doing this until no swaps are performed during a pass then the array is said to be k-sorted. Obviously a k-sorted array isn't fully sorted unless k=1. So our improved method is to sort the array for decreasing values of k until we reach k=1. This method is called a *Shell sort* after the man who invented it. The Shell sort is still a bit of a mystery in that the values of k that you should use for best performance are unknown, but 31, 15,

7, 3 and 1 seem to be good choices. If you use this sequence of k values then Shell sort isn't too bad. So I suppose the moral is that if you must bubble use a Shell!

If you would like to compare a Shell sort with the bubble sort given in Chapter 3 then use the two subroutines listed below in place of SortArray and Scan:

```
SUB ShellSort (a())
k% = 31
DO
    DO
        noswap% = 0
        CALL scan(a(), noswap%, k%)
    LOOP UNTIL noswap% = 0
    k% = (k% - 1) / 2
LOOP UNTIL k% < 1
END SUB

SUB scan (a(), noswap%, k%)
FOR i% = 1 TO UBOUND(a, 1) - k%
    IF a(i%) > a(i% + k%) THEN
        SWAP a(i%), a(i% + k%)
        noswap% = 1
    END IF
NEXT i%
END SUB
```

SHELL.BAS

» Quicksort

After you have tinkered with basic sorting methods such as insertion or Shell sort it can be something of a shock to meet your first really sophisticated and efficient sorting method. *Quicksort* is an amazing algorithm in that it takes quite a while to convince yourself that performing all of its strange manipulations really will sort an array. It isn't uncommon to find programmers who think that Quicksort is some kind of magic. It isn't and it is fairly easy to understand, given time. The method was invented in 1962 by C.A.R. Hoare and it is still one of the fastest sorting methods that we know of.

Quicksort is a great improvement over simple bubble sorting methods, when the number of items to be sorted is large. For very small numbers of items simple sorting methods may actually be faster than the more complicated Quicksort but as the number of items increases it doesn't take long for Quicksort to live up to its name.

The fundamental operation of Quicksort is a rearrangement of the array that produces a division into a right-hand part that contains items greater than a given value x and a left-hand part that contains items less than or equal to this value. The value of x is arbitrary but life is easier if we assume that it is one of the values actually in the array. In other words, the partition that we are trying to achieve looks like:

x<=	>x

A partitioning of this type doesn't result in a sorted array but the array is more ordered in that during subsequent sorting no elements will have to be moved between the two halves. This of course suggests that the two halves can be sorted independently of one another and we have succeeded in splitting the task of sorting N items into two tasks of sorting N/2 items. The next stage should be obvious in that further applications of the partitioning method would reduce the task further. Repeatedly partitioning the array finally results in partitions of single elements which need no additional work to sort. That is, the array can be completely sorted by use of nothing but the partitioning method recursively.

To construct a Quicksort program the easiest thing to do, first of all, is to assume the existence of a partitioning procedure part(d(),l%,r%,i%,j%) where l% and r% are the right- and left-hand ends of the region of the array to be partitioned, and i% and j% are the position of the division between the two regions of the array. That is, the portion of the array from d(l%) up to and including d(j%) contain values less than or equal to x and the portion from d(i%) up to and including d(r%) contain values greater than x.

```
        l%              j%   i%                r%
        ↓               ↓    ↓                 ↓
       ┌────────────────┬────┬─────────────────┐
       │      x<=       │    │       >x        │
       └────────────────┴────┴─────────────────┘
```

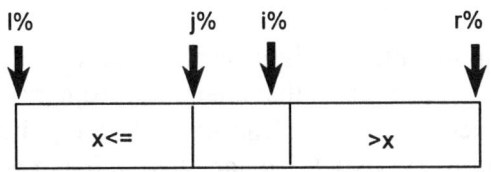

Given that this procedure can be called recursively, a Quicksort program is simply:

```
SUB Qsort(d(),l%,r%)
CALL part(d(),l%,r%,i%,j%)
IF l%<j% THEN CALL Qsort(d(),(l%),(j%))
IF i%<r% THEN CALL Qsort(d(),(i%),(r%))
END SUB
```

The recursive part of this routine is just a matter of it calling itself to sort the left and right portions of the array that result from the partitioning, as long as there are at least two elements in the portion. Notice the use of brackets to ensure that the variables are passed by value.

The only problem that remains is how to write the partitioning procedure. There are a number of ways of doing this but it is worth saying at this point that procedure Part is one of the most difficult to write well in the whole of computing.

Most versions of the partitioning method use a simple scan with two pointers, i% and j% say. First a scan to the right is performed using i% to find an element bigger than x:

```
i%=l%
DO UNTIL d(i%)>x
   i%=i%+1
LOOP
```

Clearly this data item is in the wrong portion of the array and should be moved. To find somewhere to move it to, a scan to the left is performed using j% to find an element smaller than or equal to x:

```
j%=r%
DO UNTIL d(j%)<=x
   j%=j%-1
LOOP
```

Clearly, this data item is also in the wrong portion of the array and a neat solution to both mis-locations is to swap the values:

```
SWAP d(i%),d(j%)
```

After the first swap the left and right scans continue from where they left off and as they find elements that are in the wrong portion they are swapped. This process continues, cleaning up the array into the desired partitioned form, until the inevitable happens - the two pointers meet. When this happens the partitioning is complete and all the elements to the left of the meeting place are less than or equal to x and all the elements to the right of the meeting place are greater than or equal to x. Putting all this together gives us our first attempt at subroutine Part:

```
SUB part(d(),l%,r%,i%,j%)
i%=l%
j%=r%
CALL pick(x)
DO
   DO UNTIL d(i%)>x
      i%=i%+1
   LOOP
   DO UNTIL d(j%)<=x
      j%=j%-1
   LOOP
   IF i%<j% THEN
       SWAP  d(i%),d(j%)
       i%=i%+1
       j%=j%-1
   END IF
LOOP UNTIL i%>j%
END SUB
```

If you try this version of Part you will find that it fails for two reasons. The first is simply that there is nothing to stop the i% value falling off the end of the array during the scan. The j% value doesn't fall off the end of the array because it will stop when it reaches the x value. It is easy to stop the i% value from falling off the end by including another test but it turns out that the solution comes free with the method used to solve the more difficult second problem. Even if you stop i% falling off the end of the array you will find that the whole sort program still fails to sort the array in some cases. The reason is very subtle and it is to do with the type of partition with which we have chosen to work. Consider the partition applied to the values 1 2 4 6 3 5 with an x value of 6. The portion smaller than or equal to 6 is just 1 2 4 6 3 5 but the portion greater than 6 is null. This means that if by chance you pick a value of x that is the maximum value in the array the right-hand portion will be null. In this case the recursion will never end because its termination depends on dividing the array into ever smaller chunks and this division leaves the left-hand portion unaltered.

There are a number of possible solutions. You could, for example, detect this case, swap the position of the x value with the far right-hand element and then decrease the size of the portion by one i.e. i%=i%-1. After all, if x is the largest value in the portion this is where it should be after the portion is sorted. However, there is an even easier method.

If you change the definition of the partition so that the second portion consists of values greater than or equal to x, rather than just strictly greater than x, then the problem just goes away. In this case the right-hand portion is never null. It also ensures that the i% value never falls off the end of the array - because it will never go past the x value. The price of this simplicity is just the occasional unnecessary swap of two equal values. To make the change all that is necessary is to alter the test in the first DO UNTIL loop to d(i%)=>x. You also have to alter the IF that guards against making a swap after the pointers have passed. It now has to be modified to include the possibility that i% and j% point to the same element, i.e. IF i%<=j%. In this case no swap is necessary but one is performed so that i% and j% are updated and so pass each other. If you don't like the wasted swap then simply add another IF statement to take care of the increment - it's just as inefficient!

The value of x is arbitrary but for an efficient method it is desirable that it divides each portion of the array into two roughly equal sized chunks. In an ideal world this means that we would like x to be the median - i.e. the value that divides all of the data into 50% larger and 50% smaller. Finding the median would take too long, so a simpler solution is to take a value from roughly the middle of the array. This isn't likely to be the median but if the array already shows some order it might be closer than any other value.

Even if you don't quite understand the Quicksort method you can still make use of the Qsort subroutine as listed below:

```
SUB QSort (d(), l%, r%)
CALL part(d(), l%, r%, i%, j%)
IF l% < j% THEN CALL QSort(d(), (l%), (j%))
IF i% < r% THEN CALL QSort(d(), (i%), (r%))
END SUB

SUB part (d(), l%, r%, i%, j%)
i% = l%
j% = r%
x = (d((l% + r%) \ 2))
DO
     DO UNTIL d(i%) >= x
         i% = i% + 1
     LOOP
     DO UNTIL d(j%) <= x
         j% = j% - 1
     LOOP
     IF i% <= j% THEN
         SWAP d(i%), d(j%)
         i% = i% + 1
         j% = j% - 1
     END IF
LOOP UNTIL i% > j%
END SUB
```

QSORT.BAS

To use Qsort to sort an array a() simply use the call Qsort(a(),1,n%) where n% is the length of the array.

You might like to compare the speed of Qsort as compared to Bubble and Shell sort on large arrays - you will easily be convinced of Qsort's superiority. To give you some idea of just how much better, the times for sorting 5000 values using the three methods are: Bubble 3249 seconds, Shell sort 148 seconds and Quicksort 11 seconds. So you can wait for just short of an hour or for 11 seconds - it's up to you! However, Quicksort is not so good for small quantities of data or when the size of the partition on which it is working is very small - for example making a recursive call to sort two elements seems excessive! You can improve Quicksort by substituting an alternative sorting method for small partitions but in most cases the basic Quicksort is good enough.

Using the keyboard

Although the keyboard sounds a dull method of interacting with programs it needn't be. QBasic provides a wide range of programming commands that make it possible to accept user input in almost any of the sophisticated ways that you will encounter in commercial applications programs.

» Polling

The INPUT command is fine for reading in values when you can allow the program to stop and wait for the user, but it isn't useful for interactive input. For example, suppose you wanted to write a game or menu system that allows the user to move a screen pointer using the keyboard. If you use INPUT then the user would move the pointer one step at a time, pressing Enter to make the program move on. There is a way of finding out immediately what key the user has pressed and reacting to it. The INKEY$ function returns a string corresponding to the most recently pressed key. If no key has been pressed then it returns the null string. It doesn't wait for the user to press a key, it simply examines the current state of the keyboard. For example, the following program repeatedly examines the keyboard and if a key is pressed displays it on the screen:

```
DO
   A$ = INKEY$
   IF A$ <> "" THEN PRINT A$;
LOOP
```

Notice the way that a loop is necessary to keep on examining the state of the keyboard until a key is pressed. This technique of repeatedly looking at the state of some item of hardware, keyboard or whatever, is usually called a *polling loop*.

There are two complications concerning the use of INKEY$. The first is that it doesn't actually examine the current state of the keyboard but the state of the *keyboard buffer*. This is an area of memory that stores key presses until a program asks for them. What this means is that

INKEY$ can return a key that was pressed some time before and given that the auto-key repeat is on there may even be a lot of repeats of a given key in the buffer. The solution is to write a simple routine that clears the keyboard buffer by reading from it until it is empty:

```
SUB ClearKey
DO
   A$ = INKEY$
LOOP UNTIL A$ = ""
END SUB
```

Use ClearKey before and after keyboard polling to make sure that there are no leftover key presses.

The second problem with INKEY$ is that for some keys, the cursor keys for example, it returns a two-character string. The first character is null and the second is the *key scan code*. You can find a complete list of key scan codes in the QBasic Help - just select Keyboard Scan Codes from the contents list. Alternatively, you can use the following program to display either the ASCII or scan code where appropriate:

```
CLS
DO
   A$ = INKEY$
   SELECT CASE LEN(A$)
   CASE 0
   CASE 1
      PRINT "Standard key - ASCII code ="; ASC(A$)
   CASE 2
      PRINT "Extended key - Scan code  ="; ASC(MID$(A$, 2, 1))
   END SELECT
LOOP
```

KEYS1.BAS

» Key events

The biggest problem with polling is that the user can only interact with the program at times set by the occurrence of the INKEY$ instruction. An alternative method is to define event handling routines that are automatically called any time that a key is pressed. The basic idea of event handling was described in Chapter 9 but it is such an important method when used in combination with the keyboard that it deserves further explanation.

The ON KEY(*n*) statement can be used to respond to any one of 31 keys as events. Notice that keys 11, 12, 13 and 14 refer specifically to the cursor keys on the numeric keypad.

n	Key
0	All of the keys in this list
1-10	Function keys 1 to 10
11	Cursor up
12	Cursor left
13	Cursor right
14	Cursor down
15-25	User definable by the KEY command
30, 31	Function keys 11 and 12

To use a key event you first have to associate the key with a subroutine using:

    ON KEY(n) GOSUB line

You can then enable or disable event handling using:

    KEY(n) ON/OFF

In most programs it is important to make sure that you enable and disable key event handling to control the interaction with the user. If you want to suspend event handling while making sure that any events that occur during the suspension period are handled when the key is turned back on, then you can use:

    KEY(n) STOP

This causes QBasic to remember, but not respond to, events.

If you want to trigger events on keys other than the standard cursor and function keys, then you have to make use of the facility to assign event key numbers 15-25 to any key on the keyboard. This is done using the command:

```
KEY n, CHR$(shift)+CHR$(scan code)
```
where *n* is the event key number, *shift* is the state the generalised 'shift' keys including Ctrl, Alt etc., and *scan code* is the normal scan code that the key produces. The shift state is given by:

Shift	Shift keys pressed
0	No shift
1,2,3	Either left or right Shift key
4	Ctrl key
8	Alt
32	Num Lock
64	Caps Lock
128	Extended keys on a 101 key keyboard

You can also add shift values together to indicate that more than one shift key has been pressed, e.g. 4+8 would indicate that both the Ctrl and the Alt key were pressed.

The scan code that a key produces isn't the same as the ASCII code of the character that it produces. Each key has a unique and unchangeable scan code but it can produce more than one ASCII code depending on the state of the shift keys. Keys can even be deprogrammed to produce different ASCII codes but their scan codes never change. You can see a list of scan codes in the QBasic Help - just select Keyboard Scan Codes from its contents list.

For example, to assign event code 25 to the key combination Ctrl, i.e. code 4, and Cursor right, i.e. scan code 77, you would use the command:
```
KEY 25,CHR$(4)+CHR$(77)
```
Following this ON KEY(25) would respond to the right cursor key only when Ctrl was also pressed.

You can see an example of using the keyboard via polling in Listing 10.1 and you can see the same task using event handling in Listing 10.2. Notice that both programs use subroutine Update.

You will find a more realistic example of event handling of the keyboard in the Qtress program listed later.

» Function keys

The KEY statement can also be used to define the action of the function keys and list their current assignments. The command:

> KEY ON/OFF

turns on or off a display of the function key assignments on the 25th line of the screen. If the 25th line is used for this purpose then it is unavailable for normal text display - it doesn't scroll with the rest of the screen and any attempt to use it causes an error. You can discover the current assignments of the function keys using the command:

> KEY LIST

The statement:

> KEY *n,string*

sets function key *n* to return the given *string* when it is pressed. The string can be up to 15 characters. Function keys 11 and 12 can be programmed using *n* equal to 30 and 31. For example:

> KEY 1,"Help"

programs function key F1 to return the string Help. Using the function keys as an alternative to writing subroutines that display custom menus has advantages and disadvantages. For example, the KEY ON command produces a single strip display at the bottom of the screen listing all of the function keys even if you have used only one. Also, the input to the program takes the form of the complete string that you programmed for each function key. This makes decoding what the user wants more difficult but it also allows the user to by-pass the function keys and type the same strings directly.

Listing 10.1
Keyboard Polling

```
SCREEN 2
CLS
x% = 10
y% = 10
CALL update(x%, y%, 0, 0)
DO
   a$ = INKEY$
   IF LEN(a$) > 1 THEN
      SELECT CASE ASC(MID$(a$, 2, 1))
      CASE 75
            xinc% = -1
            yinc% = 0
      CASE 77
            xinc% = 1
            yinc% = 0
      CASE 72
            xinc% = 0
            yinc% = -1
      CASE 80
            xinc% = 0
            yinc% = 1
      END SELECT
      CALL update(x%, y%, xinc%, yinc%)
   END IF
LOOP
END

SUB update (x%, y%, xinc%, yinc%)
LOCATE y%, x%
PRINT " ";
x% = ((x% + xinc% - 1 + 80) MOD 80) + 1
y% = ((y% + yinc% - 1 + 25) MOD 25) + 1
LOCATE y%, x%
PRINT CHR$(2);
END SUB
```

KEYPOLL.BAS

Listing 10.2
Event handling

```
SCREEN 2
CLS
x% = 10
y% = 10
ON KEY(11) GOSUB up
ON KEY(12) GOSUB left
ON KEY(13) GOSUB right
ON KEY(14) GOSUB down
KEY(11) ON
KEY(12) ON
KEY(13) ON
KEY(14) ON
CALL update(x%, y%, 0, 0)
DO
LOOP
END

right:
 xinc% = 1
 yinc% = 0
 CALL update(x%, y%, xinc%, yinc%)
RETURN

left:
 xinc% = -1
 yinc% = 0
 CALL update(x%, y%, xinc%, yinc%)
RETURN

up:
 xinc% = 0
 yinc% = -1
 CALL update(x%, y%, xinc%, yinc%)
RETURN

down:
 xinc% = 0
 yinc% = 1
 CALL update(x%, y%, xinc%, yinc%)
RETURN
```

KEYEVENT.BAS

As an example of using the function keys and of the DRAW command the following program implements a simple 'turtle' drawing program. Turtle geometry is taught in many schools as a way of learning the basics of programming and many other skills. The idea is that you have a turtle that leaves a trail as it moves. All of the commands for moving the turtle use the turtle's 'frame of reference'. For example, the Move command moves the turtle in the direction it is facing, the Left command turns the turtle 90 degrees to its left and so on. The program's commands are:

Move n	F1	move forward n steps
Left n	F2	turn left (90 degrees) n times
Right n	F3	turn right (90 degrees) n times
Turn n	F4	turn left through angle n
Clear	F5	clear screen and return turtle to start
Record	F6	store subsequent commands
Stop	F7	stop recording
Play	F8	play recording back
Erase	F9	erase recording
Done	F10	exit program

Any of these commands can be entered either by pressing the function key indicated or by typing in the equivalent string. The program works in screen mode 9 but you can change this to any other graphics mode without worrying about making any other changes to the program.

The main program simply sets up the function keys to show the appropriate list of commands and then uses a SELECT command to process each command using a suitable CASE clause.

Using the keyboard

```
CONST TRUE = &HFFFF
CONST FALSE = 0

SCREEN 9
CONST xmax = 640
CONST ymax = 350

DIM Tape$(50)
n% = 50
VIEW PRINT 22 TO 24

CALL setkeys
KEY ON
angle% = 0
xt% = xmax / 2
yt% = ymax / 2
rec% = FALSE
replay% = FALSE
ins% = 1
CALL drawTurt(xt%, yt%)

DO
   CALL GetCommand(C$, replay%, Tape$(), ins%)
   BEEP
   CALL GetValue(C$, V$)
   CALL RemoveTurt

   SELECT CASE UCASE$(MID$(C$, 1, 4))
        CASE "MOVE"
             DRAW "C7U" + V$
        CASE "LEFT"
             angle% = (angle% + VAL(V$) * 90) MOD 360
             DRAW "TA" + STR$(angle%)
        CASE "RIGH"
             angle% = (angle% - VAL(V$) * 90) MOD 360
             DRAW "TA" + STR$(angle%)
        CASE "TURN"
             angle% = (angle% + VAL(V$)) MOD 360
             DRAW "TA" + STR$(angle%)
        CASE "CLEA"
             CLS
             angle% = 0
```

TURTLE.BAS

```
                DRAW "TA" + STR$(angle%)
                CALL DrawTurt(xt%, yt%)
        CASE "RECO"
                rec% = TRUE
                replay% = FALSE
                ins% = ins% - 1
        CASE "STOP"
                rec% = FALSE
        CASE "PLAY"
                rec% = FALSE
                replay% = TRUE
                ins% = 1
        CASE "ERAS"
                rec% = FALSE
                replay% = FALSE
                Tape$(1) = ""
                ins% = 1
        CASE "DONE"
                STOP
    END SELECT
    IF rec% THEN CALL Record(Tape$(), C$, ins%)
    CALL PlaceTurt
LOOP
```

The main program is rather long but this is typical of the use of a SELECT statement to decode commands. Notice also the way that the VIEW PRINT command restricts input and output to the lower portion of the screen. Notice also that you have to type in the command words in upper case. The following subroutines are used by the main program:

```
SUB DrawTurt (xt%, yt%)
DRAW "BM" + STR$(xt%) + "," + STR$(yt%)
DRAW "L10E10F10L10"
END SUB
```

This sets the graphics cursor roughly to the centre of the screen and then draws the first turtle shape:

```
SUB PlaceTurt
DRAW "C16L10E10F10L10"
END SUB
```

This draws the turtle in colour 16 at the current graphics cursor location.

```
SUB RemoveTurt
DRAW "C0L10E10F10L10"
END SUB
```

This blanks the current turtle by drawing it in colour 0, i.e. black.

```
SUB GetCommand (C$, replay%, Tape$(), ins%)
IF replay% THEN
   C$ = Tape$(ins%)
   ins% = ins% + 1
   IF C$ = "" THEN replay% = FALSE
ELSE
   INPUT C$
END IF
END SUB
```

This reads commands from the keyboard or from the array Tape$ which is used to store the recorded commands.

```
SUB Record (Tape$(), C$, ins%)
IF ins% < UBOUND(Tape$, 1) THEN
   Tape$(ins%) = C$
   ins% = ins% + 1
ELSE
   PRINT "Tape FULL"
   BEEP
END IF
END SUB
```

This stores the current command in Tape$.

```
SUB GetValue (C$, V$)
V$ = ""
FOR i% = 1 TO LEN(C$)
   d$ = MID$(C$, i%, 1)
   IF digit%(d$) THEN V$ = V$ + d$
NEXT i%
IF V$ = "" THEN V$ = "1"
IF INSTR(C$, "-") THEN V$ = "-" + V$
END SUB
```

This retrieves any number that is specified as part of the command. It works by using the function digit% to test each character in turn to see it if is a digit or not.

```
FUNCTION digit% (d$)
SELECT CASE ASC(d$)
CASE 48 TO 57
   digit% = TRUE
CASE ELSE
   digit% = FALSE
END SELECT
END FUNCTION
```

Finally, the subroutine that sets each function key to a command is:

```
SUB setkeys
KEY 1, "Move "
KEY 2, "Left "
KEY 3, "Right"
KEY 4, "Turn"
KEY 5, "Clear"
KEY 6, "Record"
KEY 7, "Stop"
KEY 8, "Play"
KEY 9, "Erase"
KEY 10, "DONE"
END SUB
```

You can extend the turtle graphics program but notice that if you do you will have to find a way of extending the number of function keys available. One solution is to use one function key to produce another menu by assigning another set of strings to the keys.

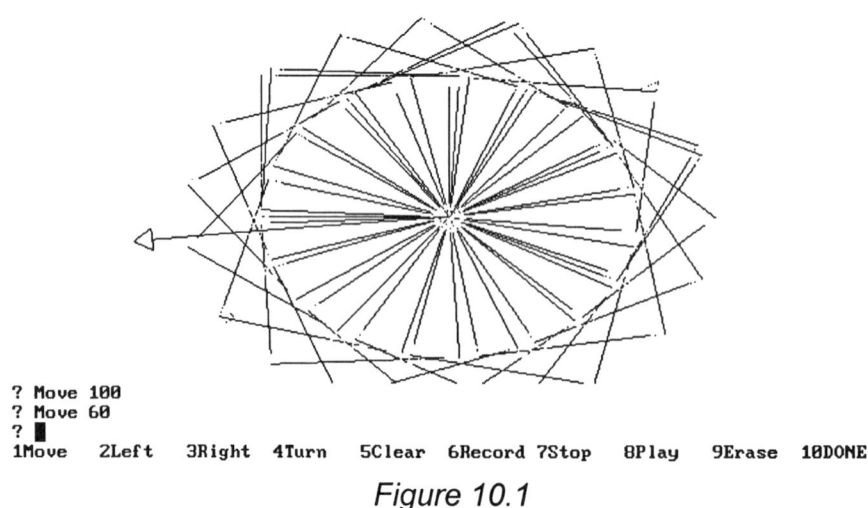

Figure 10.1
The result of repeatedly replaying a short 'program'

Qtress

This application is an example of how a complete graphics game can be created using event handling for control. Unusually this game, although it relies on movement, only makes use of a text mode. The advantage of this is that it will work quickly on any machine but the disadvantage is that the shape of the blocks changes as they are rotated. The reason for this is that a text character isn't square. Even with this slight difficulty the game is very playable. (If you would like to see a high resolution graphics version then one is included on the disk of programs that accompanies this book -HTRESS.BAS. It isn't very different from the text version.)

Qtress is based on the well known game of Tetris invented by Alexei Pazhitnov and Vadim Gerasimov who hold the copyright on that name. This QBasic version isn't as full an implementation as the original but it still demonstrates how a simple idea can result in a compulsive game! A sequence of differently shaped blocks slowly fall down the screen and the player's task is to pack them together at the bottom of the the screen leaving as few spaces as possible. Each complete row formed is removed from the screen, gaining the player a bonus score. The

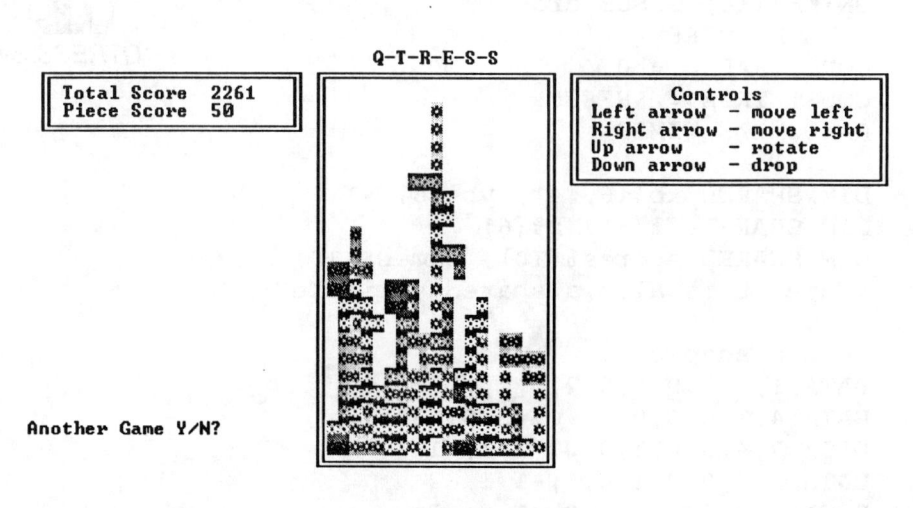

Figure 10.2
A completed game of Qtress

blocks can be moved left and right as they fall and can be rotated to give the best fit. To speed up the game pressing the down arrow key makes the block fall to the bottom at a higher rate. Points are scored for each piece packed but the number of points scored for a piece decreases as it falls and for each time it is moved left or right or rotated until it is dropped. In other words, you get the maximum score for a piece by dropping it as soon as it appears on the screen. Of course using this strategy you are unlikely to make very many full rows. The game is over when the playing frame is stacked to the top and no more pieces can be packed into place.

The actual implementation of the game uses no completely new techniques. The user interacts and controls the fall of the blocks using event handling on the cursor keys. The block shapes are stored in two arrays xb%() and yb%() which store the x and y co-ordinates of each block relative to the first block in the shape.

The main program uses a great many subroutines to make the game work. It consists of two parts, an initialisation phase and a play loop.

```
'initialisation phase
ON KEY(11) GOSUB rotate
ON KEY(12) GOSUB moveleft
ON KEY(13) GOSUB moveright
ON KEY(14) GOSUB drop
CALL KEYSOFF
CONST FALSE = 0
CONST TRUE = &HFFFF
RANDOMIZE TIMER

DIM SHARED xb%(6, 4), yb%(6, 4)
DIM SHARED f%(6), b%(6)
DIM SHARED scores%(10), names$(10)
'Note: t is also a shared variable

'block shapes
DATA 1,4,0,0,1,0,2,0,1,-1
DATA 4,1,0,0,0,-1,0,-2,0,-3
DATA 7,4,0,0,1,0,0,-1,1,-1
DATA 2,4,0,0,1,0,1,-1,1,-2
DATA 4,2,0,0,1,0,0,-1,0,-2
DATA 4,7,0,0,-1,1,-1,1,-2
```

QTRESS.BAS

```
DO
SCREEN 0
COLOR 7, 0
CLS
LOCATE 1, 35, 0
PRINT "Q-T-R-E-S-S"
CALL init(scx%, scy%, fx%, fy%, h%, w%)

'Play loop
DO
    CALL start(s%, sx%, sy%)
    d = .6
    pscore% = 50
    scoreinc% = 1
    CALL showscore(score%, pscore%, scx%, scy%)
    IF NOT (TestFree(s%, sx%, sy%)) THEN EXIT DO
    DO
        CALL update(s%, sx%, sy%, d)
        go% = TestFree(s%, sx%, sy% + 1)
        IF go% THEN
            sy% = sy% + 1
            pscore% = pscore% - scoreinc%
        ELSE
            CALL DisplayShape(s%, sx%, sy%)
            CALL StopBeep
            score% = score% + pscore%
            CALL checkrows(bonus%, fx%, fy%, h%, w%)
        END IF
        CALL showscore(score%, pscore%, scx%, scy%)
    LOOP WHILE go%
LOOP
LOOP WHILE ANOTHER%
END
```

The DATA statements in the initialisation part of the main program hold the shape data. This is then read into the arrays xb%() and yb%() within subroutine init. You can only use data statements within the main program but they can be read into variables using the command READ anywhere in the program. Data is read from a DATA statement as if it was a sort of internal sequential file. You can also read the data more than once by using the RESTORE command which resets the DATA statement so that the next READ uses the first item in the list. In this case each DATA statement records colour and shape of each piece in the format:

f, b, x1,y1,x2,y2,x3,y3,x4,y4

where *f* and *b* are the foreground and background colours and *x1,y1* to *x4,y4* are the positions of the four blocks that make up each shape.

The play loop is relatively uninteresting in its own right because most of the work is done by subroutines that it calls. The basic principle is that each time through the loop the piece is printed at its new position. Before moving the piece it is removed or blanked from the screen by printing spaces where it used to be and then testing to see if the new location that it will occupy is free. If it is then the piece is printed at its new location. If it isn't then the piece is printed at its previous location and another piece is generated and dropped.

The first subroutine to look at in detail is Init:

```
SUB init (scx%, scy%, fx%, fy%, h%, w%)
'read block data
RESTORE
FOR s% = 1 TO 6
  READ f%(s%), b%(s%)
  FOR i% = 1 TO 4
    READ xb%(s%, i%), yb%(s%, i%)
  NEXT i%
NEXT s%
'setup screen
fx% = 30: fy% = 2: h% = 22: w% = 20
CALL DrawFrame(fx%, fy%, h%, w%)
score% = 0
scx% = 6: scy% = 2
CALL DrawFrame(52, 2, 6, 27)
CALL Startmess(52, 2)
CALL DrawFrame(scx%, scy%, 3, 22)
END SUB
```

The first part of this subroutine simply reads in the shape data. Notice that the arrays have been made SHARED so they don't have to be passed as parameters. The second part of the subroutine sets up the screen by drawing frames and printing messages.

The DrawFrame subroutine makes use of graphics characters to draw a double lined frame h% high and w% wide with its top left-hand corner at x%,y%:

```
SUB DrawFrame (x%, y%, h%, w%)
FOR i% = x% + 1 TO x% + w% - 1
  LOCATE y%, i%
  PRINT CHR$(205);
  LOCATE y% + h%, i%
  PRINT CHR$(205);
NEXT i%
FOR i% = y% + 1 TO y% + h% - 1
  LOCATE i%, x%
  PRINT CHR$(186);
  LOCATE i%, x% + w%
  PRINT CHR$(186);
NEXT i%
LOCATE y%, x%
PRINT CHR$(201);
LOCATE y%, x% + w%
PRINT CHR$(187);
LOCATE y% + h%, x%
PRINT CHR$(200);
LOCATE y% + h%, x% + w%
PRINT CHR$(188);
END SUB
```

The Startmess subroutine simply prints the instructions in the frame already drawn on the screen.

```
SUB Startmess (x%, y%)
LOCATE y% + 1, x% + 2
PRINT "        Controls"
LOCATE y% + 2, x% + 2
PRINT "Left arrow  - move left"
LOCATE y% + 3, x% + 2
PRINT "Right arrow - move right"
LOCATE y% + 4, x% + 2
PRINT "Up arrow    - rotate"
LOCATE y% + 5, x% + 2
PRINT "Down arrow  - drop"
END SUB
```

The Start subroutine selects a shape at random and starts it off somewhere towards the middle of the playing frame.

```
SUB start (s%, x%, y%)
s% = INT(RND * 6) + 1
y% = 6
x% = 40
END SUB
```

The statement RANDOMIZE TIMER in the main program makes sure that the RND function gives different numbers each time you start the program.

The Update subroutine performs most of the work in moving the shape but, like all good modular subroutines, it passes most of this work over to other subroutines.

```
SUB update (s%, sx%, sy%, d)
CALL DisplayShape(s%, sx%, sy%)
CALL KEYSON
CALL mark
CALL FallBeep
CALL delay(d)
CALL KEYSOFF
CALL BlankShape(s%, sx%, sy%)
END SUB
```

DisplayShape and BlankShape are responsible for drawing and removing the shape at its current position:

```
SUB DisplayShape (s%, x%, y%)
FOR i% = 1 TO 4
  CALL Pblock(x% + xb%(s%, i%), y% + yb%(s%, i%),f%(s%), b%(s%))
NEXT i%
END SUB

SUB BlankShape (s%, x%, y%)
COLOR 7, 0
FOR i% = 1 TO 4
  LOCATE y% + yb%(s%, i%), x% + xb%(s%, i%)
  PRINT CHR$(32);
NEXT i%
END SUB
```

The DisplayShape subroutine makes use of Pblock, a subroutine which actually does the printing:

```
SUB Pblock (x%, y%, f%, b%)
COLOR f%, b%
LOCATE y%, x%
PRINT CHR$(15);
END SUB
```

The KEYSON and KEYSOFF subroutines are used to control the event handling.

```
SUB KEYSON
KEY(11) ON
KEY(12) ON
KEY(13) ON
KEY(14) ON
END SUB

SUB KEYSOFF
KEY(11) OFF
KEY(12) OFF
KEY(13) OFF
KEY(14) OFF
END SUB
```

It is important that the user cannot move the shape while it is being drawn or blanked from the screen. If this was possible then the result would be fragments of shapes left on the screen.

The FallBeep subroutine makes a high pitched sound for such a short period of time that it sounds like a click each time the shape moves.

```
SUB FallBeep
SOUND 6000, 1
END SUB
```

To give the impression of smooth movement it is important that the shape is given enough time to display on the screen before it is blanked. A simple delay subroutine would do, but it has the disadvantage that the program might be running on a machine that is so slow that the delay is not only unnecessary but actually slows the game. The solution is to use a subroutine called mark which records the time it is called in a static shared variable called t. This can then be used by a modified delay subroutine to make sure that the time between the calling of mark and delay is no more than the specified delay. In other words mark and delay can be used to fix the time that a group of instructions take to carry out.

```
SUB mark STATIC
SHARED t
t = TIMER
END SUB

SUB delay (d)
SHARED t
DO UNTIL TIMER > d + t
LOOP
END SUB
```

The TestFree function checks the location of each block using the SCREEN function to discover if it is free.

```
FUNCTION TestFree% (s%, x%, y%)
clr% = TRUE
FOR i% = 1 TO 4
IF SCREEN(y% + yb%(s%, i%), x% + xb%(s%, i%)) <> 32 THEN
   clr% = FALSE
END IF
NEXT i%
TestFree% = clr%
END FUNCTION
```

The SCREEN(y,x) function returns the ASCII code of the character at x,y and this should be 32, i.e. a space, as long as the block isn't about to land on an occupied location. Notice that testing in this way also stops the shape moving outside the frame.

If the shape has reached its final resting place then the StopBeep subroutine is called to make a pleasing (?) warble:

```
SUB StopBeep
SHARED t
CALL mark
DO
   SOUND 1000, 1
   SOUND 300, 1
LOOP UNTIL TIMER > t + .5
END SUB
```

StopBeep also uses the value of t set by the mark subroutine to establish a delay. The warble is created by repeating a very short high and low tone. After each piece has 'landed' the checkrows subroutine is called to look for completed rows and remove them if necessary:

```
SUB checkrows (bonus%, fx%, fy%, h%, w%)
bonus% = 0
j% = fy% + h% - 1
DO
        CALL testrow(j%, fx%, w%, full%, last%)
        IF full% THEN
                CALL cascade(j%, fx%, w%)
                bonus% = bonus% + 50
                CALL mark
                CALL StopBeep
                CALL delay(.3)
        ELSE
                j% = j% - 1
        END IF
LOOP UNTIL last%
END SUB
```

The testrow subroutine looks at each character in the row, tests to see if it is a space or not and sets a flag to true or false to indicate both a full row and a completely empty row:

```
SUB testrow (j%, fx%, w%, full%, last%)
full% = TRUE
last% = TRUE
FOR i% = fx% + 1 TO fx% + w% - 1
   IF SCREEN(j%, i%) = 32 THEN full% = FALSE
   IF SCREEN(j%, i%) <> 32 THEN last% = FALSE
NEXT i%
END SUB
```

Once again, the SCREEN function is used to inspect the contents of the screen at the given location.

If a completely full row is found, then subroutine cascade is called to shift all of the rows above the full row down by one row.

```
SUB cascade (j%, fx%, w%)
k% = j%
DO
   FOR i% = fx% + 1 TO fx% + w% - 1
      LOCATE k%, i%
      c% = SCREEN(k% - 1, i%, 1)
      b% = c% / 16
      f% = c% MOD 16
      COLOR f%, b%
      PRINT CHR$(SCREEN(k% - 1, i%));
   NEXT i%
   k% = k% - 1
   CALL testrow(k%, fx%, w%, full%, last%)
LOOP UNTIL last%
END SUB
```

There are two interesting techniques used in this subroutine. The first is the use of SCREEN(y,x,1) to discover the foreground and background colours at x,y. Notice the two statements following it that decode the information in c% into two separate variables, f% and b%. Also notice the use of PRINT CHR$(SCREEN(y,x)) to move the character at x,y to the current printing location.

The remaining subroutines are concerned with the finer points of implementing the game. The Showscore subroutine prints the current total and piece score at the specified screen location:

```
SUB showscore (score%, pscore%, scx%, scy%)
COLOR 7, 0
LOCATE scy% + 1, scx% + 2
PRINT "Total Score "; score%
LOCATE scy% + 2, scx% + 2
PRINT "Piece Score "; pscore%
END SUB
```

Function ANOTHER% asks the user if they would like another game, screens the input for errors and returns TRUE or FALSE depending on the answer. The line ANOTHER%=(A$="Y") sets ANOTHER% to TRUE or FALSE depending on the outcome of the test.

```
FUNCTION ANOTHER%
CALL ClearKey
DO
        BEEP
        LOCATE 22, 5
        INPUT "Another Game Y/N"; A$
        A$ = LEFT$(UCASE$(A$), 1)
LOOP WHILE A$ <> "Y" AND A$ <> "N"
ANOTHER% = (A$ = "Y")
END FUNCTION
```

At first it looks as though this function is a very neat solution to a difficult problem but it is probably best avoided in preference to a rather longer subroutine. The reason is that it results in the line:

```
LOOP WHILE ANOTHER%
```

in the main program. This is very likely to mystify another programmer reading through the main program, because it isn't clear if ANOTHER% is a variable or a function. ANOTHER% also breaks the cardinal rule that functions shouldn't cause side effects such as printing. As you can guess, ANOTHER% has been included more as a way of how not to do things if you want your programs to be clearly understood by others. ANOTHER% also needs ClearKey to make sure that all of the key presses are cleared from the keyboard buffer before the INPUT statement:

```
SUB ClearKey
DO
        A$ = INKEY$
LOOP UNTIL A$ = ""
END SUB
```

If you type in all of the subroutines as listed, then you will discover that you have a perfectly working but unplayable game! The reason is that no event handling subroutines have been defined. These are:

```
moveleft:
   CALL BlankShape(s%, sx%, sy%)
   IF TestFree%(s%, sx% - 1, sy%) THEN sx% = sx% - 1
   CALL DisplayShape(s%, sx%, sy%)
   pscore% = pscore% - 2
RETURN
```

```
moveright:
    CALL BlankShape(s%, sx%, sy%)
    IF TestFree%(s%, sx% + 1, sy%) THEN sx% = sx% + 1
    CALL DisplayShape(s%, sx%, sy%)
    pscore% = pscore% - 2
RETURN

drop:
    d = .02
    score% = score% + pscore%
    scoreinc% = 0
RETURN

rotate:
    CALL BlankShape(s%, sx%, sy%)
    FOR i% = 1 TO 4
        SWAP xb%(s%, i%), yb%(s%, i%)
        yb%(s%, i%) = -yb%(s%, i%)
    NEXT i%
    IF NOT (TestFree%(s%, sx%, sy%)) THEN
        FOR i% = 1 TO 4
            yb%(s%, i%) = -yb%(s%, i%)
            SWAP xb%(s%, i%), yb%(s%, i%)
        NEXT i%
    END IF
    CALL DisplayShape(s%, sx%, sy%)
    pscore% = pscore% - 6
RETURN
```

These subroutines have to be added after the end of the main program. The only complicated event handler is Rotate. This makes use of some tricky maths to achieve the rotation as quickly as possible. Also notice the way that the newly rotated position is tested for occupancy before the shape is re-displayed. If there is something in the way then the rotation is reversed and the shape displayed at its old position.

That's all there is to Qtress but you could go on developing it for a long time. Its major omissions are: a look-ahead facility (i.e. a frame showing the next shape to be picked) and a table of best scores. Both would be easy to implement now you know so much about QBasic.

Creating a database

A database is just a program that allows a user to store and retrieve information. Writing a simple database isn't difficult using QBasic but don't imagine that you can automate your business using it. Although it is theoretically possible to write such complex programs, in practice there are easier ways to build large databases.

In this example the information to be stored will be a name and address record with some space for notes. However, the principles are the same no matter what data you want to store in the record and if you follow the details of the construction of the database you should have no difficulty in customising it and extending it to meet your own needs.

You might think that the biggest concern in constructing a database is the way that the data files are used and organised. While this is a very important aspect, there are many others that are almost as important, in particular the quality of the user interface. A typical database program may have 10% of its instructions devoted to working with data files and the remaining 90% responsible for interacting with the user.

The first stage in any database design is to specify the record. In this case a name, four general address lines, a postcode, telephone number and notes fields should be sufficient. A little thought soon reveals that all of the fields are best represented by strings, even the telephone number, so all that remains is to decide on names and lengths. This is always a difficult job because there is a desire to allocate as much space as possible for each field, which is in conflict with a pressure to keep down the total record length to conserve disk space. A reasonable compromise in this case is:

```
Fullname   30
Add1       40
Add2       40
Add3       40
Add4       40
PostC      20
Tel        20
Notes      40
```

This translates at once into a type definition:

```
TYPE rec
    FullName AS STRING * 30
    Add1     AS STRING * 40
    Add2     AS STRING * 40
    Add3     AS STRING * 40
    Add4     AS STRING * 40
    PostC    AS STRING * 20
    Tel      AS STRING * 20
    Notes    AS STRING * 40
END TYPE
```

The next problem is how to solve the two tasks of showing users the data stored in the record and allowing them to change or add to it. The simpler, but less satisfactory, solution is to use PRINT and INPUT statements. A more sophisticated method is to draw on the screen what looks like a record card and allow the user to fill in or alter any of the fields - see Figure 10.3. Surprisingly, the methods needed to implement this aren't that different from the sort of techniques used to implement a graphics game.

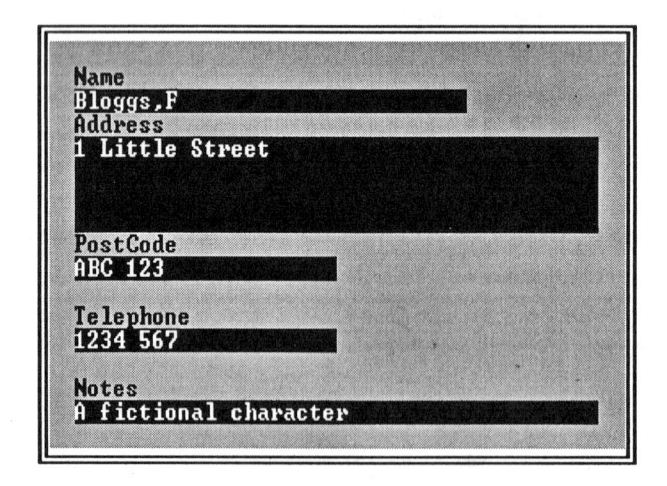

```
Tab - Next field        End - End data entry
```

Figure 10.3
The record entry screen

Creating a database

The first subroutine that is needed draws the record on the screen, complete with a blue background and an enclosing frame:

```
SUB ShowRec (id AS rec, x%, y%, h%, w%)
CALL DrawBox(x%, y%, h%, w%)
CALL DrawFrame(x%, y%, h%, w%)
CALL DrawFields(id, x%, y%)
END SUB
```

DrawBox is very simple:

```
SUB DrawBox (x%, y%, h%, w%)
COLOR 2, 1
FOR i% = 1 TO h%
   LOCATE y% + i% - 1, x%
   PRINT STRING$(w%, " ")
NEXT i%
END SUB
```

DATABASE.BAS

Notice that the area within the box has a blue background. This is used later in the program in a test to discover that the cursor is within the box.

The DrawFrame subroutine is the same as the one used in the Qtress game:

```
SUB DrawFrame (x%, y%, h%, w%)
COLOR 7, 0
FOR i% = x% + 1 TO x% + w% - 1
   LOCATE y%, i%
   PRINT CHR$(205);
   LOCATE y% + h%, i%
   PRINT CHR$(205);
NEXT i%
FOR i% = y% + 1 TO y% + h% - 1
   LOCATE i%, x%
   PRINT CHR$(186);
   LOCATE i%, x% + w%
   PRINT CHR$(186);
NEXT i%
LOCATE y%, x%
PRINT CHR$(201);
LOCATE y%, x% + w%
PRINT CHR$(187);
LOCATE y% + h%, x%
```

```
PRINT CHR$(200);
LOCATE y% + h%, x% + w%
PRINT CHR$(188);
END SUB
```

Also notice that the frame has a background colour of 0, this is used to detect when the cursor has reached the edge of the frame.

The DrawFields subroutine makes use of ShowField to place each field and its title within the frame:

```
SUB DrawFields (id AS rec, x%, y%)
CALL ShowField(id.FullName, "Name", x% + 3, y% + 2)
CALL ShowField(id.Add1, "Address", x% + 3, y% + 4)
CALL ShowField(id.Add2, "", x% + 3, y% + 5)
CALL ShowField(id.Add3, "", x% + 3, y% + 6)
CALL ShowField(id.Add4, "", x% + 3, y% + 7)
CALL ShowField(id.PostC, "PostCode", x% + 3, y% + 9)
CALL ShowField(id.Tel, "Telephone", x% + 3, y% + 12)
CALL ShowField(id.Notes, "Notes", x% + 3, y% + 15)
END SUB
```

ShowField is equally simple:

```
SUB ShowField (f$, FieldName$, x%, y%)
COLOR 7, 1
LOCATE y%, x%
PRINT FieldName$
COLOR 0, 7
LOCATE y% + 1, x%
PRINT f$
END SUB
```

Each field is drawn using background colour 7. This means that each area of the form can be identified using nothing but the background colour according to:

Colour	Area
0	Black frame
1	Blue box
7	White field

Now that we have a complete routine for displaying the current contents of the record, the next step is to write a routine that allows the user to change the contents.

The FormGet subroutine has three parts: the display; the user interaction; and the collection of the new values:

```
SUB FormGet (id AS rec)
COLOR 15, 0
CLS
x% = 10
y% = 3
h% = 18
w% = 45
LOCATE 25, 1
PRINT "Tab - Next field         End - End data entry"
CALL ShowRec(id, x%, y%, h%, w%)
curx% = x% + 3
cury% = y% + 3
DO
        LOCATE cury%, curx%, 1, 0, 15
        CALL ReadKey(EC%)
        SELECT CASE EC%
        CASE 0
        CASE 9
                CALL MoveNext(curx%, cury%)
        CASE 77 * 256
                CALL MoveRight(curx%, cury%)
        CASE 75 * 256
                CALL MoveLeft(curx%, cury%)
        CASE 79 * 256
                EXIT DO
        CASE IS < 256
                PRINT CHR$(EC%);
                CALL MoveRight(curx%, cury%)
        END SELECT
LOOP
CALL ReadRec(id, x%, y%, h%, w%)
END SUB
```

The section before the DO loop displays the current state of the record on the screen. The DO loop polls the keyboard using ReadKey and then a SELECT sorts out what should happen according to the key pressed. If the key was END, then the loop terminates and the ReadRec subroutine reads the values displayed on the screen back into the record variable.

The ReadKey subroutine returns a generalised ASCII code for the key pressed. If the key was a standard key, then the usual ASCII code is returned. If it was an extended key, then it returns 256 times the scan code:

```
SUB ReadKey (EC%)
A$ = INKEY$
SELECT CASE LEN(A$)
CASE 0
  EC% = 0
CASE 1
  EC% = ASC(A$)
CASE 2
  EC% = ASC(RIGHT$(A$, 1)) * 256
END SELECT
END SUB
```

The main movement subroutines are MoveRight and MoveLeft which respond to the right and left cursor keys respectively:

```
SUB MoveRight (curx%, cury%)
CALL getcol(curx% + 1, cury%, f%, b%)
IF b% = 7 THEN curx% = curx% + 1
END SUB
SUB MoveLeft (curx%, cury%)
CALL getcol(curx% - 1, cury%, f%, b%)
IF b% = 7 THEN curx% = curx% - 1
END SUB
```

Both subroutines make use of the GetCol subroutine to discover the colour of the screen and so keep the cursor within a region that has a background colour of 7. GetCol is simply a re-write of the lines used in Qtress for the same purpose, but turned into a subroutine:

```
SUB getcol (x%, y%, f%, b%)
c% = SCREEN(y%, x%, 1)
b% = (c% / 16)
f% = c% MOD 16
END SUB
```

The most complicated of the movement subroutines is MoveNext, which moves the cursor to the next field. There are a number of simple but tedious ways of doing this job, but MoveNext uses a general method that works no matter where in the form the fields are placed. The principle is that screen locations are examined until the next area with a field background colour, i.e. 7, is found. As the cursor starts off in a field region first step is move it off the current field using MoveRight. Then a scan for the next field is performed from left to right and top to bottom. Only the colour of the screen is used to determine the type of area that the cursor is currently in:

```
SUB MoveNext (curx%, cury%)
DO
        t% = curx%
        CALL MoveRight(curx%, cury%)
LOOP UNTIL t% = curx%
curx% = curx% + 1
DO
   LOCATE cury%, curx%, 0
   CALL getcol(curx%, cury%, f%, b%)
   SELECT CASE b%
   CASE 0
      curx% = curx% - 1
      CALL MoveEdge(curx%, cury%, -1, 0)
      cury% = cury% + 1
      CALL getcol(curx%, cury%, f%, b2%)
      IF b2% = 0 THEN CALL MoveEdge(curx%, cury%, 0, -1)
   CASE 1
      curx% = curx% + 1
   CASE 7
     EXIT DO
   END SELECT
   LOOP
END SUB
```

The only new subroutine used by MoveNext is MoveEdge which uses the screen colour to find the edge of the frame in any given direction:

```
SUB MoveEdge (curx%, cury%, dx%, dy%)
DO
        curx% = curx% + dx%
        cury% = cury% + dy%
        CALL getcol(curx%, cury%, f%, b%)
LOOP UNTIL b% = 0
curx% = curx% - dx%
cury% = cury% - dy%
END SUB
```

Once the user has finished data entry or editing, the ReadRec subroutine is called to move the screen display for each field back into the corresponding field of the record variable. ReadRec was created by editing ShowRec:

```
SUB ReadRec (id AS rec, x%, y%, h%, w%)
CALL ReadField(id.FullName, x% + 3, y% + 3)
CALL ReadField(id.Add1, x% + 3, y% + 5)
CALL ReadField(id.Add2, x% + 3, y% + 6)
CALL ReadField(id.Add3, x% + 3, y% + 7)
CALL ReadField(id.Add4, x% + 3, y% + 8)
CALL ReadField(id.PostC, x% + 3, y% + 10)
CALL ReadField(id.Tel, x% + 3, y% + 13)
CALL ReadField(id.Notes, x% + 3, y% + 16)
END SUB
```

Finally ReadField is:

```
SUB ReadField (f$, x%, y%)
FOR i% = 1 TO LEN(f$)
   MID$(f$, i%, 1) = CHR$(SCREEN(y%, x% + i% - 1))
NEXT i%
END SUB
```

This uses the SCREEN function to transfer the data into each field. Notice that the fact that all of the fields are stored as fixed length strings has made it unnecessary to pass the individual field lengths. If you are working with numeric values it would be necessary to complicate matters by recording the length of the field on the screen and performing a data type conversion.

The next stage is to write subroutines that make it possible to store and retrieve a record. Storing a record is easy enough - just a matter of creating and using a standard direct access file - however, finding a record is another matter. The simplest way of finding a record is to keep an index as a separate file. If you want to find a record on the basis of the name field, for example, you would create an index of names sorted into alphabetical order. Each element of the index would contain a name and the record number of the relevant record. It makes sense to define a new variable type to implement the index:

```
TYPE indexrec
        surname    AS STRING * 30
        recnum     AS INTEGER
END TYPE
DIM index(500) AS indexrec
```

This definition and the declaration of the array has to be entered into the main program.

In this example it is proposed to store the index in memory while the database is open, using the array index(). The first task is to write a subroutine that allows a new record to be added to the database and to the index:

```
SUB Add (id AS rec, index() AS indexrec)
CALL BlankRec(id)
CALL FormGet(id)
CALL Addrec(id, index())
END SUB
```

The BlankRec subroutine simply makes sure that there is nothing stored in the record variable id before FormGet displays it and allows the user to enter new data:

```
SUB BlankRec (id AS rec)
id.Fullname = ""
id.Add1 = ""
id.Add2 = ""
id.Add3 = ""
id.Add4 = ""
id.PostC = ""
id.Tel = ""
id.Notes = ""
END SUB
```

The Addrec subroutine is responsible for actually writing the new record to the database:

```
SUB Addrec (id AS rec, index() AS indexrec)
lastrec% = LOF(1) / LEN(id)
PUT #1, lastrec% + 1, id
CALL Insert(id.Fullname, lastrec% + 1, index())
END SUB
```

The LOF function is used to find the current length of the database and dividing this by the length of each record gives the number of records in the database. The PUT command writes the new record at the end of the database. Subroutine Insert adds the new name and record number to the index:

```
SUB Insert (n$, recno%, index() AS indexrec)
i% = 1
DO
      IF i% = recno% THEN EXIT DO
      IF index(i%).surname > n$ THEN EXIT DO
      i% = i% + 1
LOOP
FOR j% = recno% - 1 TO i% STEP -1
   index(j% + 1).surname = index(j%).surname
   index(j% + 1).recnum = index(j%).recnum
NEXT j%
index(i%).surname = n$
index(i%).recnum = recno%
CALL writeindex(index(), recno%)
END SUB
```

The index could be maintained in sorted order using one of the methods described in the sorting application - i.e. bubble, Shell or Quicksort - but, as the items are generated one at a time, an insertion sort is actually efficient. A new index entry is compared against the existing entries until its correct place in the array is located. Then all of the entries below this point are moved down by one to 'open up' a free space in the array which is then used to store the new item.

After updating the index array it is written out to disk as a sequential file using subroutine writeindex:

```
SUB writeindex (index() AS indexrec, n%)
OPEN "\address.inx" FOR OUTPUT AS 2
FOR i% = 1 TO n%
   WRITE #2, index(i%).surname, index(i%).recnum
NEXT i%
CLOSE 2
END SUB
```

Notice that this is an example of a sequential file using WRITE. An alternative to writing the index file out after each addition would be to only allow the user to quit via a menu option and to write out the index file as part of the closedown procedure. This is more efficient, but it runs the risk of the index becoming out of date because of the program being interrupted in some way. This is still possible, even when it is written out after every addition, and in a more complete database program you would have to implement an option to re-build the index from scratch.

Now that the index part of the program has been implemented, the next step is to implement the routines that make use of it to find a record. Notice that the index uses the full entry in the Fullname field of the record and this can cause problems in that an entry such as B.J. Smith would be indexed under B rather than Smith. There are a number of solutions to this problem, including splitting the Fullname field into Title, Initials and Surname. A simpler solution is to enter all names as a Surname followed by Initials. The Find a record routine is:

```
SUB Find (id AS rec, index() AS indexrec)
DIM n AS STRING * 30
CLS
CALL DrawFrame(20, 10, 2, 30)
LOCATE 9, 20
PRINT "Type the name you are searching for";
LOCATE 11, 21
INPUT "", n
h% = LOF(1) / LEN(id)
CALL BinSearch(n, index(), i%, h%)
num% = index(i%).recnum
CALL GetRec(id, num%)
CALL Browse(id, num%)
END SUB
```

Find makes use of GetRec to actually read the data into the fields:

```
SUB GetRec (id AS rec, num%)
GET #1, num%, id
END SUB
```

It then locates the specified name in the index using a binary search as implemented by subroutine BinSearch:

```
SUB BinSearch (n$, index() AS indexrec, i%, h%)
l% = 1
DO
   i% = l% + (h% - l%) \ 2
   IF index(i%).surname = n$ THEN EXIT SUB
   IF index(i%).surname < n$ THEN
      l% = i% + 1
   ELSE
      h% = i% - 1
   END IF
LOOP UNTIL l% > h%
END SUB
```

A binary search works by dividing the area of the array in which the item would have to be located in half each time. It makes use of two pointers - l% and h% - which point to the low and high limit of the array in which the item has to be. At the start l%=1 and h%= the last element in the array, because all we know is that the item is somewhere in the array. The element in the middle of the range l% to h% is examined. If this is the item required the search is finished. If it is smaller than the item you continue the search, but in the section of the array from the middle to the end. If it is bigger then you look in the section of the array from the middle to the beginning. In this way, the item is either found or the section of the array in which it must be stored gets smaller and smaller until it is found. If the item isn't in the array, the l% and h% pointers eventually cross and this is used to stop the search. In this case, the item that is found is at least close to the item searched for. Binary search is one of the fundamental algorithms that every programmer should know.

Once either the record or a near match is found the user is given the option of browsing through the records. The Browse subroutine can also be used in its own right to implement a browse option in the main menu:

```
SUB Browse (id AS rec, num%)
lastrec% = LOF(1) / LEN(id)
LOCATE 25, 1
PRINT "PgUp - Back One    PgDn - Forward One   End - End";
DO
   CALL GetRec(id, num%)
   x% = 10
   Y% = 3
   h% = 18
   w% = 45
   CALL ShowRec(id, x%, Y%, h%, w%)
   LOCATE 1, 38
   PRINT "Record Number "; num%
   DO
      CALL readkey(CE%)
   LOOP UNTIL CE% <> 0
   SELECT CASE CE%
   CASE 73 * 256
      IF num% > 1 THEN
          num% = num% - 1
      ELSE
          BEEP
      END IF
   CASE 81 * 256
      IF num% < lastrec% THEN
         num% = num% + 1
      ELSE
         BEEP
      END IF
   CASE 79 * 256
      EXIT DO
   END SELECT
LOOP
END SUB
```

274 *Applications*   *Chapter 10*

All that is needed now is a main menu:
```
SUB menu (C$)
COLOR 7, 0
CLS
CALL DrawFrame(24, 3, 5, 25)
LOCATE 1, 26
PRINT " Database Main Menu"
LOCATE 4, 26
PRINT "<A> Add record";
LOCATE 5, 26
PRINT "<B> Browse";
LOCATE 6, 26
PRINT "<F> Find";
LOCATE 7, 26
PRINT "<Q> Quit";
LOCATE 9, 26
INPUT C$
C$ = UCASE$(LEFT$(C$, 1))
END SUB
```
and a main program (note the record and array definitions have already been discussed):
```
TYPE rec
     Fullname   AS STRING * 30
     Add1       AS STRING * 40
     Add2       AS STRING * 40
     Add3       AS STRING * 40
     Add4       AS STRING * 40
     PostC      AS STRING * 20
     Tel        AS STRING * 20
     Notes      AS STRING * 40
END TYPE

TYPE indexrec
     surname    AS STRING * 30
     recnum     AS INTEGER
END TYPE

SCREEN 0
DIM id AS rec
DIM index(500) AS indexrec
```

```
ON ERROR GOTO filerr
CALL openfiles(id, index())
ON ERROR GOTO 0
DO
   CLS
   CALL menu(C$)
   CLS
   SELECT CASE C$
   CASE "A"
      CALL Add(id, index())
   CASE "B"
      CALL Browse(id, 1)
   CASE "F"
      CALL Find(id, index())
   CASE "Q"
      EXIT DO
   END SELECT
LOOP
END

filerr:
     OPEN "\address.inx" FOR OUTPUT AS 2
     CLOSE 2
     RESUME
END
```

Although no attempt has been made in this program to include error handling, the ON ERROR command has been used to detect when the index file doesn't exist. The FileOpen subroutine is responsible for reading in the index:

```
SUB openfiles (id AS rec, index() AS indexrec)
OPEN "\address.dbs" FOR RANDOM AS 1 LEN = LEN(id)
OPEN "\address.inx" FOR INPUT AS 2
i% = 1
DO UNTIL EOF(2)
   INPUT #2, index(i%).surname, index(i%).recnum
   i% = i% + 1
LOOP
CLOSE 2
END SUB
```

This is a very basic introduction to how a database might be constructed using QBasic. In practice, you would have to add many other facilities. For example, the form input routines do not respond to the backspace key and while you can type over an entry there is no way to insert new text. The database module itself lacks any facility for printing and has no way to delete a record. Deleting a record turns out to be something of a problem in that you have to re-use the space that is freed by removing a record and this can mean moving all of the other records and updating the index. A much better method is simply to use a special field in each record to mark deleted records and then write all of the routines to ignore such deleted records. In practice it would probably be easier to re-construct the index each time from the database by reading the index field into an array and then sorting it. This sounds inefficient, but recall that the Quicksort routine can sort 5000 items in 11 seconds so the inefficiency isn't of practical importance.

Armed with this example you should be able to create your own database to store whatever data interests you. There are no new techniques needed, but even the simplest real database takes a lot of programming.

Index

A

absolute co-ordinates	134
ACCESS	181
AND	139, 186
apage	148
APPEND	169
arithmetic expression	19
arithmetic operators	19
array	101, 158
array element	102
ASC	91
ASCII code	90, 240
ASCII file	159
aspect ratio	133

B

background colour	128
BEEP	154
binary file	159, 178
binary search	272
bit strings	145
BM (blank move)	135
BLOAD	207
block IF	45
block storage	158
bottom-up programming	93
breakpoint	212
BSAVE	207
bubble sort	51, 230
buffer	158

C

CALL	61
CALL ABSOLUTE	207
capitalisation	17
cascaded IFs	184
case	17
CDBL	92
CGA	120, 127
CHAIN	215
chaining	215
CHDIR	179
CHR$	91, 125
CINT	92
CIRCLE	132
CLEAR	195
Clipboard	11
clipping window	150
CLNG	92, 226
CLOSE	163, 171
CLOSE#1	208
CLS	129
COLOR	126,
colour control	128
COMMON	71
COMMON SHARED	107
conditional loop	15, 23, 32, 34, 187
conditions	44
CONST	95
constant	21
Copy	11
COUNTRY	225
CSNG	92
Ctrl key	10
CTRL-BREAK	31
cursor keys	10
Cut	11
CVDMBF	176
CVI	175
CVL	175
CVMS	176
CVS	175

D

data files	261
database	261
date base	220
DATE$	225
dates	220
debugging	209, 211
DECLARE	94, 110, 117
DEF	81
DEF FN	75
default variable type	81
delay subroutine	228
delete block	12
deleting subroutines	64
DIM	102
direct access file	159
disk storage	157
display adapter	120
display colours	13
display options	13, 32
DO	31
DO-LOOP	188
documentation	213
double precision	80
double quotes " "	5, 23
DRAW	135
dynamic arrays	107

E

Edit	9
Edit/New Function	74
Edit/New SUB	64
editing keys	10
editor	7
EGA	120
ELSEIF	184
END IF	45
End of File function	169
END SUB	61
enumeration loop	38, 187
ENVIRON	205
EOF	169
EQV	186
ERASE	108
ERDEV	203
ERDEV$	203
ERL	203
ERR	203
event driven programming	199
event handling	199, 203
exceptions	198
EXIT statement	13, 32, 36, 198
exit condition	37
EXIT FOR	188
exit point	36
exporting data	168

F

FALSE	32
fields	122, 166, 174
file number	162
FILEATTR	177
File menu	13
FILES	179, 204
Find	12
fixed length record	167
flag	52
FOR-NEXT loop	38, 106, 188
foreground colour	128
FREEFILE	162
function keys	241
functions	77, 92

G

GET	138
global variables	66
GOSUB	199
graphics cursor	128
graphics mode	119

H

Help Path	13
Hercules graphics adapter	120
hexadecimal	95

I

IF	44, 117, 184
IF ... THEN	32
IF..THEN..ELSE	44
Immediate window	213
IMP	186
indenting	31
index	102, 105, 160
indexed sequential file	160
infinite loop	31, 34
INKEY$	237
INP	207
INPUT	22, 237
input prompt	22
INPUT#	163, 208
insertion sort	229, 270
INSTR	90
integer constant	95
integer division	83
integer variables	82
interrupt	199
IOCTL	209

K

key	160, 239, 241
keyboard buffer	237
keyword	11
KILL	179

L

large programs	214
LCASE$	91
LEFT$	89
LINE	130
LINE INPUT	166
line numbers	5
linear search	159
literal string	23
local arrays	107
local variables	66, 195
LOCATE	125
LOCK	180
LOF function	177, 270
logical colours	142
logical expressions	186
long integer variable	82
LOOP	31
lower bound	105
LSET	175, 177
LTRIM$	177

M

main menu	7
marking blocks	9
MGA	127
MID$	86, 175
MKD$	175
MKDIR	179, 204
MKDMBF$	176
MKI$	175
MKL$	175
MKS$	175
MKSMBF$	176
MOD	227
modular programming	59
mouse	9
movement keys	10
MSHERC	121

N

NAME	179, 204
named constant	95
near pointers	207
networks	180
New	13
NOT	186

O

octal	95
offsets	207
ON	199
ON ERROR	203, 275
ON KEY	199, 239
Open	13, 161, 208

opening subroutines	63	RETURN	77
OR	139, 186	RIGHT$	89
OUT	207	RMDIR	179, 204
output screen	6	RND	115, 254
		RSET	175, 177
P		RTRIM$	177
PAINT	138, 144	Run menu	5
PALETTE	129, 142 -143	RUN	214
parameters	67		
Paste	11	**S**	
Path	13	scan code	238
patterns	144	scope	70, 84, 107
physical colour	142	SCREEN	121, 148, 256
PMAP	152	scroll bars	13
POINT	153	sector	158
polling loop	199, 237	SEEK	177
PRESET	139	select	30, 185
PRINT	2, 13, 23	sequential file	270
print list	24	Set Next Statement	212
PRINT#	162, 208	Shaker sort	230
Procedure Step	212	SHARE.EXE	181
program	2	SHARED	216
PSET	129, 139	SHARED arrays	107, 252
PUT	139, 171, 270	shared scope	71
		SHELL	180, 204
Q		shell sort	230
QBasic editor	4	shortcut keys	6, 9
QBASIC.EXE	3	side effects	67
Quicksort	231	single precision variables	82
		single quotes	21
R		Single Step	212
RANDOM	170	SLEEP	228
random access file	159	SOUND	154
records	112, 166	stack space	195
recursion	190	Start	6
REDIM	108	STATIC	72, 107
relative co-ordinates	134	Step	212
REM	213	stepwise refinement	64
remark	213	STR$	84
repeat	30	STRING	111
Replace	12	string	81
reserved word	11	string constant	95
RESUME	203	string functions	86

string variables	80	**V**		
structured programming	57	VAL	92	
SUB	61	variable length record	167	
substring	85	variable parameters	69	
SWAP	117	variable type	80	
syntax checking	11	VARPTR	206	
		VARSEG	206	
T		VGA	120	
Tab key	13, 31	VIEW	149	
testing	210	VIEW PRINT	153	
text cursor	9	VIEW SCREEN	150	
text file	159	View/Split	63	
THEN	44	Viewing SUBs	62	
time conversion	226	viewport	149	
time wasting loop	228	vpage	148	
TIME$	227			
TIMER	228	**W**		
TRACE	212	WHILE	36	
TRUE	32	WordStar control keys	10	
Turtle Graphics	244	world co-ordinate system	152	
two-dimensional array	103	WRITE	271	
TYPE	112	WRITE#	166	
U		**X**		
UBOUND	115	XOR	139, 186	
UCASE$	91			
UNLOCK	180	!		
UNTIL	36	'	21	
upper bound	105	""	5, 23	

Other books of interest

Foundations of Programming by Mike James   ISBN 1-871962-04-8
This book could radically change the way that you think about programming. It presents a language independent view of what programming is all about and how best to go about it. It is packed with new ideas and novel ways of looking at old ideas. If you are a practising programmer this book will change your style. If you are a programming student it will help you to understand what your lecturers are, or should be, teaching you. If you teach programming it will help you raise your sights from the details of a particular language or method to a broader view of the principles and philosophy.

Rough Guide to Languages by Mike James   ISBN 1-871962-28-5
This guide gives you the essentials of a comprehensive selection of programming languages - enough to enable you to read a program and starting writing your own. Short program examples are given together with a specific example demonstrating the best features of each language. Languages covered include many different Basics, C, C++, Prolog, Forth, Cobol, ADA and PostScript. An indispensable book for all programmers.

The C++ Windows Laboratory by Don Asumu   ISBN 1-871962-34-X
The Turbo Pascal Windows Laboratory by Don Asumu   ISBN 1-871962-32-3
A pair of soft media titles (disks plus book) that provide an express route to becoming an expert in object oriented methods for Windows programming. Load each of eighty-two complete "experiments" to see how it works and read the extensive commentary to discover how the effects were achieved and how you can use the same techniques.

The 386/486 PC (Updated 2nd Ed) by Harry Fairhead   ISBN 1-871962-22-6
The 386 family of processors (which now ranges from the 386SX to the Pentium) has rapidly come to dominate the PC world, and this extensively revised and expanded edition tells its success story as well as answering any questions you may have about extended and expanded memory, LIM, hard disk seek rate, wait states, caching, memory interleave, shadow RAM and other highly technical topics. This edition covers the Pentium chip, the local bus, superscalars, Windows NT and OS/2 Version 2 and provides advice about configuring and optimising your system's hardware.

For more information on any of these titles or our latest catalogue contact:

**I/O Press, FREEPOST, Leyburn, North Yorkshire, DL8 5BR
Tel: (01969) 624402 Fax: (01969) 624375
Email:Infomax@Cix.compulink.co.uk**